R the

Royal

F amily

the Royal Family

The Story of the British Monarchy from

Victoria to Elizabeth

by Pierre Berton

 New York   Alfred A. Knopf   1955

THIS IS A BORZOI BOOK,
PUBLISHED BY
ALFRED A. KNOPF, INC.

L. C. catalog card number: 53–9456

PUBLISHED MARCH 8, 1954
SECOND PRINTING, MARCH 1954
THIRD PRINTING, NOVEMBER 1955

TO MY MOTHER

Much of this material first
appeared in *Maclean's*, Canada's
National Magazine, to which
the author is deeply indebted.

CONTENTS

page

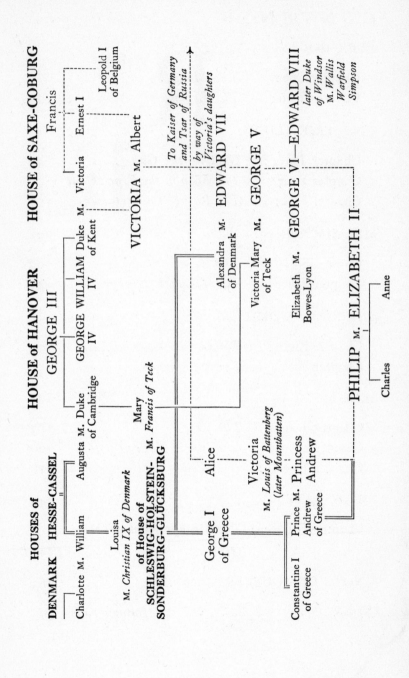

HOUSES of   HOUSE of HANOVER   HOUSE of SAXE-COBURG

DENMARK HESSE-CASSEL GEORGE III   Francis

Charlotte M. William   Augusta M. Duke GEORGE WILLIAM Duke M. Victoria Ernest I Leopold I
        of Cambridge IV IV of Kent   of Belgium

   Louisa   VICTORIA M. Albert
M. Christian IX of Denmark

of House of
SCHLESWIG-HOLSTEIN- Mary   To Kaiser of Germany
SONDERBURG-GLÜCKSBURG M. Francis of Teck   and Tsar of Russia

                   by way of
                  Victoria's daughters

Alice   Alexandra M. EDWARD VII
        of Denmark

Victoria   Victoria Mary M. GEORGE V
M. Louis of Battenberg of Teck
(later Mountbatten)

George I Prince M. Princess Elizabeth M. GEORGE VI—EDWARD VIII
of Greece Andrew Andrew Bowes-Lyon   later Duke
   of Greece   of Windsor
                M. Wallis
Constantine I   PHILIP M. ELIZABETH II Warfield
of Greece   Simpson

           Charles Anne

the Royal Family

BUCK HOUSE

It was a white elephant from the start. George III bought it from the Duke of Buckingham for twenty-one thousand pounds and he and his heirs spent two hundred and seventy thousand more trying to make it livable. But it was never quite livable. John Nash, the dour, snub-nosed little architect who rose from designing jails to designing Regent Street, remodeled it, but it still had some of the aspects of a jail. Blore, who had built Scott's famous home of Abbotsford, replaced Nash, but he did not succeed in pleasing his employers.

They all hated it. William IV, who never lived in it, wanted to turn it into the House of Commons. Victoria, who was the first to occupy it, fled it for the towers of Windsor, the tartans of Balmoral, and the Garter-blue alcoves of Osborne. She stands in front of it today in effigy, with her back resolutely toward it. Edward VII suffered fits of depression in it. He called it "the Sepulchre" and sometimes thought he saw his mother's ghost in the corridors. George V thought it too gaudy and wanted to tear it down, sell it for scrap, and use the funds to refurbish Kensington Palace.

It is drafty, rat-infested, expensive, and archaic, full of weighty mahogany furniture, fat pillars, heavy ornamental doors, overpowering chandeliers, and ponderous paintings in great gilt frames. Elizabeth, when she moved in as a child, looked down the long hallways and remarked dryly that people needed bicycles to navigate them. The light switches are often two yards down the halls from the bedroom doors, and the dining-room is half a mile from the kitchen.

3

It does not even look like a palace. It has no turrets, battlements, or minarets. It does not soar and it does not sparkle. It squats at the end of its Mall, a long, gray classical bulk, faced in Portland stone, girdled by a wrought-iron fence, guarded by sentries with no ammunition.

And yet to this great barn of a palace the nation turns in its moments of chaos, desperation, sorrow, victory, and transport. When kings die at Sandringham, the people go to Buck House, and there they wait in silence and in patience. There is nothing to do and nothing to see except the guardsman mechanically walking his beat. But the building itself seems to bring its own sense of comfort.

It is mansion, office building, apartment house, royal hotel, and national rallying-point all rolled into one. The crowned heads of Europe and Asia, past and present, have all stayed here at one time or another. It has six hundred rooms, two hundred and sixty servants, two hundred and fifty telephones, and ten thousand pieces of furniture. Fifteen thousand letters pour into it every day from nooks and crannies of the realm. The aura of history hangs over it; but the aura of mystery is stronger. There is always a crowd outside the gates, standing in a loose little group, trying to pierce the stone veil. In moments of great pageantry the crowd swells out until the Mall is choked. Then the veil parts for a moment and the family within comes onto the balcony and smiles and waves and is caught fleetingly in the telephoto lenses. The veil closes again, the family goes back inside its palace, but the crowd remains. As long as there is a family and a palace the crowd will be there, watching and waiting and drawing its own peculiar sustenance from the gray old mansion on the Mall.

Chapter 1: *The Blood*

The scattered British realm, whose jig-saw puzzle parts have often very little in common except an allegiance to an extraordinary family living in a gilded palace, tends to look on the members of its royal dynasty with a certain ambivalence. On the one hand, it expects its sovereigns to be human. On the other, it is constantly surprised when they are.

An unceasing cataract of newspaper trivia daily brings home the point that the people within the palace are actually mortal: that a fairy prince likes to drink pink gin and drive a sports car ninety-two miles an hour; that a fairy princess can wink at a soldier and go mad about Danny Kaye records; that a fairy queen plays a mean game of canasta and is crazy about as plebeian a pastime as square dancing. And yet when a middle-aged prince charming rejects a throne for the most fundamental of mortal emotions, the shock to his subjects is so great that it must be cushioned by the daily repetition of the phrase that "after all, he is human."

For the common round of kings and queens is such that it is never easy to think of them as altogether real. They appear either as jeweled deities, framed momentarily in the twenty-carat gold leaf and Cipriani panels of a state coach, or as highly efficient automatons: walking Union Jacks, machines for shaking innumerable hands, human phonographs for the mouthing of other men's speeches. When a Princess discards her state coach for a Lincoln convertible, the children cry out in disappointment. When the human phonograph starts broadcasting its own irrevocable decisions, the adults cry out in dismay.

The reaction is akin to that experienced by a young waiter in Voisin's, a Parisian restaurant frequented during the nineteenth century by princes of the blood, including

Albert Edward of Wales. The waiter bored peepholes in the doors of the private dining-rooms because, as he explained, "I wanted to find out how princes made love."

"Alas," he added, with both astonishment and regret, "their love-making is no more different than any other mortal's."

If the members of the House of Windsor are mortal, they are certainly anything but dull. In their private lives and times, there is plenty of the raw material out of which great fictional family sagas are concocted. Indeed, the ingredients are more than faintly Galsworthian:

There was Grandmamma, the rapier-straight matriarch, of whom everyone was a little terrified, clinging to the old ways as fiercely as she clung to her toques and tulles, unchanging as the English climate, her granite character standing like a Gibraltar among the eroding tides of family dissent and family tragedy;

There was Grandpapa, her sailor husband with his gusty temper, who ran his family like a ship, frightening and antagonizing his sons, yet choking up with emotion whenever he mentioned them or the rest of the family to strangers;

There is the "wicked uncle," the remittance man, who married beneath him and whose name is only whispered in the family circle; and there was his younger brother, the shy, stuttering, rather backward boy who seemed so weak and turned out to be so strong;

There is the younger generation: the pretty little younger sister, so witty and so talented and so lonely that everyone is trying to find a husband for her; and her dedicated elder sister, the shy, rather nervous girl who

6

had to grow up so quickly when at the age of twenty-six she found herself head of the family.

In the background like graven images stand the shadowy figures of the ancestors: Great-grandfather, a stout, spade-bearded man whom everybody liked even though he gambled and ate prodigiously and (another whisper) took mistresses; and his curious father, Albert of Saxe-Coburg, that paragon of paragons who was so strict with his son because he was haunted by the thought that the blood of his wife's ancestors, the wicked princes of Hanover, might make itself felt.

And last, but by no means least, was Albert's wife, Victoria, who was herself half Hanover and threatened to exhibit several alarming Hanover tendencies until she cast herself in the likeness of her husband to become, after his death, as much of an Albert Memorial as the grotesque piece of statuary that bears his name.

But the hot red blood of the Hanovers still mingles with the chill blue blood of the Coburgs in the veins of Victoria's descendants. How else to explain the astonishing human contrasts that are the most striking feature of the British royal house?

Edward VII, with his love for plovers' eggs, baccarat, professional beauties, and Duminy triple sec '83; Edward VIII, with his tastes in night clubs and propensity for playing the drums in jazz bands; the fashionable Princess Margaret, who likes to read racy French novels, drink pink champagne, and dance until dawn—how can these be equated with George V, that most domestic of monarchs, who preferred his stamp collection and his morning bowl of soup to more esoteric pursuits and was always in bed by 11:10 p.m., or George VI, whose heart lay in the pheasant and grouse coverts of Sandringham and Balmoral, or Elizabeth Regina, that consecrated young Queen, whose serious, preoccupied face bears the Coburg stamp of duty?

For the story of the family in the palace starts with their predecessors, the Wettins of Coburg and the Guelphs of Hanover, two great dynasties that stretch back through the mists of history to the Middle Ages and have their common meeting-ground on the English throne. It would be hard to find two more totally disparate family groups. In every sense, from their physical appearance to their emotional structure, they were entirely at odds.

The Coburg tale is pure Cinderella. The tiny principality of Saxe-Coburg, a sovereign duchy of sixty thousand people, had been wrung dry of its resources by Napoleon's armies. The branch of the Wettin family that ruled this postage stamp came as close to starvation and beggary as archdukes can get. And yet within a generation they had attained four thrones. The key figure in the rise of the Coburgs was Leopold, the archduke's brother, a solemn, unbending and ambitious prince who became King of the Belgians. Leopold's sister became Victoria's mother, and his nephew Albert became Victoria's husband. Another nephew became consort of Portugal, a daughter became Empress of Mexico, and a grand-nephew, Tsar of Bulgaria. Saxe-Coburg exported royalty as other nations export drygoods. They seemed a weak group, but the weakness was quite deceptive. They slid onto their thrones quietly and without much fanfare, but they clung to them with grips of iron. It was Charlotte of Coburg who talked her husband Maximilian into accepting the ill-fated throne of Mexico. Ferdinand of Coburg married the Queen of Portugal and was soon trying to run the country. A later

8

Ferdinand was put on the throne of Bulgaria by a strong-man, and ended up deposing the strong-man entirely and proclaiming himself Tsar. As for Albert, who arrived in England, as he put it, "the husband but not the master in this house," he was king in everything but name before his death.

It was the Coburgs who devised the modern concept of the constitutional monarchy in which the sovereign reigns but does not rule. The two chief Coburg thrones, in Belgium and England, stood like gilded blockhouses when the revolutionary prairie fires of '48 swept over Europe. The English monarchy to this day still runs on Coburg principles, laid out by that strange triumvirate of Leopold and Albert and their mentor, the Baron Christian Friedrich Stockmar, a dyspeptic physician of Swedish parentage who padded ceaselessly on tiptoe between the two courts, whispering and advising, designing and maneuvering, writing endless memoranda and staying always in the shadows.

They were a queer crew, the Coburgs, by any man's lights. They much preferred to lurk in the wings, pulling strings for those who occupied the footlights. Their abiding ambitions were varnished by the high gloss of selflessness. They were obsessed by the idea of doing good, and while some men struggle for power, wealth, or recognition, these sought the filmier goals of morality, right, and propriety. In the Coburg background there lurk ancestral shades with names like Ernest the Pious, John the Constant, and Henry the Illustrious, which manage to suggest the cast of the Coburg character. There are a whole series of Fredericks—the Wise, the Gentle, the Magnaminous, and one Frederick called the Bitten, because his mother, in a paroxysm of love, scarred his cheek forever with her teeth. This last-named Frederick died of an attack of melancholy brought on by seeing a morality play depicting the flinging into hell of a group of foolish virgins. For the Coburgs were nothing if not moral. Only one of their number is ever recorded as having married an actress, and he taught her to make cookies.

There is a slight hint of fanaticism in the Coburg attitude. One cannot help suspecting that had they lived in the America of the twenties some of them would have been in the ranks of the more ardent prohibitionists. They were, as a rule, somber men who preferred dark clothing, and the personalities of two of them, Leopold and Stockmar, were tinctured with hypochondria. The latter used to wear a wig for fear of catching a cold in the head and had adopted the interesting if puzzling habit of sleeping with his mouth propped agape by golden wedges. He once supped at the table of that outspoken Hanover, William IV of England, where he made the mistake of drinking water. "What's that you're drinking, sir?" cried William. "Water, sir," replied Leopold. "God damn it, sir!" roared the Hanover, "why don't you drink wine? I never allow anybody to drink water at my table!" The Victorian age, which followed, with all its stern morality, was largely the invention of these Coburgs, who never blustered or swaggered or wore bright spangles, figuratively or literally, who preferred to creep quietly about, contracting their advantageous marriages and aspiring to a power that often enough turned out to be quite tenuous.

They were everything the Hanovers were not. The Coburgs were sparse, dry men; the Hanovers were gross giants. The Coburgs' prevailing uniform was black; the Hanovers wore loud and often vulgar clothing: violet satin dressing-gowns, ornate embroidered waistcoats, spangled coats, and pink shoes. The Coburgs sheltered their carefully controlled emotions behind graven faces; the Hanovers wore their hearts and temperament on their brocaded sleeves. The Coburgs always maneuvered carefully around any obstacle; the Hanovers knew only one method of attack: directly frontal. The Coburgs followed the chill light of their intellect; the Hanovers were slaves to the hot dictatorship of their blood. The Coburgs were discreet, taciturn, upright, and frugal; the Hanovers were tactless, outspoken, lusty, and prodigal.

The first of the Hanoverian kings of England was George I. The last was William IV, a man with a monumental lack of public presence, who could be observed waving and smiling cheerfully to his friends at the funeral of his brother and predecessor, George IV. William and his brothers, all sons of the blind and insane George III, were in a perpetual state of dissent and turmoil. Their politics ranged all the way from those of the Duke of Kent, who professed to Robert Owen's socialism, to those of the Duke of Cumberland, who was the worst reactionary in the kingdom. Between the lot of them they brought the British monarchy to its nadir. Mobs followed Cumberland in the streets, jeering and catcalling and dragging him from his horse. William himself leaned from his carriage and spat on his hooting subjects. "I feel the crown tottering on my head," he said, and indeed it was only the calculated Coburg morality of the succeeding generation that saved the throne.

They were like children, these Hanovers, with their love for practical jokes and bright plumage, with their incessant squabbling and incredible public *faux pas*. They had a craze for expensive toys (some of which were women), and all but one were continually and hopelessly in debt. Kent, who always kept six footmen standing at his front door to receive visitors, had a house jammed with musical clockwork birds, and organs with dancing horses, and halls lit with hundreds of colored lights. Sussex had eighteen watches all ticking together in a glass case, and clocks that played marches and anthems every hour on the hour.

They were a passionate lot, living among a welter of mistresses and illegitimate offspring. Scandals blew across their thresholds with the regularity of tradewinds. Cumberland, who was known far and wide as "the Ogre," was popularly supposed to have seduced his own sister and murdered his valet, though in point of fact he did neither. York got into a scrape of classic dimensions when it was discovered that his mistress, Mrs. Clarke, had been accepting bribes to influence army promotions. The passion often found its outlet in outright cruelty. Cumberland, the Ogre, retained the torture device known as "picqueting" for recalcitrant troops under his command: the unfortunate soldier had to balance for hours at a time on a sharpened stake fixed in the ground. Kent, a martinet who provoked his men to near mutiny, thought nothing of awarding a man 999 strokes of the cat. And there is the grisly story of his treatment of Private Draper in Quebec, whom he sentenced to hang. Draper was dressed in his shroud and marched with his coffin to the field of execution while the band played appropriate funeral dirges. Then in the shadow of the gallows, and at the last moment, the Duke reprieved the terrified man.

Beside the prim Coburgs, the Hanovers look like creatures from a comic strip: George IV, his obese figure imprisoned in corsets and his purple jowls sticky with greasepaint, confidently insisting that he and not Wellington had

won the Battle of Waterloo; Cumberland, with his single
evil eye, his ragged beard, and his scarred cheek, with his
neck swathed in yards of cravat, defying the mob that re-
viled him; Cambridge in his odd blond wig chattering un-
ceasingly at the top of his voice and enraging parsons with
his running commentary on the church service from his
seat in the front pew. (When one minister read out the
commandment: "Thou shalt do no murder," Cambridge
is supposed to have cried in a loud voice: "No. I leave that
to my brother Ernest.")

They were all of them stubborn leftovers from the
eighteenth century, that roistering and vibrant English era
when extravagance and eccentricity were as common as
Chippendale tables, and a man could erect a ruined castle
in his back yard without exciting comment. But they had
no place in this new century into whose moods the Coburgs
slid so easily. Lusty they were, but they left no living issue
until Kent was persuaded (for a sum) to give up the Mme
St. Laurent, his mistress, who had been his wife in everything but name for twenty-seven years and marry into the
Coburg dynasty. His wife, who was Leopold's sister, had
all the ambition and all the morality of her breed, and
when Kent died, two years later, leaving a small daughter,
Victoria, she brought her up to avoid the Hanoverian
court as she would the Black Death. But Victoria had the
Hanover blood as well as the Coburg, and though she and
her descendants have worn the Coburg face, the emotional
brew that is a Hanover heritage still simmers within them.

For the Windsors (who changed their name from the
Coburg "Wettin" in World War I) are an emotional
people who have learned to hold their emotions in check.
Each of them, from Victoria to Elizabeth, has worn the
iron mask of royalty—that peculiarly blank, heavy-lidded,

expressionless stare that can be seen gazing so coldly from the official portraits, effigies, bas-reliefs, stamps of the nation, and coins of the realm. Only occasionally has the frozen guise slipped momentarily to reveal a swift glimpse of the face behind it, but when it has, the glimpse has been a fascinating one.

There is the glimpse of Queen Mary as a Princess, hiding behind pillars at a grand ball and sticking out her foot to trip up passing guests, and there is a later glimpse of her as a Queen whistling music-hall numbers in the corridors of the palace.

There is the glimpse of the grave-faced George V trying to say good-by to his family, as revealed in the clipped phrases of his own sparse diary: "It is horrible saying goodbye to the sweet children. . . . Very much affected and could hardly speak. The leave taking was terrible. I went back with them to the yacht when I said goodbye and broke down quite. . . ."

There is a glimpse of Victoria, alternately wide-eyed and giggling as she watches her Albert shaving, and there is a later glimpse of the decorous and proper Albert dashing up a hill at Balmoral to dance a wild witch's dance around the fires that celebrated the victory at Balaclava.

There is a glimpse of Edward VII as Prince of Wales, aged fifty and still lurking behind a pillar, the sweat glistening on his terrified brow because he has committed the unpardonable blunder of being late for one of his mother's affairs.

And there is a glimpse of a later Prince of Wales, now Duke of Windsor, with his brother Kent, flinging gravel at a lady's window, and later bribing a butler and turning up dressed as waiters at one of her dinner parties.

There are other glimpses behind the mask: George VI

14

falling panting on the floor after a family square dance; Alexandra squealing with delight because a servant has dropped a tray of crockery; Elizabeth II's eyes filling with tears as Joe Smallwood, the cocky little Premier of Newfoundland, refers in an emotional speech to her ailing father.

But in public the Windsors have always worn their masks, and this has been especially noticeable whenever they have been in danger. If they have the Coburg reserve they also have the Hanover courage. None of the sons of George III ever shirked a fight, whether it was physical or verbal. Kings and princes no longer indulge in squabbles or fisticuffs, but the Windsor stoicism is part of the pattern. Victoria sat quite still when a madman cut at her face, and again when she was well along in her pregnancy and an assassin tried to shoot her. Once, when Albert detected a menacing motion in the crowd, the two of them went out again in their carriage purposely to lure the attacker into the arms of the police. In the seven attempts made upon her life she flinched only once, when she was well on in years and very nervous. Edward VII and Alexandra were reading the newspaper in a Belgian railway car when a youth fired a pistol at them. The bullet passed between the two of them, but Edward's only reaction was to look up casually, remark *"Pauvre fou!"* and return to his paper again. When George V and his Queen were enthroned at the Delhi Durbar of 1911, fire broke out in the vast marquee, threatening death and panic to hundreds. The King never moved or so much as glanced at his wife, but calmly continued to pin on decorations.

"I am not of a demonstrative nature," Albert of Saxe-Coburg once remarked, and this has been true of each of his descendants. It is the best explanation of the striking lack of communion that has marred the relationship of parent and child down through the generations. Victoria's rejection of her mother on the day she became Queen is one of the dramatic moments of royal history. For years the two were hardly on speaking terms. It was Albert who in the end brought them together, but he in turn was never able to tune in on the wave-length of his heir, who became Edward VII. The boy reacted so violently to his father's disciplined upbringing and his mother's scorn that he became the living antithesis of the age that bore her name. And Edward, who tried to give his sons a normal upbringing, was never really close to George V, who stood in such awe of him that intimacy was difficult. As for the relation between George and his own sons, it was so lacking in rapport that it was necessary for them to make appointments in advance in order to see their father. This too had violent and unhappy consequences. One son, David, rebelled against it until his life became one long rebellion. Another son, Bertie, withdrew so far within the protecting shell of his own personality that it became a torture for him to come out again when kingship was thrust upon him.

Only in the most recent generation has there been anything approaching a normal family relationship among the Windsors. Between Elizabeth II and her parents there was certainly a closer bond than there has been for a century. This was due largely to Elizabeth's mother, a warm personality, as Alexandra was, with no trace of Coburg blood in her veins. For George VI, like those who came before him, was not a demonstrative man and it sometimes used to embarrass him when his little daughters climbed upon his knees to put their wet lips against his face.

Outward reserve is often the hallmark of shyness, and

the Windsors, with the single exception of Edward VII, have been remarkably shy people. Inward nervousness has been as much of a family trait as outward stoicism. Victoria's journals are alive with constant references to her own nervousness before a speech or a function and, indeed, she burst into tears before appearing at her own Jubilee. The others, right down to the present Queen, have had it too. Much of it comes from the necessarily confined existence that royal offspring must suffer, from the inability to meet on equal terms, and sometimes on any terms, with children of a like age, from the constant and often repressive companionship of adult mentors. But some of it must be regarded as inherent.

The shyness and nervousness have been accompanied by another quality of temperament which is common to people whose emotions lie just below the surface of their personalities. This is the quality of passion. In private the Windsors have had a Hanoverian temper. The violent coughing that racked Edward VII's last hours and helped to hasten his end was brought on as a result of a fit of rage. George V had a propensity for sudden gusts of anger and for swearing great round oaths in a loud voice. George VI could go white with anger if official functions did not run like clockwork.

Into this emotional fabric has been interlaced a certain strand of family sentimentality, which again hardly shows in public but which has endured through the generations. The break in Elizabeth's voice when she referred in a speech to Queen Mary's famous carpet as "the work of my grandmother's hands," and the mists in her eyes when, during her father's illness, the national anthem was played, hark right back to Victoria, whose voice breaks and whose eyes mist up every time she refers to members of her family in the pages of her journals. It is paradoxical that within a family where the gap between parents and children has often been publicly observable there should also be this strong and sentimental feeling of kinship. It is most highly accented in George V, who, though he could never get close to his sons, or they to him, could get so emotionally worked up when taking his leave of them. One can almost see the solemn shades of his expressionless Coburg ancestors struggling with the ghosts of the passionate Hanovers.

It is the Coburg blood that has in the main won out. It shows itself in the almost deliberate lack of ostentation which has also been a family trait from Queen to Queen (though it skipped a generation with Edward VII). When George V met anybody he felt was putting on too many airs, he would start referring to Buckingham Palace as "my house in Pimlico." The Windsors have the Coburg chameleon ability to adapt to their surroundings, and each of them has gauged correctly the new mood of the times. The ermines and the emeralds are reserved for state occasions and the family don them almost reluctantly. For they have much preferred to play the role of a group of upper middle-class country squires, fond of shooting parties and racing meets, not too keen on the sophisticated pleasures of the city, at home in the music hall but a little uneasy at the opera, and quite out of depth in a picture gallery. The artistic discrimination of George IV, the intellectual curiosity of Albert, have not filtered down to succeeding generations, and the family background is well larded with anecdotes that attest to it. Victoria's attitude toward a painting was one of immense practicality. The riband of the Garter was of a definite and observable blue, and when it appeared in her portrait she insisted that it be the exact shade. In vain the harassed von Angeli tried to explain that color changes in certain lights. She would have none of it. There was the Garter; they could see it. That was how it was to be.

George VI once commissioned six paintings of Windsor Castle from the English modernist John Piper, who is noted for his paintings of stormy scenes. Piper did the paintings and was paid for them but heard nothing more about it. Finally, consumed with curiosity regarding the royal reaction to his work, he decided on the occasion of a palace garden party to approach the monarch on the subject. The King at first seemed to have some difficulty recalling the matter at all, but finally he remembered the paintings. "Ah, yes . . . Piper," he said. "Pity you had such bloody awful weather."

His father, George V, was once led by the Earl of Stanhope down a long line of magnificent portraits of the day. The King gazed at each with some concentration and then made his only comment: none of them seemed to be wearing the Garter. The Earl, somewhat taken aback at this unexpected piece of art criticism, replied that none of them *had* the Garter, whereupon the King announced he was conferring it immediately upon Lord Stanhope, who would then be able to have his portrait painted with it on.

The absence of highbrowism, the embracing of middle-class rather than aristocratic traits, again go back to Victoria, who was England's first middle-class Queen. She was almost ostentatious in her lack of ostentation, and this was notable in her appearance at Westminster Abbey on the occasion of her 1887 Jubilee. Here among the scarlet uniforms, the ermine robes, the shining breastplates, the plumed headdresses, and the bright jewels that flashed all about her was silhouetted a lonely and rather dumpy little old lady in a black satin dress with a white front, and a white bonnet bordered in velvet. This was stark, naked drama, and her appearance in this manner struck her people so forcibly and emotionally that all the unpopularity brought on by her long hermitage within the battlements of Windsor melted away, and she became almost overnight the transcendent figure in her realm.

It is a German quality, this almost Wagnerian sense of the dramatic moment, which this outwardly undramatic dynasty has always unconsciously maintained. And this is not surprising, for the family is still largely German in its background. Elizabeth II is almost half German, and her successor Charles will be a good deal more than that, for his father's blood is also heavily Teutonic. Once when an acquaintance was criticizing the Boche to the Duke of Windsor, the Duke (he was then Prince of Wales) remarked: "You forget I am three-quarters German myself." The German blood still shows in a number of small ways: in the sense of the meticulous, the stress on uniform, dress, and decorations which, by and large, has always been a family characteristic; and in the almost fanatical insistence on punctuality, which kept the Sandringham clocks running half an hour fast for two generations. It is perhaps significant that the two fabulously unpunctual Queens, Alexandra, and Elizabeth, the present Queen Mother, have also been the only non-German additions to the family.

And yet this German family is totally British. The bottling up of emotions that has been its notable trait has become over the years a markedly British quality—the quality of the stiff upper lip, which has been lampooned so much by the non-British world. The British, like their sovereigns, are essentially a sentimental people, but they do not like to show it and they would be embarrassed if the ruling family showed it. For they like the ruling family to be a mirror-image of the national character; or perhaps, conversely, the national character mirrors the personality of its ruling family.

The genius for unconscious drama has come to be a British quality too. It shows again and again in the great pageants in which the family in the palace must always take the chief roles. It showed most recently during one remarkable moment of George VI's funeral procession, as the long column of slow-marching mourners passed Marlborough House, the home of Queen Mary. In this square and classical Wren mansion, as stern as a Coburg face, the blinds were all drawn but one, and to this single unshuttered window every eye was pulled as if by a magnet. As the coffin passed, a dark figure appeared in the window and waved its hand slowly in grave salute. Now every eye turned back to the procession and to the carriage bearing two Queens and two Princesses, swathed in black veils. As if by unspoken order, the four black figures bowed in unison to the figure in the window. Behind them, marching in line came the four royal Dukes. And again, as if by silent word of command these four turned their eyes to the window and saluted. The procession moved on in utter silence, broken only by the slow but inexorable thump of marching feet. Then, as the figure of the dowager Queen slid into the shadows, a wave of uncontrollable emotion spread through the crowd. So great was it that radio broadcasters found difficulty in speaking.

"We are not a family," George VI once remarked dryly, "we're a firm," and to this family firm, with its checkered heritage of Coburg and Hanover, Elizabeth II now falls heir. The ghosts of her lineage march with her daily down the white and gold corridors of her palace; the graven busts stare at her from their marble plinths; the stern, painted faces gaze down from their great baroque frames.

From childhood she has been steeped in the background of her family, which is also the background of her country's history. Does she sometimes rise up against it? Perhaps. Her sister Margaret was once asked to name her favorite King and she gave an unexpected answer. "I think perhaps Charles II," she said, "because *he* wasn't my grandfather." Elizabeth herself broke the succession of Edwards and Georges, which have been the tradition of the Windsor house for so long, when she christened her first-born. And shortly after her reign began, when a new portrait of her was brought in, finished, for her inspection, she gazed at it long and thoughtfully and then, turning to a courtier, she made a simple plea:

"Please!" she said. *"Don't* say it makes me look like Queen Victoria!"

Chapter 2: *The Legend*

How cold and expressionless they both look, the legendary pair who founded the present royal house of Britain, staring out from the effigies and the statues, the stone memorials and the daguerreotypes and the Winterhalter paintings that clutter palace and castle, textbook and public place: Albert, serious, proper, and severe; Victoria, absolutely devoid of expression. In her black satin dresses and white tulle caps and elastic boots she reminded the painter von Angeli of a plump little mushroom. But behind that blank mushroom expression there was a heart that beat with a wild and exuberant passion.

There is a faint hint of it in one lone photograph, taken when both had reached middle age, when Albert was growing paunchy and bald and the little Queen was taking on the features and dimensions of a German *Hausfrau*. Albert is as formal as ever, but there is the whisper of a look on Victoria's face as she stares up into his eyes that is almost impossible to describe but that has in it some of the elements of longing, terror, desire, and supplication. It was not long after this that Albert was taken from her and the face again became a mushroom. But the terror, the longing, and the passion remained, to boil within her for almost half a century until she too, with a bridal veil for a shroud, went on her long journey to meet the man who, living and dead, governed her existence.

When she was young, she had the rippling Hanover laugh. The tiny bud of a mouth opened wide, the heart-shaped head was flung back, and the bell-like voice pealed out at the jokes and puns and risqué stories that, despite the legend of "we are not amused," she thoroughly enjoyed. She was a spendthrift in the Hanover tradition. She enjoyed her meals and had a tendency to gobble them. She loved to gallop at top speed over the moors on horse-

23

back. She was sometimes subject to fits of helpless laughter and she did not like what she called "a Sunday face." She loved company and she loved gossip and she loved her pony, her dogs, her piano, and her dolls. She loved to dance, tirelessly and vivaciously, to the violins of the elder Strauss until dawn pinked the Carrara marble of Nash's great Roman arch before the palace, and she confessed that the quadrilles made her feel "quite frantic."

Her pompous martinet of a father had died when she was eight months old and her mother brought her up a Coburg. She was forced to wear a sprig of holly at her throat at mealtimes to keep her chin up. She was not allowed to descend a staircase without someone holding her hand. No one, except her mother or the Baroness Louise Lehzen, her governess, was ever allowed to be alone with her. Until the day she was Queen she had no room of her own. She loved melodramatic novels but she was forbidden to read them, for she must attend to sterner texts which she hated. If, in later years, she treated those around her as if they were dolls, it is not to be wondered at, for her dolls were her closest friends. Even her cousin, who was her only childhood companion, could not address her familiarly by her first name.

She grew up a demure, expressionless child, never revealing her feelings, while all about her were violent personalities who never hid theirs. Her mother quarreled openly with King William at the climax of a dinner party, but Victoria said not a word. She gave no hint of the steel within her character until the morning when she was brought down from her bed and told that she was Queen. She never returned to that bed. With a poise that sent shivers down the backs of her courtiers she banished her mother to the shadows of the palace, demanded a room

of her own, and took over the reins of queenship. At her
first privy council, as the Duke of Wellington said, "she
not only filled the chair, she filled the room." Those who
had tried to steer her in her girlhood got short shrift. The
meddlesome and ambitious Irish comptroller, Sir John
Conroy, who had connived with her mother to establish
a regency, was swiftly sent packing. Uncle Leopold in
Belgium, who had been pouring out a stream of chattering
letters of suggestion and advice, with half the words un-
derlined and capitalized for emphasis, found himself
politely but firmly ignored. It was as if the child had been
transformed into an adult in the first moment of her
queenship. But when she died, and the great mysterious
trunks that were crammed into her castle at Windsor
were opened, it was found that she had kept everything
from that vanished childhood—all the muffs and mittens
and little girl's frocks and parasols, and all the dolls she
had loved so much.

All her life the fatherless child sought a father-image.
She sought it in Uncle Leopold whose letters had heart-
ened her until they grew tiresome. (But she learned her
habit of underlining words from him.) She sought it in
Melbourne, the handsome, black-browed prime minister
of her early queenship, with the mellow voice and the calm
mien which was never ruffled, even when his wife was
openly seduced by the poet Byron. In later years she
sought it in other disparate characters: in the queer Indian servant called the Munshi, whom she allowed to read
secret papers; in John Brown, the bearded Scots gillie
whom she allowed to insult her; and in Benjamin Disraeli,
whose own particular brand of soothing syrup was among
the stickiest ever countenanced.

She needed a male confidant, for her youth had been entirely dominated by those of her own sex. Melbourne she saw almost daily for four years, and the longest lapse between them was eleven days. He acted as her secretary, rode with her in the streets, sat at her left at dinner, and talked with her until after eleven p.m. She wrote down everything he said in the journal which she kept so faithfully all her life, and when she was crowned she remarked expressly on the fatherly look he gave her. Her enemies hissed at her as "Mrs. Melbourne," and Charles Greville, the acid diarist of the day, who described her as a willful and obstinate girl, thought her feelings were sexual. If they were, she did not realize it. She took the advice of Stockmar, who, with his alert little face that missed nothing, told her to regard Melbourne as her father, and she wrote that these "were quite my feelings."

It was to Albert she gave all the affection and the passion that had been bottled up inside her since birth. She gave it so completely that she had little left for her children, and her forty-year immolation on the altar of her consort's memory is one of the more extraordinary chapters in royal annals. But then, Albert of Saxe-Coburg-Gotha was one of the most extraordinary men who ever guided the hand of a Queen.

From the skeptical vantage point of a later century this paragon among paragons still seems almost too good to be true. An observant diplomat, Count Mensdorff, remarked that "from the earliest infancy he was distinguished for perfect moral purity both in word and deed," and all the evidence supports it. From his toddling days he wore the dark-hued vestments of morality as a constant cloak. As a little boy he would confess his sins to his diary —his refusal to recite poetry, a quarrel with his brother —then add in firm tones: "That was not right. Naughty!"

At six, he was raising funds to build a house for a poor man who had lost his possessions in a fire. At thirteen, he was framing a stern and all-embracing timetable for his own study. It began at six a.m. and took up most of the day.

At three, he was told by a nursemaid that he would marry the future Queen of England and from this age onward he never questioned his duty. For with Albert, duty came before pleasure and pleasure seldom came. It was not surprising that Victoria fell passionately in love with him, with his sloe-eyes and his straight features, for he was noble, he was moral, and he stood ready to fill the vacuum that Melbourne, moving toward the twilight of senility, was eventually to leave behind him. She wished Albert would propose to her, for it hurt her pride to take the lead in so delicate a matter, but she understood her Coburgs and she knew that in this instance he would never take the initiative.

The enraptured Queen was now all atremble with delight and ecstasy, but Albert's attitude was more that of martyr than of lover. Women had always embarrassed him. At the age of five at a children's party a little girl had been brought up to him and he had screamed in disgust and anger. Now, after his betrothal, he wrote to his stepmother that "life has its thorns in every position and the consciousness of having used one's powers and endeavors for an object so great as that of promoting the good of so many will surely be sufficient to support me." It was not the letter of an ardent swain.

It is not too surprising that he should have viewed his new life with some dismay, for the two had very little in common. Victoria liked the city; Albert couldn't stand it. Victoria liked to stay up late at night; Albert was nodding by ten or eleven p.m. Victoria was at home in the company of courtiers; Albert detested them and preferred intellectuals. Victoria was frivolous and light-hearted in her temperament and tastes. Albert was somber, dedicated, and bookish. And yet in the end she drew closer to his image and he in his turn came to have a deep and very real affection for her.

At first he was frustrated in his new environment. Victoria had once dreaded the thought of marriage, for she was accustomed to having her way and, as she put it, she "thought it ten to one I shouldn't agree with anybody." In the early days of her marriage she had her will with Albert. She chose his entire household without his seeing them. He complained that he was "only the husband and not the master in this house"; he could not select his own private secretary; his wife did it for him. She even denied him the intellectual companionship he sought so thirstily, for she was jealous of anyone who stole him from her. Nor would she let him share her own work. He had nothing to do except to catalogue the royal art treasures.

But little by little a subtle change was wrought in the management of the household. Little by little, the serious Prince in the frock coat, who wore the blue riband of the Garter across his chest from morning until night, became not only master but King. "Be you the constitutional genius of the Queen," Stockmar had advised him, and soon the Queen had moved her desk next to his so she might be near him while she worked. It was the thin edge of the Coburg wedge and before Albert's days were done he was reading every state document, attending every state audience, dictating his wife's letters, revising her speeches, and prompting her policy. When she received a report on the condition of workhouses it was Albert who sat up all

28

night composing her comments, and when the East India Company wanted to give medals to brave soldiers it was Albert who dictated her answer: "There must not be two fountains of honor in the Realm." All of this the self-willed Queen accepted passively. "We women are not *made* for governing . . . we women . . . are *not fitted to reign,*" she wrote to her uncle.

Soon the household had forsaken city palace for country castle and found itself trooping off to bed before eleven. Artists and musicians began to appear at court and in the evening, while Albert nodded sleepily in his chair, there were musicales. The gaming tables of the Hanover era melted away as Albert and the Queen stood over the piano and sang while Herr Mendelssohn played for them.

The consort's consuming desire was not only to better himself but also to better everybody around him. "Never relax," Stockmar whispered to him, and he never did. He focused the cold light of his methodical mind on the chaos of the household and soon he was into everything, substituting hot noonday meals for cold luncheons, peering into the palace kitchens which he found "hot, unhealthy and altogether unfit," devising a new kind of filing system for the royal papers, paring costs, untangling the endless red tape of royal bureaucracy, and forever economizing, changing, advancing, and reforming.

Soon he had the palace on a working basis and had saved enough money to purchase two estates: the home of Osborne on the Isle of Wight and the Castle of Balmoral on the Deeside in Scotland. He designed their reconstruction right down to the furniture and the landscaping, to the chairs of solid coal in Osborne, and the tartanned carpets and wallpaper in Balmoral, where the granite turrets took on some of the character of a Rhineland *Schloss.*

The results gave him great satisfaction but everyone did not agree. Lord Rosebery once remarked reflectively that he thought the drawing-room at Osborne was the ugliest in the world until he saw the one at Balmoral.

The consort's industry was enormous. "To me," he said, "a long, closely connected train of reasoning is like a beautiful strain of music." He was at his desk by seven each morning, his green-shaded lamp illuminating the pallor of his face as his sharpened quill scratched out the endless memoranda that characterized each of his days. He worked for two hours before he would eat breakfast and he managed to churn out fifty volumes of memoranda before the filament of his being burned itself out. In his spare time he composed music of a mathematical and pious nature: a Jubilate, a Sanctus, a Te Deum and a Chorale. He puzzled out chess problems, sketched landscapes, and played melancholy music on the organ. There were those who said that only the organ really knew what was in him.

And still he worked. His was the moving spirit behind the Great Exposition of 1851, whose Crystal Palace, a monstrous edifice of glass, seemed to epitomize the entire Victorian age with its craze for gewgaws and gingerbread and its conservatories full of rubber plants and aspidistras. On the crown estates of the Duchy of Cornwall he built flats and took the progressive but novel step of equipping them with bathrooms. Despite this folly they made money, boosting the annual income of the duchy from sixteen thousand to sixty thousand pounds a year and making possible his son's purchase of the Sandringham estate.

But this estimable Prince, with all his estimable qualities of duty, piety, morality, and learning, never established any sort of rapport with his adopted countrymen. He never understood them any more than he understood their climate, nor they him. They suffered him but never warmed to him. For he was not one of them. He spoke German to his wife by preference and he took Prussia's side on international problems. He was stiff and he was formal and he never walked about in the streets but always rode in a carriage and then with an equerry beside him. He seemed to lecture at people rather than talk to them and it was perhaps true that, as his brother once remarked, "of mankind in general he was contemptuous."

He had worse faults than these in English eyes. He neither gambled nor raced, and he persuaded his wife to make dueling a crime. He preferred chess to cricket and Mendelssohn concertos to foxhunters' horns. He hated wild parties, bawdy stories, and gossip, and he seemed very womanish with his after-dinner piano music and his sketchbook. With his filing-cabinet mind, his professorial mien, his inherent shyness, and his absolute lack of frivolity he seemed as foreign as his accent. And yet he founded a dynasty more English than the Union Jack, made his Queen over in his own image, and laid the cornerstone of the Victorian age's stern moral structure. On his deathbed he performed his last service to the nation by softening an angry note to the United States that could easily have plunged his country into war. Thirty years after he went to his grave he was still, in effect, King of England, for his wife predicated her every decision on the simple question: "What would dearest Albert have done?"

Over his final years there hung a dark smog of melancholy brought on by the bitter awareness that his countrymen did not recognize his worth. His Queen could give him love, but not the intellectual communion which he craved so badly. His heir, Bertie, was, in his eyes, little better than a dunce and only his daughter Vicky he felt understood him. They grew to be close companions, but Victoria remarked that Vicky was really a very plain girl. For she did not care to have anyone monopolize her darling. The children were always secondary to her. "I find no especial pleasure or compensation in the company of the elder children," she wrote. In her husband's absence, she said, they were as *nothing* to her.

Duty consumed Albert and duty killed him. He inspected some buildings at Sandhurst one rainy day and got soaked to the skin. He was already fatigued and this lowered his weakening resistance. Then Bertie got into a scrape at Cambridge involving a woman and Albert felt he had to go up and administer a lecture of moral reproof. Here he suffered the chill that hastened his end. He did not struggle very hard to live. His wife wept beside his bed, watching in terror while his features, so cold and so rigid in life, grew colder and more rigid in death. Then she burst from the room, crying out that he was gone, and her cries continued to echo and re-echo down the long decades of her lonely reign.

With the loss of her husband, all of Victoria's emotional currents were channeled into a vast and morbid preoccupation with the grave. There had been a hint of this special form of hypochondria in her early childhood, for in her youthful journals she had occasionally luxuriated in the details of the deaths of people she hardly knew, setting down lengthy accounts of the funeral with that careful eye she had for minute and accurate observation. She learned to flirt more seriously with grief at the death of her mother, whom she had once snubbed so coldly. On this occasion she had wept almost solidly for two weeks.

But all this was as nothing compared to the intensity of her mourning for Albert. She clung to her grief with such tenacity that it became her friend and constant companion. She cut off her daughters' hair and put the locks in "the dear coffin." Above her bed she hung a picture of Albert's face in death. His rooms were closed off from the rest of the castle and preserved for the remainder of her lifetime just as they had been when he occupied them. His clothing was laid out freshly each day and new water poured each morning into his basin. The glass from which he had taken his final dose of medicine was left undisturbed on his bedside table. His desk and his pictures were left just as they had been in his lifetime.

She had made a monument of Albert's memory. Now plans went on apace for further monuments, mausoleums, memorials, and effigies. His letters, his speeches, his memoranda, his childhood diaries, and his biography— all ten volumes of it laboriously prepared over the years by Sir Theodore Martin and edited of course with constant changes, additions, and interpolations by Victoria herself—all these must be placed before the public so that they might finally know what manner of man he was. Her children were astonished and disturbed by what they felt was a want of reserve in all this, but the Queen was adamant. All must be known; then Albert would be appreciated.

There must be other monuments. All the children and grandchildren—indeed, all succeeding generations of males—must bear the name of Albert. The official court painters should be German, for Albert was German; Prussia must be treated with great sympathy, for a strong

Prussia was Albert's ideal. But the greatest monument of all, as it turned out, was Victoria herself. She became a sort of female Albert. The city-lover now clung to the sheltering bosom of the countryside. The girl who once danced until four now refused to serve refreshments at court receptions for fear they might be thought of as amusements. She came to abhor smoking and the men in her household had to puff their cigars up chimneys so the telltale evidence would not assail her nostrils. She came to abhor drinking and would not allow her male dinner guests to linger more than fifteen minutes over their port before they joined the ladies. (This practice she had begun in Albert's day when she was jealous of his enjoying the company of others without her.) She provided carriages from the royal mews for guests under her roof on the strict condition that they would not use them to go to balls, or the theater or any other place of amusement. She refused a peerage to Sir Alexander Cockburn because, she said, he had been immoral in his private life. She would on no account receive the King of Milan because his conduct was "very disreputable." And she declared that when she went on to the next world she could not of course allow herself to be presented to King David because of "his inexcusable conduct to Uriah."

Her sorrow never quite left her. For years she retired to Windsor, until she became little more than a legend to her subjects who so seldom saw her. Her court was almost perpetually in mourning for various obscure relatives, each of whose deaths was marked with an unswerving fidelity. She did not feel she could attend privy council meetings in person, so she remained hidden behind a door in an anteroom, and when it became necessary to give her assent, a clerk would peer around the door and the melancholy Queen would nod her head and the clerk would say "approved." A year after his death she sent copies of Albert's speeches to his friends inscribed with the phrase "from his broken hearted widow Victoria." Two years after that she was still signing letters to her children "your unhappy mamma" and referring in each one to "your darling papa."

"He was my entire self, my very life and soul, yes, even my conscience if I can describe it thus," she wrote the Empress of Prussia. "My thoughts were his, he guided and protected me, he comforted and encouraged me." Six months later she was still on the same theme: "All I look forward to is future union with Him; my only comfort is in the constant spiritual communion with Him and in the endeavor to fulfill His wishes. To work for Him, to honour His memory more and more, to have memorials raised in His name. Here is my only consolation, or rather the only encouragement that helps me to do what lies in my power! I can do no more!" The capitals are Victoria's and they refer to Albert and not the Deity.

And yet, for all the grotesquerie of her sorrow, it is— as one turns the pages of her journal—impossible not to feel a pang of compassion for the little Queen who had once roamed so gaily over the Highland moors with her consort, stopping incognito at inns, pretending to be a wedding party, picnicking along the river banks, holding her husband's hand, sketching the countryside with him beside her, and noting it all down brightly to the last tiny, irrelevant detail. There is a sentence in her journal a year after his death which for all its melodrama has the cry of a wounded animal about it: "August 21, 1862. . . . The view was so fine, the day so bright, and the heather so beautifully pink—but no pleasure, no joy! all dead!"

35

Her attitude to Bertie, the Prince of Wales, which had never been one of great warmth, was warped by her sorrow. The Queen believed with conviction that Albert had died of worry as a result of Bertie's escapades. "It quite irritates me to see him in the room," she told Lord Clarendon, and for the rest of her days her relations with her son were tinged with a certain contempt. She never would allow him to see secret papers or foreign-office dispatches, and her whole attitude to him continued to be that of an exasperated mother ticking off a small and errant boy. She gave the impression that she could not trust him and as a result he remained untrained in the tasks of kingship. In all this there was a faint whisper of the jealousy that shows in her diary when she wrote: "Everyone says that the difference when *I* appear, and when Bertie and Alix drive, is *not* to be described. Naturally for *them* no one stops or *runs* as they always did, and *do* doubly now for *me.*"

For years she basked in the warm sunlight of her own self-pity. She referred to herself as "the poor, nervous shaken Queen" and talked about her "poor birthday" and her "thorny crown." The Hanoverian tendency toward insanity seems to have bothered her, for she would tap significantly at her head and cry "my reason! my reason!" The opening of parliament she compared to an execution and she said she could not undertake it. She imagined herself continually on the brink of breakdown or death—indeed she longed for death—but this consolation was denied her. In the end she outlived all her ministers. "The Queen alone is enough to kill any man," the long-suffering Gladstone remarked to Lord Rosebery.

For with all her nervousness and misgivings, the five-foot Queen had the stamina of an ox. At fifty-seven she could walk for miles across the moors. Before Albert's death she thought nothing of proroguing parliament when she was well along in pregnancy. In her final years, despite failing eyesight and joints wracked by rheumatism, she would still sit up until one or two in the morning, even while on holiday, to get all her work done. She signed her name sixty thousand times a year, twice as often as the present Queen does. She signed two and three hundred documents at a time, always scorning a stamp which would have made the job simpler but less personal. She wrote all her own letters and of course she wrote them by hand. When she died she left behind her twelve hundred folio volumes of them together with one hundred volumes of her journal. She published sections of her journal (*Leaves from a Journal of a Life in the Highlands*) in two volumes and they became best-sellers.

She took good care of her health, which was always robust. She liked plenty of fresh air and she seldom felt cold, though others around her shivered. She rarely had a fire in her room, a thing her husband had never got used to, for he felt the dampness of the English climate keenly.

Nervous she was, but in moments of crisis she had that same self-control which had been so noticeable in her childhood. Once, in Scotland, the carriage in which she was traveling turned turtle and the Queen was sure that she and her daughter would be killed. But her thoughts were mainly ones of matter-of-fact annoyance : there were still some things she had not settled and wanted to do. And when a demented army officer slashed her face with his cane she sat motionless with the blood streaming down her face until he was taken away.

But though she showed so little emotion, she was for all her life guided by her emotions, and in this respect she could not emulate her dead husband. For she was all woman, subject to the strengths and weaknesses of her sex. Personal sentiment colored her thinking. Her relations with Ireland grew cold when the city of Dublin refused to raise a statue to the Prince Consort. She said she would never forgive the country and she was loath ever again to set foot on its shores. Her own political views had a habit of being colored by the charm of her ministers. With Melbourne, she was a Whig; with Disraeli, a Tory. The latter knew exactly how to handle her. "Everyone likes flattery," he told Matthew Arnold, "and with royalty you should lay it on with a trowel." He called her "the Faery," made her an Empress, and managed to suggest that the Suez Canal was her own personal property. She sent him valentines and books and her picture. "Gladstone treats the Queen like a public department," Disraeli once remarked. "I treat her like a woman."

She had a childlike naïveté about her. When a friend remarked that Cecil Rhodes disliked all women and could be very rude about it, she replied: "Oh, I don't think that can be so, because he was very civil to me when he came here." The Greeks at one period tried to secure her son, Prince Alfred, as their king. "It is a high compliment paid to our child," Victoria wrote, "which the Queen *cannot* but believe is *chiefly* owing to the respect and admiration for our beloved great Prince and to the confidence in the education which his father must have given to his children." But all the Greeks really wanted was the Ionian Islands which Britain held.

It is a tribute to the fiber of her being, then, that this sentimental and lonely little woman, who at times seemed more like a small girl, with her dolls hidden away in trunks and her birthday book that everybody must sign and her "present table" loaded with gifts that delighted her so much, should be held in such awe, nay, in such terror, by those around her. In the first months of her reign she had singlehandedly defeated the doughty Peel when he had tried to choose her women of the bedchamber on political grounds. Years later she was to terrify the iron Bismarck, who entered her presence shaking with agitation and departed it mopping his forehead and remarking: "There was a woman! One could do business with her." She kept her staff in a perpetual state of shivers. When she appeared unexpectedly around a corner at Osborne or Windsor, they would leap into hedges. When she sat down she never looked behind her, for she knew a chair would always be there. And no man sat in her presence.

She sought affection, consideration, and personal comfort, for she had had little enough in her childhood, and Albert was no longer present to tender it to her. Ensconced among the monkey-puzzle trees at Osborne on the Isle of Wight, she waited while her aging ministers suffered the torments of seasickness to come to her with state matters. She was terribly put out when Lady Augusta Bruce, one of her women of the bedchamber, decided to marry and leave her service. She thought it was most unnecessary and wrote that it was "my greatest sorrow and trial since my misfortune." She would brook no argument. When she yielded at last and allowed the installation of electric lights in the palace, Colonel R. E. B. Crompton, who made the installation, tried to argue with her that concealed lighting would be the best. At this the Queen told him he was being impertinent and punched him on the shoulder. She would allow no servant to address her directly. On one occasion when an explosive ember burst from a fireplace and landed on the Queen's skirt, a maid ventured so bold as to point it out to the Queen. For this impudence she received a sharp rebuke. For Victoria believed that those of the blood royal were on a higher plane than the rest of the human species and she felt that she reigned by God's express desire.

She could be indomitable. When Ladysmith was threatened by the Boers she said its capture would be quite impossible and should be prohibited. And she grew indignant when the waves struck roughly at her ship on a trip to Ireland. She called Sir James Reid, the doctor who always attended her on these sea voyages. "Go up at once, Sir James," she said, "and give the Admiral my compliments and tell him this thing must *not* occur again."

Her soldiers were as precious to her as her dolls and she thought of them as her personal property. The Boer War casualties would cause her to break down and cry. She had all the photographs of all the officers who had been killed pasted into albums (for she was fond of albums of all kinds), and wrote each widow and mother a personal letter of condolence. During the Egyptian campaign she sent, in one day, a total of seventeen notes to the ministry of war regarding the army and the troops.

Her character was a confusing blend of contradictions. The woman who cried over her soldiers' deaths did not want to abolish flogging them for their misdeeds. She was strongly against the ill treatment or vivisection of dogs and horses, but she was strongly in favor of whipping human beings. She could see a man lying by the roadside in a state of exhaustion and immediately order that henceforth her carriages should be equipped with a bottle of whiskey so that this tragedy might not occur again. She could defray anonymously the expenses incurred by an official accepting a peerage because she felt he deserved but could not afford the honor. But after his fifty-eight years of service as a member of parliament she could not bring herself to thank the aging Gladstone upon his retirement, for she thought him "an old, wild and incomprehensible man." In all her years of dealing with Gladstone, she never once asked him to sit down, and she succeeded in breaking the heart of this dedicated statesman whose only wish was to serve his nation and his Queen. When he died the best thing she could say of him was that he had many good qualities, though many bad ones. And yet in this there was consistency. She could not bring herself to say more than what she felt to be the truth. Anything else would be hypocrisy and, whatever else Victoria may have been, she was no hypocrite.

Her beliefs were fixed on Albert's death and like her movements, she did not stray from them. Her day was charted to the instant, and her engagements and her migrations were immutably fixed. Her tastes were fixed, too (in music, Mendelssohn; in landscape painting, Landseer; in literature, Marie Corelli), and so were her opinions. She cried out against "this mad, wicked folly of women's rights" and she lumped radicals, republicans, and socialists together with democrats as dangerous revolutionaries. She lived in an era of industrial horror which mired men's souls and racked children's bodies—but she was never aware of this. When somebody told her of conditions which forced seven persons to sleep in one bed she remarked dryly that if she had been one of them she would have chosen to sleep on the floor. For she was a woman not given to imagination. She assessed a portrait by its likeness to the subject and she treated the Impressionists as a joke.

And yet through all her eccentricities there ran a bright

skein of common sense which was her saving grace. Arrogant she most certainly was, selfish, uncomprehending, and insensitive, but she had forgotten more about diplomacy than her ministers knew. It was she who urged that, as the Empire grew, the truest economy would be to be always prepared for attacks or wars somewhere in the world. Her attitude toward India was always one of good sense. She did not at all like the first draft of the document for the reorganization of the Indian Government in 1858, for she thought it far too harsh. "Such a document," she noted, "should breathe feelings of generosity, benevolence and religious tolerance." And in 1891, after an outbreak in the Indian hill state of Manipur, she urged the avoidance of "bloody revenge," pointing out that "our dealings in India should be dictated by straightforwardness, kindness and firmness or we cannot succeed." After the Kaiser sent his memorable telegram to Krueger of the Boers congratulating him on withstanding the raid in the Transvaal, led by Sir Leander Starr Jameson, the administrator of British South Africa, the nation rose in arms and the Prince of Wales urged his mother to give the Kaiser "a good snub." But she replied that cutting remarks were only an irritant and that "calmness and firmness are the most powerful weapons in such cases."

She seemed to be eternal. Her experience went back into the realm of the history books. Henry Campbell-Bannerman, when he was secretary for war, once tried to persuade her to withdraw her opposition to a government measure. "I remember Lord Melbourne using the same arguments many years ago," Victoria retorted, "but it was not true then and it is not true now." Campbell-Bannerman felt like a small boy talking to his grandmother.

As Queen she came to wield more personal power than

any sovereign has dared use since. And this, too, was Albert's legacy. Together they had conspired to help oust the bland Palmerston as foreign secretary in 1851. Now she was influencing the choice of British representatives in foreign countries, writing continual memoranda on everything from details of uniform to naval beards, trying to veto cabinet appointments, getting bills introduced into parliament at her request, changing the words in speeches from the throne, prompting Lord Wolseley in his ambitions to govern the Sudan (against the desires of her ministers), attacking the qualifications of men appointed to high office, and always insisting on seeing everything, reading everything, approving everything until her eyesight dimmed and her fingers ached from holding a pen.

Through the sheer stamina of her existence she won the hearts of her subjects. The wave of republicanism that had swept the country in mid-century ebbed and expired as the Queen lived on. She became the universal mother, the symbol of everything that was great in her era. It was unthinkable that she could die. Cities were named for her, parks and states, a water lily, a railway station, a carriage, and in the end the age itself. The crowned heads of Europe looked upon her as the head of a vast interlocking directorate of kings and princes. She was the only living person of whom the Kaiser stood in awe, for she was always "Grandmamma" to him and he was "little Willy" to her. She sent him finger-wagging notes from time to time and he replied humbly.

In the end she did die and a tremor of stupendous proportions shook her realm. Her death, as the Duke of Argyll put it, was like a great three-masted ship sinking. She kept rallying and sinking . . . rallying and sinking . . . as if in the final moments she was grappling with that same dark figure who had been so long in her thoughts. She breathed her last in the arms of the Kaiser, confident to the end that she was going to meet her Albert. But it was not Albert's or Willy's name that crossed her lips when the moment came. It was to that son who was to follow her on the throne, whom she had for so many years treated as a naughty boy, and who now stood beside her, the tears starting from his eyes, that in this final moment she turned. "Bertie!" she whispered; and she was gone with her era.

THE JERSEY LILY

She came from the island of Jersey in the channel to London in 1877 with an obscure husband and a single black evening gown, and within a week she had taken the city by storm. She had classical features, a translucent skin, straight fair hair, a white throat, and eyes that no one could forget.

She did not tighten her waist in the fashion of the day. "To see her walk," Lady Oxford later wrote, "was as if you saw a beautiful hound set upon its feet." When she entered a drawing-room all conversation ceased.

She was the greatest feminine phenomenon of her age. When her portrait was hung in the Academy they had to rope it all around to protect it from the enthusiastic crowd that constantly surged about it. She herself had to give up walking in the streets because of the mobs who surrounded her.

One day a woman wearing a similar black dress in a public park was mistaken for her. So great was the press of people that she was whisked, suffocating and insensible, to St. George's Hospital.

Men fought over her. She was to be seen of an evening in a polished silk hat and a skin-tight riding-habit mounted upon a spirited chestnut in Rotten Row. One evening she was riding with the Earl of Lonsdale when she noticed a man of her acquaintance at the railing and stopped to speak to him. The Earl was infuriated. There were words. The Earl leaped from his horse and over the railing, sprang upon his rival, and knocked him down. It enhanced the Jersey Lily's reputation.

45

Whistler, Millais, and Burne-Jones all painted her portrait. Oscar Wilde wrote a poem to her and later a play for her called *Lady Windermere's Fan*. Women wore Langtry shoes and Langtry hats, which she unconsciously inspired by twisting a piece of velvet into a toque and sticking a quill through it.

The old Queen had received a present of a beautiful white she-ass from Egypt and she wanted to give it a suitable name. She wrote Lord Cromer and asked him what the Egyptians usually called these animals. Lord Cromer replied that every she-ass in Cairo was called Mrs. Langtry.

The old Queen simply had to see her. She astonished all her court by staying up late at a reception instead of turning the presentations over to a daughter. Then the reason was espied. Mrs. Langtry was at the end of the line.

Mrs. Langtry captured London.

Albert Edward, Prince of Wales, captured Mrs. Langtry.

Chapter 3: *Guelpho the Gay*

"We all feel motherless today," Henry James wrote to a friend in Paris. "We are to have no more of little, mysterious Victoria but instead, fat, vulgar, dreadful Edward."

Fat he most certainly was. In an age of gargantuan appetites, he was king of the trenchermen. He could look up from a monstrous dinner and say, plaintively: "What—only five savories?" He could stride into the Hôtel du Palais in Biarritz, seat himself at a table announcing he wasn't hungry, then trudge steadily through course after course, leaving those about him gasping for breath, to inquire with a wounded air when the fruit came round: "Is there no cheese?" At night it was the custom to leave a cold chicken or a plate of sandwiches beside his bed. They would be devoured by the time morning tea with its accompanying platter of biscuits arrived.

But he was not vulgar and he was not dreadful. His succession came as a breath of tropical air to the chill and arid atmosphere of the Victorian court. In his youth they had called him "Guelpho the Gay," and he was all Hanover.

He came to the throne an old and ailing man in the twilight of his days, subject to deep periods of melancholy, bitterly mortified by the years of rebuffs from that same mother who had whispered his name on her deathbed. From her he had never known the respect which he was to insist on from others. "She does not much like the child," Greville the diarist had written, and when he was still in his frocks she had scooped him up and slippered him while the court watched. For the rest of her life she continued to submit him to various public slipperings of one form or another. When he was thirty-three and setting off to tour India, she lectured him on the details of what he should eat and how he should behave on Sunday, and ended up by admonishing him to be in bed by ten. After Albert's death she developed what Lord Palmerston called "an unconquerable aversion" for him. To the end of her reign clerks in the foreign office were employed altering copies of the dispatches she had signed to keep all delicate or important matters from him, and he, like the lowliest of her subjects, had to depend upon the press for his information. She did not even bother to inform him that she had been made Empress of India, a breach which was heightened by the fact that he was in India at the time. She told Gladstone that she doubted her son's fitness for high estate.

His upbringing was so badly handled that it can stand as the classic textbook on How Not to Rear a Child. Albert and his punctilious mentor Stockmar were terrified that the boy would develop the pleasure-loving instincts of the Hanovers and as a result he was kept in a state of protective custody for all his formative years. At the age of seven he was taken from his governess and from then on he was denied all feminine influence and all companionship with boys of his own age. Albert personally supervised his training (with the gloomy Stockmar at his elbow) and one of the first things he banned was toys, for he felt they contributed nothing to a child's development. Bertie's first tutor was a young man named Birch who did not see eye to eye with these dictums and was therefore quickly and summarily dismissed. Bertie was despondent: he had liked Birch so much that he was in the habit of writing him affectionate little notes and hiding small presents under his pillow. The new tutor, Gibbs, was cut from different and more mediocre cloth. He believed in manners, dress, morality, and duty, and not much else.

The Coburg blueprint for Bertie's education was simple: he was to spend every waking hour of the day improving himself or being improved. Walled off from the outside world in White Lodge, Richmond Park, he was surrounded by a bleak company of aging soldiers and graying clerics who forbade him to speak to anyone outside the immediate household. He must keep a daily diary which was read regularly by Albert and Stockmar. They had a habit of inserting biting comments on its composition and making suggestions for rewriting portions that did not appeal to them. He must write regular letters to all his royal relatives in which were to be inserted proverbs or Biblical quotations. He was not to lounge or slouch or put his hands in his pockets or make jokes or read novels, even those by Sir Walter Scott. He was to study music and art and have poems, plays, and improving books read to him at all hours. In other words, he was to have everything a growing boy should have, except love, freedom, and gaiety. It is not surprising that when he grew older he went off in pursuit of all three.

Bertie's third tutor, Colonel Bruce, a disciplinarian, arranged his day like an army syllabus: Before breakfast he was to memorize classics and prepare exercises; after breakfast he was to take lessons in Italian; between eleven and twelve came the study of the classical languages, and after lunch he was steered through museums and art galleries. He studied French from five to six and music from six to seven. All of this was supposed to produce a model youth, a second Albert. But Bertie was strangely stubborn in his resistance to it all. He was a frail, nervous boy, subject to fits and tantrums that nobody professed to understand. When he was fourteen his parents commented bitterly on his obvious lack of knowledge. When he was sixteen he asked to be allowed to join the army, but Albert wouldn't hear of it and spoke at length of "the temptations and unprofitable companionships of military life." When he was seventeen he received a birthday present of another lengthy memorandum which began with the words "Life is composed of duties. . . ." Bertie read it and burst into tears. Metternich saw him about this time, when Bertie was in Europe, and remarked that he had a pleasing personality but "an embarrassed air and is very sad."

He was packed off to Oxford and then to Cambridge. The memoranda regarding his conduct increased in detail and in length. The terrible vision of George IV still hung like a ghostly ogre over all of Albert's dictums. As Prince of Wales, this Hanoverian rake had gone about in a black velvet coat glittering with pink spangles and shoes with high scarlet heels. Bertie therefore must wear somber clothing. And the former Prince of Wales had been addicted to practical jokes, so Bertie must be cautioned against such frivolities. And he had played cricket. Bertie must not play cricket. It was far too democratic a game anyway, for it tended to place a prince on the same level as the rest of the world and that would not do. There were only two games he could play: croquet and tennis. There were other precepts. Bertie must not smoke. Bertie must wear a special academic gown so that his fellow students would know who he was. Bertie must sit in a special seat at lectures. Bertie must not mix with his fellows. He must live by himself, surrounded as always by the dry old men who were his only boyhood companions.

Occasionally Bertie managed to evade his jailers. Once he escaped from Cambridge, boarded a train, and headed for the freedom and anonymity of London. But his ab-

sence was discovered and his route traced. Albert was
telegraphed and when Bertie got off the train he found a
royal carriage waiting for him with orders to proceed directly to the palace.

Yet through it all Bertie continued to resist every effort
to cast him in the Coburg mold. They sent him to Italy to
improve his mind, but the only thing that intrigued him
was a trio of portraits of beautiful women in an artist's
studio. They sent him to Egypt to see the pyramids, but
he sat on the cold stone, plunged into a copy of *East
Lynne,* and spoke bitingly of "moldering stones" and
"tumbledown old temples." They gave him such a diet of
improving books that he never again picked one up. They
made him concentrate so hard that in later life he was
never able to stay with any subject for more than half an
hour. They made him so lonely that in his after years he
could never bear to be alone again.

He began to look and act suspiciously like a Hanover.
He had the Hanoverian eyes and the Hanoverian tendency toward plumpness. He had the Hanoverian passion.
He had a charm and ease of manner and a complete absence of that shyness which was a Coburg quality. He did
not wear spangles, but in his adult years he affected a
variety of advanced dress that became popular style. And
almost to the end of his days he was addicted to practical
jokes—to the hiding of dried peas in friends' beds and
the thrusting of burning cigars into their outstretched
hands.

For Albert the Good, who had succeeded in making his
Queen and his eldest daughter over in his own image, had
failed utterly with his heir. It was not the only failure
of the Coburg training plan. Albert's daughter, Victoria,
who became Empress of Germany, tried it with her son,

with similarly lamentable results. "The dream of my life was to have a son who should be something of what our beloved Papa was, a real grandson of his in soul and intellect," she wrote her mother. The son turned out to be willful, hot-headed, and mischievous, with an appetite for flattery and an almost unbearable pride. At the age of four he was crawling about sinking his teeth into the bare shanks of his kilted relatives, and later, as Kaiser Wilhelm II, he continued to bite off more than he could chew.

After Albert's death it was thought proper that Bertie should be married. He did not particularly want to wed, but his mother felt that he should become domesticated as soon as possible, before any more regrettable Hanoverian tendencies began to appear. A list of suitable royal young women was drawn up, but Bertie never got past the first one, Alexandra of Denmark, a Princess of great charm, great simplicity, and dazzling beauty. They were married in 1863 and Bertie was on his own at last, but it would not be quite accurate to say that he settled down. Released from his gilded cage, he soared on full wing in pursuit of forbidden pleasures.

His great town home, Marlborough House, and later his country estate of Sandringham, became an axis around which a new society revolved within the larger perimeter of Victorianism—a society that was known at first simply as "the Marlborough House set," but was later to take on the permanent label of Edwardian. It was a loose and lively society dedicated to aristocratic pleasures—to enormous pheasant shoots, yachting parties, twelve-course dinners, and masked balls; to baccarat, billiards, good cigars, fast horses, and dazzling women. Needless to say, it did not play chess. Everything it did was on a prodigious and exotic scale and at its head was the bearded and debonair figure of Albert Edward, whose name was already invading the music halls:

*As I stroll along with big cigar and promenade the
   Strand,
The ladies say "How grand! Oh doesn't he look
   gay?"
And in upper ten society, I hold a mighty sway.
I'm the bosom friend of Albert, Prince of Wales.*

He set the fashion. The Norfolk coat, the Homburg hat, and the dinner jacket all swept into popularity because he was among the first to wear them. Paris overflowed with Prince de Galles cigars, suspenders, wines, and brandies. When Albert Edward began to drink an obscure German wine called "hock" it became popular almost overnight. When he got rheumatism in his shoulder and began to shake hands with one elbow close to the waist everyone started to shake hands that way. He invented a cocktail which everybody drank: rye whisky, crushed ice, square of pineapple, piece of lemon peel, dash of Maraschino, some champagne, and powdered sugar. The boy who had been prohibited from smoking now puffed on Egyptian cigarettes especially put up for him by Laurens. And when he entered White's club and found that smoking was prohibited he simply organized a club of his own, the Marlborough, opposite his own home. Here, if not at his mother's court, he was king.

"His menus for breakfast were almost appalling in their length and solidity," a commentator wrote in 1885. At one breakfast he consumed mutton chops, oysters, and asparagus. His sideboards groaned of a morning with galantines, cold pheasants, grouse, ptarmigans, hams, and tongues which his guests could sample between the hot courses of porridge, omelets, whiting, and deviled kidney. His dinners ran up to twelve courses. Lamb would follow quail and chicken and turkey would follow lamb. There would seldom be less than three desserts (peaches and cream, soufflé, Venetian ice). In the middle of the meal there would be a breathing-space and Albert Edward would eat a *sorbet* to clean his palate and smoke a Russian cigarette. Then he would plunge in again and after the cheese and fruit he would smoke an enormous Corona-Corona.

In the field, portable stoves were trundled out to keep the luncheon dishes hot, and steaming cups of turtle soup were brought round to the hunters. For hunting was the great love of Albert Edward's life, and he came to be one of the better shots in the realm, though his accuracy was marred by a certain restlessness and impatience which characterized his entire life.

The Edwardian hunts were as prodigious as the Edwardian meals. Every year ten thousand partridges were raised from eggs and set loose in the Sandringham coverts. The Prince's larder held six thousand birds and was exceeded in size only by that of his friend, the Baron Hirsch in Hungary. In a single shoot, the Prince and his friends would knock down three thousand birds or six thousand rabbits and in 1885 sixteen thousand birds were killed in one season on the Sandringham estate.

The Prince shot stags in Berzencz, bears in Slavonia, crocodiles on the Nile, flamingos, spoonbills, and storks in Egypt, and an enormous bat in the tomb of Rameses IV. He stuck pigs in India, bagged a tiger in Nepal, and an elephant in Ceylon, and sent them all back, mounted, skinned, and tanned, together with sloths, cheetahs, leopards, and deer, to England. When he went to India in

54

1875 he took along three horses from his stable of sixty that had been especially trained, by a series of visits to the zoo, to take no notice of wild beasts and reptiles. His hunting camps on this occasion were like great cities, populated by twenty-five thousand souls as well as a variety of animals: two hundred and fifty camels, a hundred horses, sixty teams of oxen and more than a hundred elephants.

It was hard to keep pace with this indefatigable Prince who was filling the vacuum in his life with an enormous capacity for luxury. Lord Hardwicke, the inventor of the polished silk hat, tried to keep up with him on his tours of India and Africa and as a result lost a good portion of his fortune. Another long-suffering crony, Christopher Sykes, actually went bankrupt through entertaining the Prince, as his nephew later recounted, and the Prince had to pay his debts for him. For it was a costly matter to satisfy his tastes. The Duke of Sutherland once gave a Nile party in his honor and the liquid provisions placed upon the steamer for this occasion included three thousand bottles of champagne, four thousand bottles of wines and liquors, and twenty thousand bottles of soda water.

The entertainment of the Prince at a country home required an enormous outlay. A complete suite of rooms had to be placed at his disposal, including bathroom, dressing-room, bedroom, and sitting-room, and it was the custom to call in upholsterers and decorators to transform these to the royal taste. Telegraphic arrangements had to be made as well as arrangements to house the rest of the Prince's considerable entourage. He brought his own chef, two valets, and always a footman in scarlet livery who personally served him at the table. The Prince himself chose the guests and the menus and, from the moment he arrived, he, and not the owner of the house, acted the part of host.

In the great rambling mansion of brick and stone that was Sandringham, the tiger skins and boars' heads mingled with the yachting and racing trophies against a background of crimson silk screens, dusty gold hangings, upholstery of blue brocade, and the inevitable conservatory stuffed with palms and wickerwork. Long into the night the guests danced while the Prince pumped a barrel organ, and sometimes there would be sleigh-ride parties with Albert Edward and his friends tobogganing down the great staircase on tea trays.

For Bertie of Wales was seeking the childhood he had never known. He was an avid tricyclist and one of the first royal personages to buy a motor car. He loved to pour a bottle of brandy over the head of his somber companion, Sykes, and roar with laughter as this unfortunate and snobbish man, without changing expression, let the liquid trickle slowly through his beard and remarked quietly: "As it please Your Royal Highness." There were other amusements involving Sykes. He was hurled under a billiard table and prevented from escaping by the Prince and his companions who poked at him with billiard cues. He was dressed in a suit of armor for a fancy-dress ball, then locked out and left to clank about in the public thoroughfares. The Prince watered his bed with a sprinkling-can and soaked his head with a soda siphon and thought it all capital fun. There were other jokes involving animals which the Prince and his great crony, Lord Charles Beresford, indulged in: poultry doped and tied to bedsteads; live donkeys hoisted into private chambers, dressed up, and slipped under the blankets.

In Paris, which became his favorite city, there were

more erotic amusements. "The Prince of Wales is leading a very dissolute life here," Lord Clarendon reported to the Ambassador in Paris, "and so far from concealing it his wish seems to be to earn for himself the reputation of a roué."

His portly figure, perfectly turned out, became a familiar sight along the boulevards and in the Moulin Rouge, where his incognito was respected and the star attractions were Yvette Guilbert and La Goulue, later to be immortalized by Toulouse-Lautrec. From his headquarters in the staid Hotel Bristol he made his way to the Café Anglais and its famous private dining-room, "le Grand Seize," with its crimson wallpaper and golden hearth. He even appeared on the stage in Sardou's *Fédora,* taking the part of a corpse half hidden from the audience while the great Bernhardt wept across his body.

Back in London his little single horse brougham clip-clopped discreetly over the London cobbles as he sought out the kind of womanly affection that had been denied him in his boyhood. He found it in a galaxy of professional beauties of whom Lily Langtry was the crowning ornament.

After Mrs. Langtry there were other conquests, and some defeats. One high-bred beauty refused to be seen with him when he came calling in his little brougham. In vain he urged her not to mind the gossip. People, he said, were always saying things about him and he didn't care a bit. "Perhaps not, sire," came the cool reply, "but so far they say nothing about me and I don't mean that they should."

He needed the company of attractive and brilliant women and, although his wife, Alexandra, filled the first requirement, she did not fill the second. She was an unworldly and almost childlike woman who had been brought up with great simplicity in the little yellow palace of her father, Prince Christian, an impoverished cavalry officer. There, in Copenhagen, Alexandra knitted her own stockings, sewed her own dresses, and always waited on her parents' guests. Occasionally Hans Christian Andersen came and read aloud to her from his fairy tales. Now, in her fairy-tale existence with a Prince of England she never quite lost her simplicity of being. She loved to turn cartwheels, which she accomplished with great elegance, and she was fond of simple jokes. She was delighted when one of Lord de Grey's footmen dropped a tray of valuable china, and it became the custom on subsequent visits for Lady de Grey to have a tray of cheap and brittle china ready that could be smashed by a footman, to Alexandra's great glee. In Marlborough House, in the middle of a wall of bookshelves, she had a secret door installed behind the false façades of books bearing such names as *Look Within, The Hidden Door,* and *Open Sesame.*

Her generosity was as fabulous as it was naïve. She was a target for any charlatan, for she would answer any letter begging for money with an immediate check, regardless of its authenticity. She had a drawer stuffed full of five-pound notes which she dispensed on impulse. She was told once that one such letter was from a professional beggar who made a habit of preying on the gullible. "If that is the case and no one else will help him, I must send the poor man ten pounds," Alexandra replied. She was equally kind to animals and would stop her carriage to upbraid anyone she saw mistreating a horse or a dog. When her own pets died she buried them soberly in the grounds of Marlborough House and erected small tombstones to

58

their memory. She had a way of treating crowds as if they were all personal friends and she would often appeal to the people closest to her carriage to look after their children when the throng pressed close.

She was fabulously unpunctual, a failing that drove her meticulous and fanatically precise husband into towering rages. She even kept him waiting for his coronation until, it is said, he hammered on her door and cried: "Alexandra —if you persist in being troublesome you shall not be crowned at all!" Generally, she was twenty to thirty minutes late for dinner, and in later years, when she lived alone as a widow, her household was in a state of perpetual chaos. Often she would not sit down to lunch until three thirty in the afternoon. Her room and her desk presented a similar spectacle of confusion, littered with books and pictures and miniatures and curios, bottles of scent, gold pencils, souvenirs, and bric-a-brac. For everything she was given, no matter what its intrinsic value or beauty, she formed an attachment, and could not part with it. It was the same with her children. She could not bear to see them grow up and leave her and when they did she could never quite get used to the fact that they were adults. When her eldest son died suddenly of typhoid fever she followed the Victorian tradition of locking up his room and keeping it exactly as it had been in his lifetime.

She was a dazzling beauty, even in later life when she had grown deaf and lame. Her brows never wore a frown nor bore a wrinkle. She had a perfect oval face, sloping shoulders, and an exquisite carriage and she wore jewelry as if she had been born with it on. She was perhaps the most popular woman in the realm and it was because of her Danish background that the Prince could never see eye to eye with his pro-Prussian mother on the question of

Bismarck's annexation of the Danish provinces of Schleswig-Holstein. It helped turn him against the Germans and it was the wedge that broadened the gap between himself and his nephew, the Kaiser.

But Alexandra, beauty though she was, did not fill the vacancy in Albert Edward's life. All his days he pursued the will-o'-the-wisp of feminine companionship. It is possible that he found it at last in Alice Keppel, a woman described by Hugh Walpole as "a sergeant-major with a sense of humor." This genial, handsome woman, who seemed to have no enemies, became his constant companion and whist partner, keeping up a brilliant line of conversation which ran all the way from the politics of the day and the price of stocks to the latest scandal.

The Prince's defections from Victorian proprieties, while they were always discreet, could not but become matters of public knowledge and discussion, and it is ironical that in each of the two public scandals in which he was involved he should have been cast in a minor role.

The first came in 1871 when Sir Charles Mordaunt of Walton Hall, Warwickshire, applied for the dissolution of his marriage with Lady Mordaunt on the grounds that she had committed adultery with Viscount Coles, Sir Frederick Johnstone (both friends of the Prince), and "some person." That person was the Prince himself. He was summonsed as a witness in the court case where a series of perfectly respectable and innocuous letters between himself and the lady in question were produced. This, coupled with the fact that Lady Mordaunt was found insane, served to clear him of any culpability. But his very presence in the witness-box created an unfortunate impression in the public mind and added fuel to the fires ignited by the republican clubs then springing up all over England, attacking the Queen and her family. It was, curiously, another accident that restored the Prince to popularity. He came down with an attack of typhoid fever that almost took his life and the Queen came out of her self-enforced seclusion to stay by his side until the crisis passed. This sentimental spectacle of a mother's vigil and a son's anguish struck the imaginative nation, and when the Prince finally came out of his coma and was reported to have asked for a glass of beer, this completely English action caused universal rejoicing.

A much more notorious scandal was the so-called "Tranby-Croft affair," which took place twenty years later, in 1891. It took its name from the country residence of a wealthy shipowner named Arthur Wilson. It was here, during a game of baccarat at which the Prince was a player, that Sir William Gordon-Cumming was accused of cheating. Sir William signed a paper promising never to play cards again and the others thereupon undertook to keep the incident a secret. But the story leaked out and Sir William brought an action for slander against the principals in the baccarat game. In the subsequent court case, Albert Edward again appeared as a witness and it was his testimony that largely influenced the jury to find in favor of the defendants. The Prince had not observed Sir William cheating, indeed he had hardly been brought into the matter, but he said he believed the testimony of his friends. Sir William's defeat had a Victorian air of melodrama about it: he was ruined forever socially, but his sweetheart, who had stood stoutly at his side throughout the affair, married him at once. The trial was almost as disastrous for the Prince. The general public considered it monstrous that he should gamble at all. The great journalist, W. T. Stead, in his *Review of Reviews* invented what he called a prayer gauge by which he calculated the exact number of fervent "amens" that had been voiced in the churches of the land, on the Prince's behalf, during the half century of his life—all apparently to no avail. The Archbishop himself felt called upon to ask the Prince to renounce gambling. Victoria summoned him for one of those icy, earwigging interviews he dreaded so much. Worse still, the Kaiser, who was forever seeking a chance to be one up on his uncle, sent along a sickeningly moral little note on the evils of gambling that drove its recipient into a white rage. When he visited the Duke of Richmond's home he was met with a polite request: "You can do as you like, sir, when you are under my roof; but no baccarat!" It was at this time that the public prints announced, with raised eyebrows, that he had attended thirty plays, twenty-eight race meetings, and forty social affairs in the space of nine months. And yet there was little else for him to do. He could not take his proper stance beside the throne because the occupant refused to permit it. When he came to the throne, at last, it was almost too late.

He was not a profound man, but he fitted the mood of the age that took his name. He knew everything, as Gladstone remarked, except what was in books. He placed more emphasis on outward and visible signs than he did on inward and spiritual graces. He was a fanatic on matters of dress and appearance, on decorations, ribbons, orders, and medals. He could spot a faulty decoration instantly, no matter how obscure. A motion picture, one of the first, was made of his coronation and during its showing his picture was thrown on the screen, reversed. Instantly his guttural German voice could be heard booming out his only comment: "Decorations on the wrong side!" Once, when a Swedish diplomat wore one of his orders the wrong way, the King, on saying good-night to him, whispered a single phrase in his ear: "Hunt and Roskell, 25 Old Bond Street." The puzzled minister visited the premises of these court jewelers and at once discovered what was wrong.

As Prince, and later as King, he kept two valets working full time and he insisted that those around him observe all the properties of attire. (He himself used up two dozen pairs of gloves a year.) At one affair an admiral's daughter appeared in a dress that showed about an inch of ankle and he administered a husky reproof: "I am afraid you must have made a mistake. This is a dinner, not a tennis party."

He believed in discretion. As Prince he once gave a dinner at Marlborough House in the course of which a member of the company told a bawdy story. In the middle of it two women slipped in to listen. At once the Prince invoked the frigid punishment of sending for the man's carriage. On another occasion a companion made a joke involving the Deity. He replied icily that "that is a name which should never be mentioned in jest." When Leopold II arrived for his coronation with a retinue of mistresses, the King let it be known to the Belgians, through his prime minister, that he would never again receive their monarch.

For he was a believer in etiquette and good form. He loved the race track but never on Sundays. He knew a great many divorcees, but he would not receive them at court. He had a violent temper but he never let it show in public. His rages came like sudden gusts and vanished as easily. He is supposed on his accession to have seen a bust of John Brown, his mother's gillie, and smashed it in a fit of temper, for Brown had once been rude to him. At card games he would often swear violent oaths at his partners on losing a hand, for though he played rather badly, it depressed him to lose. Once, on shipboard, he grew suddenly angry at the design of a special star which was supposed to accompany the Order of the Garter being presented to a non-Christian prince and he threw the whole thing out of a porthole.

But in public he was always pleasant. He was a stickler for etiquette and propriety and for the outward preservation of those Victorian values which seemed to him to be eternal. Women were important to him, but he always regarded them as playthings. It horrified him to think they might get the vote and he was even reluctant to eat venison if he thought the stag had been shot by a huntress. He was punctilious about the dignity of his own position. The story that he sent for Mrs. Langtry's carriage and ended his alliance with her because she dropped a piece of ice down his neck is only a legend, but if she had performed this breach of etiquette that is certainly what he would have done. He never opened any of his vast correspondence; a servant stood behind him with a knife and decorously slit each letter. He never handled used money, only newly minted coins, a situation which sometimes caused embarrassment when he was gambling for high stakes. He was once playing billiards with a friend and asked him to hand him a package of cigarettes. The friend complied, whereupon Edward at once reproved him. "You should have handed me that on a tray," he said.

He had the grand manner and could freeze a man with a glance—but he preferred to be amiable. His courtesy was unfailing. To people who he knew would not accept a tip he would offer his "portrait" on a new gold sovereign. He had the carefully developed ability to walk between two lines of men, shake hands with each one, and pass a word or so with those he knew best without ever breaking his stride. One of his most treasured possessions was a solid-silver inkstand presented to him anonymously when he was Prince of Wales. He had been walking in Piccadilly when he saw an aged and blind beggar trying to cross the road. No one paid any attention until the Prince happened along, took the man's arm and steered him through the traffic. The following day the inkstand arrived engraved with the words: "To the Prince of Wales from one who saw him conduct a blind beggar across the streets. In memory of a kind Christian action."

He was a born diplomat. He could make pretty compliments in three languages and he never had the slightest trouble making graceful little extemporaneous speeches. The quality of being able to look amused and diverted at all times made his first tour of Canada and the United States as a young man an instant success. Half a million people gave him a frenzied ovation in New York and when he left a man in the crowd shouted: "Come back in four years and run for president!" He had no racial or religious or national prejudices and he numbered Jews, Catholics, and Americans among his friends, a radical procedure at that time for a Prince of the blood. These friendships often stood him in good stead. One close crony was Sir Ernest Cassel, the great Jewish financier who had risen up from bank clerk. He loaned the Prince half a million pounds at two and a half percent, then told him how to invest it and as a result brought him to the throne solvent.

The giving of presents was Edward's greatest joy, and the finest present he felt he could give was a medal or decoration. It pleased him to see men wearing as many as possible. He was a considerate host, always placing books and hanging pictures in his guests' rooms chosen carefully to fit their tastes. For he was a man who liked life to slip by smoothly and easily. He wanted everybody to be friends, with him and with each other. When he was attacked by republicans like Sir Charles Dilke and Keir Hardie he went to see them and won their friendship through sheer charm. (He read the radical paper *Reynolds News* every week of his life.) He had a knack of resolving arguments among his companions and it is not surprising that after he ascended the throne he brought this happy facility into world politics. They called him Edward the Peacemaker.

He earned this title through three diplomatic turning points in his reign: the peace with the Boers, the Entente Cordiale with France, and the Triple Entente with France and Russia. His own part in these matters has often been overrated, for it is probable that they would all have come about without his presence; but in each instance he did play his part. It was he who opposed a policy of unconditional surrender, therefore making possible a practical ending to the Boer War. His own cordial treatment of the Czar, which included investing him as an Admiral of the Royal Navy, helped cement relations with Russia. But it was in Paris that he enjoyed his greatest triumph. His state visit to France after his accession to the throne met with a chilly and hostile reception and there were cries of "Vivent les Boers" as he passed by. He got an equally frigid treatment when he went to the theater, but an incident during the entr'acte melted the ice. He purposely left his box to mingle with the hostile crowd, where by chance he espied an actress whom he had seen perform in England. He made his way to her, extended his hand, and in a voice that all could hear he said: "Oh, mademoiselle, I remember how I applauded you in London. You personified there all the grace, all the *esprit* of France!" The story raced through the city and next day all Paris was at his feet.

But if he is to be credited with the *ententes,* he must also be charged with his part in the alienation of Germany, for since the Schleswig-Holstein incident he had developed a strong dislike for the Prussians and a congenital distaste for that arrogant posturer, the Kaiser. Yet even here he did not let his feelings show in public. The Kaiser had been made an Admiral of the Fleet by Victoria and this had caused him to strut so much that the yachting season at Cowes was rendered all but unbearable for his uncle. In June, 1904, the Kaiser, wearing his British admiral's uniform, gave a banquet at Kiel aboard the Imperial yacht *Hohenzollern* at which the King was guest of honor. In the course of a toast to his uncle's health, he made a sword-rattling speech in execrable taste about the greatness of the German fleet, which all present expected would inflame the King to a white incandescence. But instead of a stinging reply he spoke to his nephew almost paternally, with an unruffled air of great condescension. "The interest . . . which for many years I have taken in" (here he paused slightly) *"yachting* . . . exercised too great an attraction to allow me to miss the opportunity of convincing myself how successful Your Majesty has been in inducing so many to become interested in the sport in Germany."

It is ironical that the reign of the Peacemaker should have ended on the eve of war. The dawn of this brief eleven-year period had been marked by the King's own depression at his mother's refusal to let him serve, and the last-minute postponement of his coronation by a sudden attack of appendicitis. ("Will my people ever forgive me?" he cried as he was taken into the operating-room.) The twilight of the reign was marked by even deeper melancholy. Acute and unexpected attacks of gloom had been marring his health for some years and now in 1910 he entered upon a struggle with his prime minister, Asquith, who wanted him to create enough Liberal peers to ensure the passing of the budget by the House of Lords. This increased his morbidity and it is said that he was dissuaded from abdicating only with the greatest difficulty.

He was occasionally superstitious and it was always his habit on midnight of New Year's Eve to order his house cleared of guests and servants just before midnight struck. Then he would be the first to enter the door, leading Alexandra by the hand. But in the opening moment of 1910 he was forestalled in this custom by one of the younger members of the family. "We shall have very bad luck this year," the King said. It was a gloomy prediction but an accurate one. Before the year was out, he was dead.

Like his mother before him he stubbornly resisted death when it came. "I shall work to the end!" he declared as his strength failed. Now his Queen, who had been a philanthropist all her life, performed one crowning act of philanthropy. She sent for his mistress, Alice Keppel, and led her by the hand to the dying man's bedside so that in his last moments he might be happy. But he was already too far gone to recognize either woman and before the day was ended, the Peacemaker was at peace. Halley's comet was in the sky and throughout the realm people were preparing for the end of the world. In a way they were right. Gathering on the horizon were the clouds of a war which would destroy forever the measured, voluptuous, easy world of Guelpho the Gay.

Chapter 4:
The Man in the Frock Coat

The son who now succeeded to the throne was as different from his father as plum pudding from crêpes suzette. In interests and habits they were a hemisphere apart. Edward VII, with his guttural, Teutonic r's, his delight in foreign travel, his propensity for mistresses, and his gourmet's tastes, had been more European than English. He did not even care much for roast beef and when he ate it at all he liked it well done.

The shy little man with the dark spade beard who followed him had hardly more than a spoonful of English blood in his veins, yet he seemed more British than any of his fellow countrymen. He hated travel and he couldn't abide foreigners. German, in which his father had conversed fluently, he referred to as "this rotten language." As for roast beef, its consumption was a weekly rite. A friend, Sir Walter Lawrence, once came to Sunday dinner when the King was Prince of Wales, and refused the proffered dish. "You call yourself an Englishman and do not eat roast beef?" the Prince roared at him. "You cannot be an Englishman!" Lawrence remarked later that the eyes of the children around the table stared at him as if he were a renegade.

The new King grew quite pale when he was told in 1917 that people were calling him pro-German because of his background, and had his surname, Wettin, changed at once to Windsor. (In Germany the Kaiser immediately ordered a performance of *The Merry Wives of Saxe-Coburg und Gotha*.) A cabinet member came upon him about this time angrily flinging a copy of H. G. Wells's *Mr. Britling Sees It Through* onto the floor of his study. "That's mean!" he was shouting. "That's not fair!" He pointed to a statement in which Wells had remarked that

England was stumbling along under "an alien and uninspiring court." "I know I'm uninspiring," the King cried, "but I'm everlastingly damned if I'm alien!" It is probable that had he lived in Albert's day he would have regarded his grandfather with the same suspicion as did the rest of his countrymen.

His attitude to the national anthem was one of veneration. He never grew tired of hearing it played and when, after a long illness, he was re-introduced to it, he referred to it as "that good old thing." He once attended a concert in the Albert Hall and after it was over came around to pay his respects to the artists. They had been expecting a compliment, but instead the King said, rather shortly: "I do wish you musicians would not play *God Save the King* so quickly. You hurry through it as if you wanted to get it over." There was a flabbergasted silence and the King hastily added that this was not a specific, but a general criticism of all orchestras and bands. Then he said: "You see to me it means a great deal. I look upon it almost as a hymn." Sir Landon Ronald, the conductor on this occasion, had been given exactly opposite instructions by Edward VII. "Hurry it up!" the old King had told him.

The new monarch came to the throne in an atmosphere of crisis, suspicion, antagonism, and apathy. The year was 1910 and the hot breath of Asquith was already on his neck, seeking guarantees that new peers would be created if the Lords did not come to heel. The court looked at him askance. They had derisively called him "young square-toes" in his earlier days because of his Spartan simplicity and morality, so different from the character of his voluptuous father. The public did not know him well, for his formative years had been spent away at sea. "He is not loved, he is not feared, the man with the receding beard," ran a popular jingle of the day. He himself was largely unprepared for kingship, for the crown was intended for his elder brother, the Duke of Clarence, who died suddenly of typhoid fever. When he was crowned at last, the crowds were noticeably smaller than they had been at his father's funeral.

Two whispering-campaigns dogged his first months on the throne. One was that he was a drunkard. Actually he had a delicate digestion and had to be careful of both his food and his drink. One day he was out shooting on the moors with a noted physician and, in one of those feats of markmanship for which he was noted, brought down four birds in succession and so quickly that the last one was dead before the first hit the ground. He turned to his companion and with a bitter laugh remarked: "And they say I drink!"

The other whisper was more evil. It was said that in his naval days he had morganatically married the daughter of Admiral Sir Michael Culme-Seymour, who was the commander of the British naval stations at Malta, and that there had been children by this marriage well before his official betrothal. Two years after he came to the throne this scandal was actually published in a republican paper called *The Liberator,* which circulated in England but was printed in France. The King promptly sued the author, Edward Mylius, for libel and would have gone on the witness-stand himself had it been constitutionally possible. He was able to prove that his path and that of Miss Culme-Seymour's had never crossed. Mylius was given a year in jail.

These stories sound preposterous today. For before his twenty-six-year reign was ended, this simple and unpretentious man had brought the monarchy to a new zenith of popularity. His reign, like his era, had none of the glitter of the previous one, but he himself gained the respect of his subjects by cleaving without deviation to the values he had accepted as a child. He was born a Victorian and a Victorian he remained until his dying moment.

His childhood differed radically from that suffered by his father. Edward VII was determined that his sons should not be fed on a diet of improving books as he had been, and as a result the pendulum swung the other way. In his middle age George V was still trying to catch up on his reading and his spelling. (It surprised him to learn, late in life, that George III was the grandson, not the son, of George II.) He was never at home with big words and to the end of his days many English classics, such as Shakespeare, were foreign to him.

As a youth he worshipped his father but held him in such awe that the two were never close. The older man had a habit of loudly chaffing his sons, a trick that served to disconcert them. Years later George V himself fell into the same habit with even more disastrous results. He was much closer to his mother. She was his confidante and they were devoted to each other. Alexandra would have been quite happy spending her entire life with her children. She liked to bathe them and tuck them into bed herself. Long after her heir was grown to manhood he was still "my darling Georgie boy" to her.

He was a high-spirited but obedient boy and he acquired early in life those characteristics which in later years he carried almost to the point of eccentricity. Queen Victoria sent him a watch, "hoping that it will serve to remind you to be punctual in everything and very exact in your duties," and from then on he made a fetish of punctuality and exactitude. His father warned him that "it is very hard work being a prince; you must think all the time that other people matter more than yourself," and he took this dictum to heart. He was asked to put something in the fly-leaf of a family Bible and he wrote: "The secret of life is not to do what one likes, but to try to like what one has to do." And one evening he confided in his mother: "I cried because I couldn't have another cake for tea tonight. Don't tell Daddy. Princes oughtn't to cry." In later years he was often to feel the need for tears but seldom to show them. His mother made him promise to read a passage from the Bible each morning when he arose and for the remainder of his life he never deviated from this pledge. His tutor, an Anglican curate named John Neale Dalton, instilled in him a passion for neatness, order, and duty which remained with him all his days.

His father, with wry memories of his own tortured upbringing, was determined that his sons should be surrounded by companions of their own age and accordingly he packed the two of them off when George was twelve and his elder brother Eddie fourteen, to begin naval training on the old wooden ship *Britannia* at the mouth of the river Dart. The younger boy was among the youngest ever admitted to this "den of two hundred ravening wolves," as a contemporary called it. Here he began a fifteen-year naval career which cast his personality into the disciplined and unpliable mold of habit. The cadets rose at exactly six thirty a.m. for a cold tub, answered roll-call at exactly seven ten, said their prayers at exactly eight fifteen and went on from minute to minute, eating, working, playing, and studying until at exactly eight thirty p.m. they rolled into their hammocks and dropped off to sleep. To his dying day George V remained the naval cadet, rising and eating, working and sleeping to a time-table that never changed.

The three-year training cruise on which the brothers shortly embarked must have caused convulsions in Albert's tomb at Frogmore. There were no aides, no equerries, and only one tutor. There were few lessons and no heavy books. The boys were not addressed as royalty but by their more familiar nicknames of "Sprat" and "Herring." "Well, Georgie," one midshipman said to him once, "how's your royal ma?" "She's A-1," came the reply. Before the three years were up, the future monarch had seen most of his future monarchy and much of the world besides. But he remained the incurable Englishman. When he reached Spain he inscribed in his diary the conviction that "one Englishman will do more in one day than ten natives."

He spent fifteen years in the navy and would undoubtedly have remained in it all his life if his elder brother had not died suddenly in 1892. Reluctantly he prepared to fill his shoes. The aging Queen Victoria summoned him to her presence and in a long interview, which was almost a command, urged him to marry his late brother's fiancée, the Princess May of Teck, a shy, handsome girl with an hourglass figure who was a particular favorite of the old Queen's. The marriage, like the prayers and the meals and the reading of the Bible, took place in 1893 on schedule. But when Victoria tried to get him to change his name to Albert, he politely but firmly refused. ("May" was to become Queen Mary.)

He was now the typically typical Englishman, the retired naval officer living in the country, reading his books on naval strategy, drinking his occasional whisky and soda, eating boiled dinners and suet puddings, playing poker, and teaching his wife billiards, but eschewing all ostentation. His table was bare of vintage wines, and Wagnerian opera left him cold. His favorite tune was *Annie Laurie,* and at his wedding he had had them play *A Bicycle Built for Two.* He did not understand the meaning of the word "highbrow," which for a long time he thought was spelled "eyebrow." He thought Shakespeare's plays were "sad stuff" and is said to have declared that he would rather abdicate than witness for a third time a performance of *Hamlet.* The treasures of the palace he largely ignored. He thought one golden timepiece was far too ostentatious and said it made the palace look like a super-cinema; and when visitors to Windsor Castle would admire the Wedgwood or Chippendale he would turn them over to his wife with the words. "Now, May, you know about this." He was appalled to find that his eldest son proposed to address the British Association for the Advancement of Science. "Good God," he said. "You evidently don't seem to realize, my dear boy, what you have taken on. The last member of the family, indeed the only one, who ever felt equal to the task was your great-grandfather the Prince Consort *and he was an intellectual.* These people asked me to address them. I refused." For he was not an intellectual and, as Bernard Shaw once remarked, somewhat acidly, it was perfectly proper that he should attend a cup final rather than "the greatest event in his reign"—the opening of the Shakespeare Memorial Theatre at Stratford.

His chief pursuits were yachting, philately, and shooting. He followed them all in deadly earnest. He kept a double-barreled shotgun by his bed at all times to practice arms movements and as a result became the best shot in the Kingdom. A photographer once accompanied him on

76

a cruise on his J-class sailing yacht *Britannia* to get some pictures but he met a signal lack of success. It turned out to be a good yachting day and the King put him to work pulling and hauling until the light failed. The *Britannia* took part in five hundred contests and won two hundred first prizes. His stamp collection became the envy of philatelists the world over. In 1904 he got a phone call from his equerry, Sir Arthur Davidson: "Did you happen to see in the papers that some damned fool has given as much as fourteen hundred pounds for one stamp?" Back came the restrained tones: "I was that damn fool." The collection so absorbed him that for thirty years, come war or crisis, he regularly spent three afternoons a week in his stamp room. He gave himself over so completely to these sessions that his aides could only remember two occasions on which he interrupted them to ring for a servant.

His mind and his life were as carefully and tidily ordered as the two hundred and fifty thousand stamps neatly hinged into their three hundred and thirty red Morocco-bound volumes. It would be monotonous to detail his life in sequence, for each year was a carbon copy of the one preceding. His orbit took him from London to Sandringham for pheasant shooting in January, back to London in February, to Windsor at Easter and again in June for Ascot Week, to Cowes in July for yachting, to Balmoral in the fall for grouse and deer, to London in October, to Sandringham for Christmas. It was an unalterable schedule. He would leave for the next fixed point on the exact day, and indeed at the exact hour, on which he had left the year before.

A prayer out of place in the Anglican liturgy, an order worn the wrong way, a clock running slow—all these things disturbed the precise symmetry of his mind. Any deviation from the rulebook sounded as a discord in the harmony of his being. Aboard the royal yacht he came upon a man wearing the Order of St. Michael and St. George the wrong way around. "You're improperly dressed," he barked. "Go back and dress the right way." During his coronation celebrations one of the diplomatic missions asked if it might be received earlier than the appointed time, as one of its members had to go to Manchester. The King was furious. "They shall pass last," he said.

His day was run with an exactitude that sometimes maddened his household. As Prince it had been his habit to join his father at Sandringham exactly on the stroke of three. Now, as King, he would cut off a conversation on the moors in order to be back on the dot for five o'clock tea. He would invariably walk in to breakfast as Big Ben was striking nine and he went to bed at exactly eleven ten p.m. His after-lunch nap took fifteen minutes, no more, no less, and he awoke from it as if a bell had rung inside his head. He lived with seven hundred clocks but he was never once seen to hurry; his day was so ordered that his pace could always be leisurely and unruffled.

The consultation of his barometer, the reading of his Bible, the inscribing of his journal, the phoning of his favorite sister, the consumption of his midmorning bowl of soup: all these rites were as inflexible as a Hopi rain dance. In 1932 a new drydock was to be opened at Southampton and the ceremony was to be effected by the royal yacht sailing in and breaking a ribbon with her bows. Crowds swarmed over the great stands that looked down on the scene, expecting momentarily to see the King appear on deck. Unhappily he could not be found. Finally his officers came upon him wandering below decks crying out: "Where's my soup? I want my soup!"

In his journal, which was more of an index than a diary, and which he kept faithfully for fifty-six years, he rendered a statistical accounting of his life: the times at which he took his meals, the places he had been, the number of birds he had shot, the condition of the weather, the direction of the wind. His mind itself was a neat filing-cabinet in which he kept carefully pigeonholed a multiformity of statistical fact: the exact day on which he and his brother had joined their ship, the exact fluctuations of wheat and barley prices over a ten-year period, the exact date on which he had been tattooed.

When he and his wife went on a tour of the Empire in 1901, he returned with a careful arithmetical account of the journey. They had, he calculated, been absent 231 days, traveled twelve thousand miles by land and forty thousand by sea, made twenty-eight speeches, laid twenty-one foundation stones, received 544 addresses, made fifty-eight replies, inspected sixty-two thousand troops, presented four thousand war medals and shaken exactly 24,855 hands. When the King finally died, they found his life literally tied up in neat packets, his letters and his effects sorted into linen bags of envelope shape, each tied with red tape and clearly marked as to contents.

Is it surprising then that this man, who counted the number of hands he shook, who wore a pedometer when out hunting to clock the number of miles he trudged, who timed his walk to the second from room to room and hallway to doorway—is it surprising that he should have resisted change as if it were an enemy?

George V's reign saw more changes than any quarter-century span in history. It saw the flowering of mass production, female emancipation, and socialism; its emblems included the movie palace, the radio set, the airline hostess, and the traffic cop; it was an age of vitamins and aspirins, insulin and Coca-Cola, boogie-woogie and electric razors. But the man on the throne continued to wear his frock coat and his beard and to cling fiercely and possessively to the ordered ways: to curly brimmed bowlers, cuffless trousers pressed sideways, white gloves with black stitching, tightly rolled umbrellas, boots cobbled in Ballater, shirts tailored in Belfast, cravats drawn gracefully through a golden ring; to ancient jokes from the music halls, hymns sung at his mother's knee, stories by Captain Marryat, music by Gilbert and Sullivan, handwriting with character, and the gray pages of *The Times,* which he read religiously each morning from cover to cover, methodically marking those passages which interested him. He wore the same collar stud and he used the same hairbrushes for fifty years. He played whist but resisted auction bridge. Nobody could get him into an airplane. Everyone who visited him wore a frock coat, and his staff members always had one hanging on a rack in their offices to slip into when the King summoned them. Sometimes, as one of them put it, the halls seemed to be filled "with genial undertakers." And when the King spotted Lord Derby wearing a pair of trousers with cuffs on, he barked that he did not know that the corridors of his palace were muddy. He himself was always perfectly turned out. He had seven hundred suits in airtight boxes and he was never seen without his white carnation.

His sitting-room at Windsor, with its red leather chairs and mahogany cabinets was just as his father had left it. Once a new housemaid cleaned it up and rearranged everything in the wrong order and the King's reaction was the same as it had been when he saw the man wearing the decoration backwards. After that his housekeeper had the room photographed so that everything, every picture on the wall, every book in the bookcase, the position of every piece of furniture, might be preserved in the exact position that it had always been. At Sandringham the carpet in the dining-room slowly wore out, but he would not have it changed, any more than he would have the pictures moved about on the walls. His office at Buckingham Palace endured in the same manner. It could in no sense be described as "modern," a word the King disliked. The color scheme was nondescript. The ends of the room did not match—nor did the chandeliers. The floor was covered by a patchwork of rugs. The desk was crammed with dozens of small objects and lit with a clumsy twin-light reading lamp. But everything on that desk brought back a memory to the man who worked at it. Each object represented a person or an incident locked away in the card indexes of his mind. "Whatever does the King do with all these presents he receives on his official visits?" someone once asked, and a member of the household answered: "He keeps them in his room."

The national anthem he regarded as sacrosanct as his office. Once an acquaintance suggested substituting a new verse written by a Canadian. The King was horrified and enraged: "It's been good enough for me and for all of us for years and I can't understand your extraordinary ideas!" He was a man given to old-fashioned homilies. Mottoes lined the walls of his Sandringham study ("Teach me to be obedient to the rules of the game") and he was much given to ancient expressions such as "keep your hair on."

He did not concur with the symbols of his age. He did not care for psychologists or motorycycles any more than he cared for dinner jackets or low-necked daytime dresses on women. His Queen wore a high collar on her day frocks all her life to please him. And when his daughter Mary came down one day in a medium low collar he ordered her back upstairs again. Painted fingernails, jazz, cocktail parties, bobbed hair, newfangled dances, press reports of divorce cases, and, tragically, his eldest son—all these things disturbed him. He did not know exactly what a nightclub was, and when a picture appeared in the London *Daily Mirror* showing the Prince of Wales dancing in one, the King, who was at Cowes, stormed out of his cabin aboard the royal yacht and cried to his valet: "Look at this. What's David up to now? A nightclub. What *is* a nightclub?" The valet did not know either, so the officer of the watch was consulted and he, in some embarrassment, defined the term.

The social turmoil of his day was past his comprehension. A suffragette once disturbed the tidy ceremonial of a royal garden party by falling down on her knees in front of the King and crying out: "For God's sake, Your Majesty, stop torturing women!" The King remarked afterward, with a certain distraction, that he did not know "what we are all coming to!" A woman's place he always felt was in the background and he once compared the talk at women's committee meetings to "the chattering of geese."

He had a favorite expression when change loomed up. "Well, we never did that in the old days," he would say. He seemed always to be gazing wistfully back to the quiet times when his mother, combing out her long hair, read to him from her Bible, to the days before his German cousin became an enemy and his Russian cousin a corpse, when bombs were not thrown at kings in Spain nor pistols fired at archdukes in Serbia. In the final winter of his life, King Christian of Denmark visited him with the only present he said he wanted: a pot of *öllebröd,* a peasant soup made of beer and bread-crumbs which they used to drink as children. It was heated in the palace kitchens and the two old men sat together silently enjoying it again until tears came into the King's eyes and he closed them and said softly: "We are boys again, Christian. I can see Grandmamma, Mamma, and Auntie Dagmar, and all the old faces of Fredensborg. . . . We are boys again."

For behind the grave, bearded features, behind the loud and often profane seamen's bluster, beat the heart of a sentimentalist who liked sugary music by Romberg and romantic novels by Elinor Glyn. He was his mother's son. He venerated her, and when he was parted from her to join the navy he wept bitterly. She was always "mother-dear" to him and long after he had reached maturity he was still signing his affectionate letters to her "your loving little Georgie." His favorite sister, Victoria, was always "my sweet angel of a sister," the children were invariably "the sweet children," and his wife was always "darling May." He phoned Victoria every morning of his life at exactly the same time. It was an intimate and personal period and sometimes Victoria would pick up the receiver and say: "Hello, you old fool," until one morning the voice of the operator broke in with the words: "I beg your pardon, Your Royal Highness, His Majesty is not yet on the line." When Victoria died, the King was so overcome that he had to cancel his state opening of parliament. In the mornings that followed he would by habit reach for the telephone at nine thirty only to realize that she was

83

gone. After her death he never again appeared in public.

He was a domestic monarch. In the early days of his marriage he would invariably enter his home of York Cottage on the Sandringham estate, and bound up the stairs calling out: "May—where are you, May?" and she would invariably reply: "Here I am, George." He was the first British sovereign to employ the phrase "The Queen and I." When he made his speech to the House of Commons at his Silver Jubilee he asked that the references to his wife be placed at the end of the address, for, he said: "I can't trust myself to speak of the Queen when I think of all I owe her." When he came to this final paragraph during the actual reading of the speech his voice broke and he could hardly continue. He felt the same way toward his children, and when he set off on his 1901 tour he wrote in his diary about "the terrible moment" when the ship pulled away leaving them behind. "We feel terribly sad, leaving all our darlings," he wrote. And, at his coronation, when his eldest son knelt before him to do homage, he again confided to his journal that he almost broke down.

Like the others of his clan, he wore his emotions close to the surface. Tears came easily to his eyes. His was a high-strung personality, though this aspect of his temperament did not appear on his face. He appeared always in repose in public. His speeches were prepared for him in large type because his hand shook so uncontrollably when he read them. His annual Yuletide broadcast, which became his greatest bond with his subjects, effectively spoiled his Christmas Day. He often saw public occasions as "ordeals." The opening of parliament, he wrote, was a "terrible ordeal" and when he called his first council, it was "the most trying ordeal I have ever had to go through."

84

It is a tragedy and a paradox that this sentimental and emotional man, who could never mention his family without a catch in his throat, should never have understood his sons any better than he did the rest of the modern generation. His relations with them were marked by a curious diffidence—as if he were hesitant of revealing the emotions he felt. They waited on him at breakfast, "sirred" him the rest of the day, and, unless they wanted a stiff dressing-down, made an appointment with a page-in-waiting before they went to see him.

On one occasion the King was waiting at Sandringham to greet the Duke of Gloucester, who had been away for some time attending the coronation of Haile Selassie in Ethiopia. The King had prepared a ceremonial luncheon-party to welcome him on his return. As the guests assembled, a phone call came from the Duke announcing that he would be delayed as his car had broken down. The rest went in and sat down to the meal. Presently the Duke arrived. No word of greeting passed between father and son save for the King's brusque challenge: "Why are you late, Harry?"

When his second son, Albert, later George VI, was serving as an officer aboard HMS *Collingwood,* the King arrived to inspect the ship. Later, as was the custom, he received the officers on the quarterdeck. Each was introduced in strict order of seniority and Albert, being a junior, came almost at the end. Father and son had not met for some months but no word was spoken and no sign of recognition passed. The Prince clicked his heels and saluted and the King passed on in silence.

He sometimes tended to think of his boys as miniature editions of himself. He perched his eldest child on his knee when he was two years old, explained various naval matters to him, and tried to get him to look at maps of the sea in a large picture book. When his little terrier barked at the baby and the child cooed instead of crying, he remarked with relief: "Thank goodness he's a sportsman."

He felt that young people were constantly in need of correction and sometimes remarked that "nowadays they don't seem to care what they do or what people say of them." His attitude to his boys when they were children was one of bluff but distant heartiness, as his father's had been to him. The rough chaff and loud questions were not calculated to rest easily upon shy boys brought up in the strict confinement which is the lot of princes of the blood.

In his domestic life he tended to be a martinet. His voice seemed more designed for shouting orders in a gale than for the quiet sitting-rooms of the palace. He punctuated his phrases with "damns" and "bloody's," even in the presence of the Archbishop himself. He hated flattery but he got so used to people agreeing with him that in the end he would brook no argument. He was inclined to be dogmatic in his opinions, which he voiced with more emphasis than necessary, perhaps as compensation for his shaky educational background. Sometimes his wife would prod him a little with her parasol, when he became too loud and too long, and murmur: "Now, George." He roared at his secretaries, his ministers, and his servants, but he never held a grudge. His household and his family stood in awe of him. Once he took a party of five male guests to Royal Lodge on the Windsor grounds for lunch at two p.m. They were treated to new potatoes from the Windsor farms, of which the King was very fond. These were served from a silver tureen, which was then removed and the excess food given to the pigs. Suddenly, to the horror of the kitchen staff, a servant entered with the intelligence that the King had finished his potatoes and was asking for more. The chef immediately rushed down to the pig trough, removed the potatoes, washed them in hot water, popped them back in the tureen and returned them to the royal table.

It is a second paradox in his character that this King, for all his dogma and bluster, should have been in public the great conciliator. A Tory of Tories in his personal habits, it was he who sent for the first Labor prime minister. His reign was a series of crises, each of which he tried to solve in mediatory fashion. "Will there never be an end to them?" he once remarked to the Archbishop as they walked together in the Highlands. He began with the Constitutional Crisis, which blew over when he gave Asquith the guarantees that he had to have. He moved into the Irish Crisis, which he vainly tried to solve by calling a general round-table discussion. There followed the War Crisis, the General Strike Crisis and the Economic Crisis. Sandwiched in between were personal crises: his fall from a horse in Flanders, which left him permanently weakened, and his long illness in 1928, which made an old man of him.

Each of these dangers he met with good sense and an open mind. During the war he opposed reprisals against German prisoners as being beneath the British nation. When harsher treatment was meted out to captured submarine crews during the U-boat scare he had it stopped. Nor did he approve of the sinking of unarmed merchant vessels on sight. In the General Strike of 1926 it was he who urged strongly that no extreme measures be taken which might drive the strikers to desperation and plunge the country into civil war. When the Depression struck in 1931, his was the guiding hand behind the National Government Ramsay MacDonald headed.

But he never forgot his duty as a constitutional monarch—to advise, to warn, and to counsel. "Knowing the difficulties of a limited monarch, I thank heaven I am spared being an absolute one," he told Walter Hines Page, the American Ambassador. And it was this knowledge, seeping slowly into the consciousness of his people, together with the deep feeling that this grave little King in the frock coat stood as a symbol of stability in an unstable age, that earned him an unparalleled popularity when his Jubilee Year came. Already his troops were referring to him kindly as "the old gentleman" and, as they had with his father and his grandmother before him, his subjects now thought of him as a wise and benevolent parent.

On his accession he had seemed to have nothing to commend him as a monarch. Now, as a monarch, he was everything that was commendable. He had never expected to be popular. "Do they really think so much of me?" he asked on his Jubilee Night after the great parade. It moved him to discover that they did. "I'm sure I cannot understand it at all," he said, as his subjects cheered, "for after all I'm a very ordinary sort of fellow." And so he was, with his framed mottoes, his carefully thumbed Bible, his bedroom that smelled of tobacco smoke, his stamp collection, his old-fashioned roll-top desk and his old-fashioned values. But it was these very qualities that caused the cheers.

He was a man who never spared himself in what he felt to be his duty, nor did he spare those about him. During the war he banned alcohol from the palace and kept his household on rations so strict that there was a race to the table at mealtime in case there mightn't be enough to go around. And if a man asked for an extra egg the King looked at him as if he had committed an act of treason. In his dying hours he clung with the same tenacity to his responsibilities. His physician asked if he would like to sign the necessary order setting up a council of state and he replied that he would. But he found his fingers could not grasp the pen, no matter how hard he struggled. After some moments he turned to the councilors grouped around him and, with that old-world courtesy that had always marked his manner, he said: "I am very sorry to keep you waiting for so long." He paused to gather his strength and then added: "You see I cannot concentrate."

All his life he had looked upon himself merely as a man doing his duty, as a naval officer is trained to stand watch, and he stood watch until his final moment when his pale lips formed a single question which might easily sum up his career. "Empire?" he asked. "It is absolutely right, sir," an aide whispered. And thus, with his orderly mind set finally at rest, his life moved peacefully to its close.

Chapter 5:
The Last of the Victorians

As his legacy to the nation, George V left his Queen to live on as a link between the age of Victoria and the age of the new Elizabeth. "Life," she once said, "is made up of loyalties," and this had always been her creed. It had guided her since the days when Gladstone and Victoria decided that she should marry George, Duke of York. The previous year, her first fiancé, the Duke of Clarence, had died five weeks before their wedding day. Now she prepared to become the wife of his younger brother. "Royal Princesses must sacrifice their private feelings for the good of the people," she had said the previous year. "But if the ordinary girl understood the sacrifices, many eyes would be full of pity."

Though she shared many of her new husband's qualities, their interests were widely separate. Her mother, the Duchess of Teck, had been the most popular royal personage of her time, a plump, relaxed, cheerful creature, profligate with money, fabulously unpunctual. Though she would rise at seven she often would not be ready to come downstairs before two thirty in the afternooon. Financial matters never worried her until the family found itself near bankruptcy and had to pack off suddenly for Italy where the living was cheaper. The young Princess, growing up in her mother's bulky shadow, developed a shyness, a frugality, and a sense of time that were to stay with her all her life.

She was always a neat child, her hair never in disarray, her dresses never showing a crease or wrinkle. The physical neatness was accompanied by an extraordinary neatness of mind which molded her character. In the galleries of Florence she discovered Renaissance art and it was here that the thought struck her that although she did not possess any great store of knowledge, the storehouses existed and the knowledge could be harvested by anyone with perseverance and strength of will. Until then, her learning had been so inhibited by Victorian prudery that even the plays of Shakespeare were not allowed her. "I suddenly discovered that I was not educated," she remarked later in much the manner of a criminal confessing to a felony. As a result she set herself a schedule of reading from which she never deviated until her marriage: six hours a day, every day, for more than six years. In this she was assisted by her governess, Madame Bricka, a tall and rather temperamental Alsatian woman of nondescript appearance, great culture, and firm purpose. "Be thorough!" Bricka told her, and the pupil never forgot.

As the reading persevered, the curiosity about the world burned deeper. She confessed to Robert Browning her desire "to know more of everything." She began to meet the great figures of her day, from Millais the painter to Stanley the explorer. She studied music under Tosti, took tea with Sir Henry Irving and Ellen Terry, and played in charades with another great actor, Sir Charles Wyndham.

She began to probe deeper into the world about her, to read the reports of the select commission inquiring into sweated labor, appointed by the House of Lords. The newspaper accounts were not enough; she must get out the blue-books and official reports and go through them all and then go quite white with anger that there was so little a Princess could do about it all. This inquisitive approach to the world at large, this probing into dark corners and tiny crannies remained one of her great characteristics. Even in that tortured week when her eldest son renounced the throne, the insistent proddings of her own curiosity could not be stilled: The Crystal Palace, that symbol of the Victoria age, was burning and she must at all costs view its embers, and view them she did, abdication or no abdication.

Her conscience, once pricked, was not easily quieted. In a bootmaker's shop she flabbergasted the salesmen by asking how much the cobblers were paid for making her footwear. When told it was eight shillings a week, she declared firmly: "I will not buy boots made by sweated labor." She once refused to enter a large department store because she had learned that the employees were underpaid and denied adequate rest and welfare facilities. At the palace she was forever delving into the conditions of court dressmakers and asking questions about the needle trades. All her life the blue-book of the select commission dogged her and it was no coincidence that one of her ladies-in-waiting was also a magistrate.

The first years of her marriage could not have been easy. She had become an intellectual, and a consuming interest in period furniture and antique bric-a-brac was already becoming her ruling passion. Now this Princess, who loved the city with its theaters and art galleries, found herself thrust into a ménage of country squires who seldom looked at a picture or opened a book. She and her husband occupied York Cottage on the Sandringham estate and in this small and unprepossessing Victorian-Gothic home with its tiny, dark, and airless rooms they raised six children. They were not their own masters. They could hardly pick a flower or move a stick of furniture without deferring to Edward VII or Alexandra. After the old King died, the new King continued to live with his expanding family in the little cottage, leaving his mother, whom he never questioned, to stay by herself in sprawling Sandringham with its twenty-four bedrooms. The cottage was so small that the servants had to be boarded out and George V, on being asked where they were put up, said he didn't know but rather imagined they roosted in trees. York Cottage was their country home until 1925, when Alexandra died. She was known universally as the Queen Mother and there are those who consider it significant that when George V's reign came to its end, the new Queen mother refused to assume the title.

George V's tastes were not always his wife's. She disliked the sea and during the regatta at Cowes she would flee the royal yacht for the antique-shops on the Isle of Wight. She did not care to follow the guns and when the grouse were flushed from the coverts of Balmoral she sat alone, sewing in the garden. She stood as much in awe of her husband as everybody else. He was King first, husband second. She stood up when he entered the room and disliked to hear anyone dispute his opinions. But there is no scrap of evidence to indicate that in the forty-four years of their marriage, their union was anything less than happy.

After his death she replaced him as the symbol of everything that is constant in British life, a woman of immense energy, immense curiosity, and immense frugality. "I have never been bored," she once remarked. Day after day, until old age confined her, her stoic figure was to be seen sitting bolt-upright on the jump-seat of her twenty-seven-year-old green Daimler, as much a London fixture as the monuments to her ancestors. Parasol clutched firmly in hand, she moved along the endless treadmill she had created for herself, poking through antique-shops, arriving at cinema or theater, trudging resolutely down hospital corridors and past exhibition stalls and between counters at charity bazaars, probing, examining, and questioning, and inscribing it all carefully in her neat mind for future reference. Each week a museum must be visited; each year the British Industries Fair must be taken in exhaustively. After thirty-five years it was calculated that at this exhibition alone she had clocked a hundred miles, which is more than anyone else had, including the officials themselves. After two hours in a jewel shop with her the clerks were apt to fall back exhausted, but the ageless Queen had long since got her second wind. "I'm tired," a young relative once complained as they plodded through a hospital. "Stuff and nonsense!" the Queen said sharply. "You are a member of the British royal family and we are *never* tired."

And with it all there was the same compelling curiosity to know everything. There must be duplicate instruments in the back seat of the Daimler so that the Queen could tell what the chauffeur was up to. The parasol must be pointed into dark corners in the antique-shops to make sure nothing was being missed. Books to be dedicated to her must be read thoroughly. Official documents must be scanned for errors in spelling. Every letter must be read personally.

She had seen the motion picture *The Wicked Lady* at a special showing, and afterward someone told her that they had removed all the risqué words and scenes in deference to her. Then a lady-in-waiting must go and see the film again and report back to her what she had missed; and finally, this not being sufficient, the Queen herself must sally out and pop into a small theater to see it all over again.

A woman author sent her a copy of a book she was doing about early royalty. It must be read thoroughly and two typing errors that the author had missed must be corrected. A list of Edwardian ladies whom the author described as beautiful must be amended, in one instance by a marginal phrase in the Queen's firm hand: "Lady X was *not* beautiful."

Everything must be seen to personally and thoroughly. If a picture was to be given as a present, then a man must be sent along to hang it and the Queen must come along the next day to see that it was hung properly. Was it true that there was no wedding ring on the hand of the statue of Queen Victoria on the Mall? Then someone must be sent clambering up the statue to find out, and someone must follow him with a chisel and chisel a wedding ring on. These tiny things must always be noticed and attended to, for tiny things are often very important.

Here was a new training center for domestic servants for her to inspect, all very modern and agleam with newly polished cookery-ware and appliances. But in the midst of all this efficiency she noticed a tiny thing: the girls were perspiring as they worked. In the midst of all the electric stoves and electric cookers an electric fan had been omitted. The Queen announced she would send one around the next day, and mind they had it installed at once.

Here was a fine new day-nursery for her to visit and approve, full of gaily painted walls and cut-out fairies and new devices. Down the row of cots she went, probing and examining and looking about her until her eye fell on the unshaded bulbs above the cots. "Naked lights are bad for babies," declared the Queen. Cut-out fairies were fine, but there must be shades for those lamps.

The war came and the Queen, packed off to the country estate of Badminton, attacked its problems with the same dispatch. A pig must personally be raised and watched and fattened and killed for the meat-hungry nation. Endless cups of tea must be served to troops. Endless mufflers and socks and pullovers must be knitted at all hours of the day. The Daimler must never be empty of khaki-clad hitchhikers. Ration books must be carefully adhered to and saccharin must replace sugar. For one must always live by the rules.

But this was not enough. She was poking about the estate one day, peering at trees and sniffing at flowers (she knew all their names and species) when her eye was caught by a tangled mass of underbrush. It was an affront to the neatness of her nature. It reminded her of the ivy which she disliked so much and which was forever blurring the clean classical lines of England's great buildings; she was ruthless with ivy: she snipped at it with sécateurs when she had them handy and jabbed at it with her parasol when she didn't. Now here was something more monstrous than ivy in its lack of discipline. Soon she had recruited a small army of men and children led by herself in old clothes and thick gloves, to attack this enemy, sawing and hacking and uprooting for three hours every day except Sunday—Princes and Dukes and villagers and even King George VI, himself, who happened along on an official visit and was promptly conscripted. Before her stay at Badminton was ended, order had been restored, the tangle had vanished, and a hundred and eleven acres of scrubland had been cleared and turned into tidy cultivated acreage, neatly furrowed, planted, and put to a satisfying purpose, and marked in blue on the special map of the area which she filed away with her other trophies.

All her life she brought order out of chaos. Through palace and castle, cellar and attic, her stiff regal figure plied ceaselessly, cataloguing and arranging, sorting and sifting the immense legacy of royal knick-knackery, from rotting African elephants' tusks to Ch'ien Lung vases, left behind in utter disorder by Queen Victoria, who never threw anything away but never knew where anything was. Like the underbrush and the ivy, the dowager Queen snipped away at it for most of her life.

Sloppiness and waste she could not abide. Pieces of knotted string were carefully and personally unraveled and rewound into tidy bundles to be placed with similar bundles in a specially labeled drawer. Crumpled pieces of tissue paper and creased sheets of wrapping paper were uncreased and refolded and stored away for future use. Half sheets of notepaper were preserved and used envelopes were used again. Christmas cards were pasted neatly into scrapbooks and presented to hospitals. A sample card of each year had been preserved in another scrapbook since she was five years old and this lively pictorial history of her era was presented to the British Museum. Every photograph, public or private, ever taken of her was preserved in a scarlet-and-gold album with all the details inscribed beneath in the neat royal hand.

The frugality she learned as a child was never forgotten. As a Princess she always asked her dressmaker to submit estimates before giving her an order. As a Queen she went carefully through each account before it was passed for payment. London is dotted with antique-dealers who have been the victims of her bargaining sense. All her life she was price-conscious and she insisted that the prices of goods she bought be marked clearly enough so she could read them through her lorgnette. She could not abide an unnecessary electric light glowing in her home. Sometimes, according to her habit, when asked to dinner, she sent a bottle or so of her favorite wine ahead to be served to her. But if there was any left, she frugally brought it back again. It was not surprising that by saving and investment she became the wealthiest member of the British royal family.

Time must never be wasted. The one-course midday meal (roast beef or hard-boiled eggs) proceeded so swiftly at her polished mahogany dining-table that her aides were sometimes known to wolf pre-luncheon snacks in their rooms for fear of being unable to keep up. Every moment must be put to its maximum use. On her settee she worked furiously at *gros-point* embroidery while a lady-in-waiting read to her from books of biography or Georgian diaries. In the back seat of the Daimler she took a firm grip on the window strap while the lady-in-waiting continued reading from the daily newspapers.

Tardiness was waste, and so was hurry: Christmas presents must be chosen well in advance, early in November. Sloppiness was waste: Letters must all be answered the same day, no matter how many there might be, and the sentences must all be grammatically correct. Laziness was waste: One rose promptly at seven fifteen a.m. One simply did not loll. One climbed to the top of the Memorial at Hawkesbury and wrote triumphantly under its photograph: "One hundred and forty-four steps: not bad at seventy-six!" Scntimentality was waste: It was not enough to keep piles of crumpled five-pound notes stuffed away in drawers for casual beggars. One must be practical. One must stand behind stalls at charity bazaars and one must trek ceaselessly through hospitals, checking the walls for whitewash, the windows for proper curtains, and the lamps for proper shades. And one must always return to make sure it had all been done properly.

98

Forgetfulness was waste, and the memory must always be clear and sharp. In Tasmania, during her tour of the world, a familiar face appeared out of the blur of the crowd. She identified it instantly, plucking it from the reference files in her mind. It was the curate of East Sheen where she had worshipped as a child. She visited the New Theatre and there she met Sir Bronson Albery and produced a gold pencil which she handed him. "I should like to return this to you," she said. When Sir Bronson looked puzzled she jogged his memory. It had been his mother's, and fifty-eight years before his mother had given it to her in Switzerland.

When her husband fell ill and Lord Dawson of Penn told her that his bedroom window needed to be covered with a special netting to keep out the London soot, she beckoned to Lord Dawson and he followed her down endless corridors and up long flights of stairs to a storeroom which she unlocked. There on a high shelf was a wrapped parcel containing a bundle of net curtains of the exact type Lord Dawson had in mind. Years before she had found it in one of the royal homes and brought it here and stored it away in this room, and in her mind, for future reference.

It often came as a surprise to strangers to learn that this indomitable Queen was a woman of great shyness. As a child she was overshadowed by her brilliant mother and was so retiring that she would hide her face in the older woman's petticoats when a newcomer approached, and burst into tears on meeting a friend. As a young Princess she found herself tongue-tied and unable to make small talk. She seldom made public speeches and when she did, a faint glow which was recognizable as a blush crossed her cheeks. Even in the ninth decade of her life there was always a slight, self-conscious stiffening of her figure when she met a stranger.

The temperament within was an exuberant one. It was a temperament that demanded bright colors, good wines, cocktails, and lively theater. In her younger days she made a practice of mimicry. When she was eighty and they asked her what she would like as a birthday present she replied: "Oh, a state ball." When she was Queen Consort, she and her husband used to entertain young guards officers at afternoon sherry parties. But when the King was absent from these affairs she replaced the wine with stronger drink. It was a house joke among West End theater people that when Queen Mary attended a play it was sure to be risqué. Her grandmother, the Countess Claudine Rhedey, was a Hungarian who came from a passionate line, and Queen Mary herself, talking about her almost physical need for color and her deep dislike of black, more than once remarked that "it must be my Hungarian blood." But the vitality, like the shyness, was locked away behind the impassive features veiling her emotions from the world.

For the emotions must be husbanded as carefully as the net curtains and the pieces of knotted string. A fiancé died of typhoid fever, a young Prince died in childhood, a husband died, a son faltered, two more sons passed on. But always the face the public saw remained unchanged, the lips pursed, the eyes clear, the head high, the carriage erect. The King might be dead, but that was no excuse for the Princess Royal to burst in with her hair askew. She must make sure to do it properly before she went in to see the new Queen.

Nothing ruffled her. In 1939, when she was just turning seventy-two, her Daimler struck a truck and overturned.

The entire left side of the car was crushed and they had to get a ladder before she could come out. Black-and-blue from head to foot and with one eye injured, she still climbed from the wreckage and made her way down the ladder as if it were a red carpet. "I am going to have a cup of tea and that is all I want," she said.

Once, on an inspection tour of Windsor Castle one hot evening, she opened a door and came upon a guards officer resting stark naked upon his bed. Her poise never left her. Some weeks later at a reception the same man was presented to her. "Ah," said the Queen, "I believe we have met before."

Behind the Wren façade of Marlborough House, the Victorian age breathed faintly. Her forty-seven liveried servants glided silently over the crimson pile carpets as servants had in an earlier era. Her aging figure, straight as a warning finger, invariably dressed for dinner, slid softly past the silken walls, the cut-crystal chandeliers, the Adam fireplace, Flemish tapestries, and Laguerre fresco. Here she lived in the style of the past among the relics of the past, each one collected personally and with shrewdness and discrimination, and each arranged in harmony and good order—the gold work-boxes by Fabergé, the miniature Regency furniture, the Louis XIV fans, the Battersea enamelwork, the Chinese jade, the Georgian silver, and the five thousand books, all properly bound and carefully indexed and carded so that any one of them might be produced at an instant's notice.

Everything was as it always had been: the narrow, pointed shoes which never changed for forty years, the toque-like hats, the voluminous, lacy dresses, the many-buttoned coats, the inevitable parasol, the hair piled high above the brow in a regal coiffure. Tea at five was as much of a ritual as the daily diary. Neither was ever put off. The telephone was never used, for "that instrument was not meant for royalty." The typewriter was never used. It was cold and impersonal, and letters were to be inscribed by hand. The radio was admitted, for it brought the evening ceremony of the nine o'clock news. There was never any running water in her suite. Maids brought it up each morning in cans and poured it gently into a silver basin, just as they always had. Modern art, modern music, modern poetry were all as taboo as perfume and nail polish. Gertrude Stein and James Joyce were not read, for sentences, like everything else, had to be orderly, with a verb to each. Children, including princesses, must curtsey whenever they met her, and food must never be touched by hand. Muffins and thin pieces of toast were speared on a delicate silver fork, as they were in the days of elegance and grace, when the world was in harmony and everything, like the books on the shelves, was in its proper place.

Change and decay marked her years and she watched while the human beings who wore the crown failed, faltered, and passed on. But she herself remained for eighty-six years a symbol of the royal idea in Britain: that come what may, the crown abides. She saw Victoria die and it was her great ambition to see the new Queen, her granddaughter, crowned. "Keep me alive for Lilibet's coronation," she told her doctors, and to her final moments she struggled with death as she had struggled with the underbrush on the estate of Badminton. On the very night before she died she rose up from her bed and staggered onto the floor, where her nurses found her. But in case the struggle might be unequal, as it was, she performed that final act which tidied up the consequences of her death.

She asked that the coronation, like the crown which she upheld for all her days, go on without a falter. And thus, with everything in its proper place, Mary Augusta Louisa Olga Pauline Claudine Agnes, the dowager Queen of England, came to her graceful end.

MRS. SIMPSON

Bessie Wallis Warfield was born on June 19, 1896 at Blue Ridge Summit, Pennsylvania, of poor but not necessarily humble parents.

Her father, Teackle Wallis Warfield, who died before she was born, came from a family that had for more than three centuries been pillars of Maryland society. Her mother, who married twice more, was a Montague of Virginia. An ancestor, as widely published genealogical tables were one day to show, was Sir Pagan de Warfield. Her favorite uncle, Solomon Davies Warfield, was a railroad president. Her favorite aunt was Mrs. N. Buchanan Merryman, who brought her up, and occasionally took in boarders to make ends meet. She was known as "Aunt Bessie." Her niece was known as "Wallis."

Bessie Wallis Warfield went to Oldsfield School for Girls in Baltimore. She had violet eyes, a slender figure, a winsome smile, and an extraordinary tidiness of person. She was occasionally punished for writing notes to boys, a guilt that was confessed to by all of her fifty-six classmates save two. In the evenings, she often managed to slip away to keep an appointment with a romantic and dashing young cavalry officer who went out of her life when he was shipped to Mexico to fight Pancho Villa.

On December 17, 1914, under Aunt Bessie's ægis, Wallis Warfield made her debut at the Bachelor's Cotillion in Baltimore. Two years later she married Lieutenant Earl Winfield Spencer, USN. He took her to the Far East, where she learned something of the art of hostess-ship and conversation. She could discuss politics, marine engines, and the sailing time from Hong Kong to Bombay.

In 1927 they were back in the U. S. A., and at a ball in
Coronado, California, they saw for the first time Edward,
Prince of Wales. He made little impression on Mrs. Spencer, and Mrs. Spencer made even less impression on him.
Shortly after this, Lieutenant Spencer went off to sea and
Mrs. Spencer went to Washington. Her husband was a
Navy flyer but she herself did not care for airplanes. "I
must be very old-fashioned," she once remarked. "It's not
the fear of falling or cracking up or anything like that;
it's merely the sense of being contained—of not being free
and able to move."

In Washington, through divorce, Mrs. Spencer became
free and able to move again. She was a popular belle,
never lacking for suitors, able to get dates at all hours including three o'clock in the afternoon. She always managed to look as if she were about to model the latest cre-
ation from *Vogue* and she never had a hair out of place
or a button awry. None of her closest male friends even
including her former husband, ever said anything about
her that was not in her praise. Years later when he was
interviewed by newspapermen he eulogized her, and then
added that "she has one of the strongest characters I have
ever known any person to possess."

Uncle Sol died and left her fifteen thousand dollars. She
took it and went to England, where she married Ernest
Aldrich Simpson, whom she had met in Manhattan. He
had a British father, an American mother, a Harvard
education, a Coldstream Guards training, a ship-broker-
age business, and a passion for collecting old books. He
was tall, mustached, and reserved. His new wife described

him, in a letter to a friend, as "not very sensational," but added that "happiness is worth more than anything else."

Soon the Simpsons began to move in the tight, lively circle known as "the international set" one of whose ornaments was Thelma, Lady Furness, sister of Gloria Morgan Vanderbilt, and good friend of Edward, Prince of Wales. Mrs. Simpson was a popular member of the set. She spoke with a deep, masculine voice, had a good memory for anecdotes and wisecracks, mixed cocktails expertly but preferred whisky and soda, cooked exquisite meals but ate sparingly, knew something about flower arrangements, enjoyed brilliant conversation, Turkish cigarettes, good wine, and the company of elder statesmen, and could work jig-saw puzzles twice as fast as anybody else. She argued like a man and was once heard to remark that, in her opinion, all women were bitches.

She was also known to be a good and economical house-keeper. In 1931 her friend Lady Furness persuaded her to allow herself to be presented at court. "Very well, I'll do it," said Mrs. Simpson, adding to her reputation for wisecracks, "if it doesn't cost anything."

It was about this time that she again met Edward, Prince of Wales. This time they made an impression on each other. "You will see that there will be trouble out of this," Mrs. Simpson told a friend. "Everybody will turn against me. I shall become poor and spend the last days of my life among the spinsters of Baltimore."

As it turned out, she was only half right.

Chapter 6: *The Rebel*

In 1937, on the centenary of Victoria's accession to the throne, a British newspaper published a photograph of the old Queen in her bonnet, seated at a table in the garden of Osborne with her family grouped around her. The important figures in the photograph were identified with arrows and numbers, but in the foreground, leaning against the voluminous skirts of a female relative, was a little boy in a white sailor suit who was not deemed worthy of identification. For this was the figure that everyone was trying to forget: Edward Albert Christian George Andrew Patrick David Windsor, who came to the throne one January and left it that December, who had been prince, monarch, and duke all in twelve months, and whose memory to this day still conjures up a confusing dual picture in the minds of his former subjects.

The first picture is that of a smiling Prince Charming, ambassador to the world, salesman of Empire, waving gaily to the cheering crowds. The other shows a diminutive, worried-looking Duke, biding his days in New York and Paris, and only occasionally paying lonely calls to the country of his birth. The fact that the two figures are the same man, and that for one tragic, historical moment he was King, only heightens the confusion.

Edward VIII was the only monarch ever to quit the British throne voluntarily and, in the eyes of his people, he would be King today had it not been for the romantic accident that forced his abdication. But was it an accident? Future historians will almost certainly ask one queston: if this particular accident hadn't occurred mightn't there have been others? Could this man, whose whole character, personality, and career suggest that he ran counter to the accepted pathways of monarchy, have remained long on the throne?

In contemporary Britain this is an academic question, for Englishmen do not care to recall the disturbing memory of the man they once revered. Around that memory a hedgerow of taboo has thickened. The BBC refused to allow the manufacture or sale of recordings of his abdication speech. When he made a national radio address in the United States in 1939, neither the BBC nor the Canadian Broadcasting Corporation carried it. In family circles his name, and that of the svelte little woman whom the world still thinks of as "Mrs. Simpson," go unmentioned. And yet his slight form still casts its thin shadow across the palace, and future monarchs cannot help but be haunted by the memory of the man who gave up the throne for love.

His reign lasted only three hundred and twenty-five troubled days, but the seeds of that trouble were planted in his childhood and germinated in his youth. He was born to duty in a Victorian household where little boys in sailor suits were to be seen and not heard and must never interrupt their betters, even to warn Grandfather that he was about to consume a juicy green caterpillar with his lettuce. Throughout his boyhood days he saw few other boys of his own age and was almost never alone with his parents. There were always footmen in livery, courtiers in black, aides, secretaries, ladies-in-waiting, nannies, gentlemen ushers, pages, equerries, and all the human paraphernalia with which the great palace is peopled. What he himself in his memoirs has called "the relentless formality of their lives" stood as a barrier between the two generations. There were times when he longed to be informal. He told his father he wanted to be an engine driver when he grew up and when the astonished Duke (he was not yet King) asked him why, he replied: "Because they get so lovely

108

and dirty." He had more affinity for his grandfather than his father. There was a sense of gaiety between them and he would run to the bearded old monarch with open arms whenever he appeared.

A Prince of Wales can never choose his vocation. It is settled upon him at birth. The knowledge that he would attain the throne as surely as the trees would bud, bred in his soul a confusing dichotomy. He knew he would be King and it pleased him; but it also pleased him to try to be just like anybody else. He could be one or the other. He could never be both. But this truth did not come home to him until a certain dark week in December 1936.

In his boyhood he was occasionally disturbed by the idea. He and his brother Bertie were once turning the leaves of a picture album when they came upon his photograph with the inscription beneath it: "Our Future King." Bertie pointed to it, but David pushed his finger away and swiftly turned the page in embarrassment. When he came to be invested in the purple surcoat, the white knee-breeches, and white stockings of the Prince of Wales, the whole idea made him blush inwardly and when he was given his first suit of dress clothes he was quite unhappy. Yet he was proud enough of his position at other times. "You wait until I'm King. I'll chop your head off," he once shouted at Bertie during a childhood tussle. Walking with his grandfather, he was highly indignant because the guard, having returned the old King's salute, didn't return his. And he liked to get into the carriage first, so that he and not his brother would have the seat of honor.

Later in life the confusion persisted. Returning on a visit to Oxford, where he had studied, he entered the junior common room at Magdalen College and asked everybody to sit down, for, he said, he was a Magdalen man and didn't wish to be treated ceremoniously, but as an ordinary member of the college. On his next visit no one stood up, whereupon he tartly asked if that was any way to treat the heir to the throne. It is hard to say who was more confused by this, the Prince or the Oxonians.

In one compartment of his mind he wanted desperately to be one of the boys. He rather enjoyed playing Crown and Anchor with the Tommies in the trenches and letting them slap him on the back and call him "Teddy." When his family protested, comparing him with Lord Lascelles who married his sister Mary, he made his famous remark that "Lascelles gets royaller and royaller and I get commoner and commoner." But in another compartment he knew that he was royal. Once when he was attending a private stage show in New York a magician asking for an assistant called out: "I want young David Windsor." The ancient regality asserted itself and he stalked from the room.

Throughout his boyhood he was constantly being reminded in various subtle ways that he was different. Just as he was beginning to enjoy his naval training at Dartmouth, he was packed off to Oxford, in 1912, for an heir to the throne must have a rounded education. (His brother Bertie remained behind and went off on a cruise with the rest of his classmates.) It was the beginning of a career that has been notable for its restlessness. At both Dartmouth and Oxford, the fact of his apartness was brought home to him in an annoying fashion. At Dartmouth, where he was nicknamed Sardine, he was periodically beaten up as a reminder that he was the same as everybody else. At Oxford, where he was called Pragger Wagger, he was ignored by his classmates so pointedly that he found himself almost without friends. "It was the very devil as a kid," he recalled some years later.

The war struck while he was at Oxford and it changed his life as it changed the lives of most of his generation. To him it was a bitter-sweet experience, for though it brought home to him the frustrations of his position it also allowed him to mingle with the world on terms approaching the equality he longed for.

He made his famous appeal to Kitchener to be allowed to take his chances in battle and Kitchener told him bluntly that princes could not fight in the lines for, though it would not particularly hurt to have one killed, it would be unthinkable to have one captured. He got to France, in the end, where he was watched and guarded almost as carefully as he had been at home until, with tears in his eyes he cried out: "I can't stand it! I can't stand it! They won't let me take my chance!" Then, as if to cap the insult he was awarded the Croix de Guerre and Legion of Honor, which his father insisted he wear and which he tried to resist, for he felt that he hadn't earned them. Osbert Sitwell saw him at this period as "a very slight young figure . . . with his extreme charm, his melancholy smile and angry eyes." Fritz Ponsonby, that polished and observant courtier who came over to France with George V, saw him too—a young man, silent and nervous before his father, speaking only when spoken to, weighing each word carefully before it was uttered, and exhibiting a marked dislike for being kissed on both cheeks in the French manner.

One day he came upon a senior subaltern grousing because he had been in charge of fatigue duty for three days running. "I seem to spend all my life in supervising," the officer said. "You're damn lucky," the Prince told him. "I've spent all my life in being supervised."

But all the same the war matured him. "In those four years I mixed with men," he said in one of his best-known speeches. "In those four years I found my manhood." His car was struck by a shell just after he left it, and it brought home to him the strangely comforting realization that in the face of death, at least, princes and commoners are on an equal footing. As the war ground slowly on he watched the Victorian age crumble before his eyes. The gap between himself and his parents widened. One night, in dinner jacket, he was about to slip out of the palace when he encountered his father in his dressing-gown, worried by the sounds of anti-aircraft fire outside, the bombs from the zeppelins, and the searchlights in the sky. "Where are you going, David?" the King asked. "To a dance, sir," the Prince replied. The King was thunderstruck. "To *dance?*" he asked. "You are going to dance while my people are being killed here in London?" The Prince apologized and said he had not thought of his outing in that light, and the two of them, the nineteenth-century King and the twentieth-century Prince, sat together in silence for the rest of the evening.

"I think my parents are the most old-fashioned couple in the world," the Prince remarked soberly one day, but he himself was anything but old-fashioned. When the war ended he became the symbol of everything that was dashing in the new decade and the memory of that smiling face and slight, restless figure staring out from a hundred front pages still conjures up nostalgic visions of the tinseled era he epitomized. He seemed to be everywhere, driving his golf ball in the shadow of the Great Pyramid, scoring a hole-in-one in Brazil, riding a bucking bronco at a rodeo in Saskatoon, dancing with a drugstore girl during an official ball in Panama, shooting elephants in Africa and tigers in India, beating the drums in a dance band on Long Island, dancing and smiling his way around the world and down the corridors of the decade.

His father looked upon these gyrations with growing dismay. He was a man whose whole approach to public ceremony was summed up in a single sentence. An aide suggested once that perhaps he might look more cheerful in the presence of large crowds. "We naval men never smile when on duty," the King replied abruptly. The idea of young David, running after a crippled soldier's hat when it blew off in a Toronto windstorm, skipping dances with his official hostesses in favor of younger, prettier, but usually less aristocratic girls, and learning the Charleston and Black Bottom in America, did not fit in with his own theories on how princes should behave.

The King's grave, disapproving face can be seen staring out between the lines of a letter he wrote the Duke of York when he married Elizabeth Bowes-Lyon in 1923: "You have been so sensible and easy to work with and you have always been with me to listen to any advice and to agree with my opinions about people and things and I feel we have always got on very well together." And then the bitter afterthought: "Very different to dear David."

For David *was* different. In a family fanatical about punctuality, he was invariably late. In a family obsessed by the minutiæ of dress and deportment, he was maddeningly casual. When George V, in his frock coat, suggested that his son curb his extremes of dress, the son turned up in the voluminous plus fours that became his trade mark. He seemed, at times, to be deliberately baiting his father. "My father doesn't *like* me," he would say to his friends in his more confidential moments, and sometimes he would add: "Not at all sure I particularly like him."

The steady groove of habit into which his father's life slipped so easily did not fit his own highly strung being. The continual tours that were planned for him as the unofficial ambassador of his country (and, it must be added, to try to keep him out of mischief) contributed to his restlessness. Queen Mary once remarked that if they kept up he would lose all his power of settling down. He had inherited his full share of the family nervousness. In public he was constantly fingering his tie, stroking his hair, toying with his speech notes, shifting his position in his seat, and biting his underlip. In private he had a habit of squirming around in armchairs and tossing one leg over the side. His very relaxations had a restlessness about them. He could never concentrate on a book and he found cricket and fishing too slow. He preferred fast speedboats, polo, and steeplechasing. He liked to tap dance, play the bagpipes, and strum on the ukulele.

And yet, mixed with all this there was a domestic streak. He was an expert with a needle and once made a dozen chair covers in *petit-point* for Royal Lodge. He was fond of children and liked to visit his brother the Duke of York and play snap with Margaret and Elizabeth. When he got his own country home of Fort Belvedere he became an impassioned gardener, spending his weekends with a trowel among the rhododendron bushes that lined the driveway. Sometimes it almost seemed as if his Coburg and Hanover bloodstreams were flowing in parallel channels.

As he grew older, the constrictions of the royal task became more inhibiting. "There is no use being Prince of Wales some day unless I can do what I like," he had said as a child. But he could not do what he liked, and the realization of it produced some wistful comments. He was asked once what he would wish for if he could have anything he desired and he replied: "To be let alone, if only for an hour." Someone once made a reference to his wealth whereupon he replied: "Money? I'd give it all away, if I could, for a little freedom. How would you like to be stared at from morning till night, to be followed about, to be guarded, to have everything you do made public property?" As a boy he had said that his first action as King would be to remove the bearing reins from horses, for he thought them cruel. Now he felt the bearing reins on himself.

He seemed to be trying to prove that he could do something on his own, something that had nothing to do with his lineage or his inheritance. He learned to fly a plane, but his father refused to let him solo. He soloed anyway, in secret. It was noticed that the horses he rode were seventeen and a half hands high, too big for his small frame, and that sometimes, on official occasions, he would throw aside the speech that had been written for him and make an impromptu one of his own. He seemed to be trying to show that, though he was a Prince, there were things he could do as a man.

He rebelled at the idea that things were being made easy for him. In Peshawar, during his visit to the North-West Frontier of India, there was trouble on the border and in order to protect him the official route back to Government House was changed and the royal party proceeded on its way through back streets. The Prince was furious and ordered that the original route be adhered to. The Governor, Sir John Maffey, refused point-blank, and in vain the Prince complained he was being made to appear a coward. As a result he stayed sulking in his room and declined to attend the official dance in his honor until Lady Maffey strode in and said: "Sir, you are acting like a spoiled puppy." Then he gave in.

On his memorable visit to the distressed areas in depression-wracked Wales, he was guided into what was supposed to be a typical miner's cottage. It looked suspiciously prosperous and he ran an exploratory finger down a window frame. It had been freshly painted. He turned to his titled guide, smeared the white paint across his lapel, and said, icily: "Now take me to a place that hasn't been prepared for me." Years later a journalist reminded him of the incident and a look approaching glee came into his eyes. "Ah, yes," he said, "I remember. I was on to them!"

He was suspicious of being shielded in any way because of his position. There was a memorable occasion after the war when he was visiting wounded men in a Belgian hospital. There were supposed to be twenty-eight patients but he counted only twenty-seven. Then it was he found that the twenty-eighth was considered to be in too hideous a condition for a Prince to see. He demanded to see him and when he did he kissed him on his mutilated cheek.

These incidents—together with his own considerable charm—contributed to his enormous popularity. The newspapers called him "Galahad" and wherever he went the people cheered. His picture postcard could be purchased in Egyptian bazaars and his photograph hung in the mud hut of a Dinka chief in the Sudan. Books, articles, and newspaper stories about him, larded with creamy adjectives, rolled off the presses.

His personality dazzled everyone. It was born in him. He is probably the only living man who ever made Queen

Victoria literally unbend. As a child he had rebelliously refused to pick up his toys, and the stern old Queen, after remonstrating vainly with him, finally bent over and picked them up for him. He had a habit of climbing on her knee and kissing her fondly, and from then on she was putty in his hands.

He spoke well. "Little wretch," said George V, when he was a child, "he speaks better than I do." To the procession of familiar clichés about "gallant troops," "deep and lasting affection," "distinguished tenure of high post," and "warm-hearted welcome," he seemed to give new meaning. When he said he was "profoundly grateful for the opportunity which has thus been afforded me," he sounded as if he meant it.

Once a mayor lost himself in the middle of an official address, breaking down in the middle of a sentence which began: "Not only do we welcome your Royal Highness as a representative of His Majesty the King, but we—we . . ." The Prince quickly prompted him, *sotto voce:* ". . . we welcome you for *yourself!*"

But the adulation he inspired had its own effect on him. He began to believe some of it. He became testy with those who disagreed with him. After all, did not the South Americans strew flowers in his path? Did not the Barotse of the Zambezi applaud his hunting prowess? Did not the American papers say he could run for Congress and be elected? Did not Bonar Law refer to his "sheer commercial brilliance," and other Englishmen exclaim that, were he in business, he could easily head a large corporation? These things were flattering, for they suggested he could amount to something on his own.

Yet there was one disturbing thing. Though his speeches made the front pages regularly and the leader-writers joined in the anthems of praise, nobody who counted seemed really to listen to his ideas. He was keen about trade relations with Latin America, but he got no response from the Baldwin government. He was keen to do something about unemployment and here he did get a response: he was told by inference to mind his own business. There is a story that he once received a complaint from a group of war veterans regarding hard treatment and promptly wrote a personal letter to a cabinet minister about the matter. The minister went post-haste to the palace and the Prince was sent for and told bluntly that he was a political cipher and must write no more letters. Whereupon, the story has it, he slammed the door, stalked into the hall, and cried out: "Well, if I'm ever a King, I'll *be* a King."

He began to feel, perhaps rightly, that in his own immediate social circle he was surrounded by yes-men. Though he was intolerant of criticism on one hand, he had a great fear of toadies on the other. If only he could meet one person who would treat him as a human being, who would neither dangle him on a string nor place him on a pedestal like a god! Then, on June 10, 1931, he encountered Mrs. Ernest Simpson, a trim brunette from Baltimore, of great vivacity and almost incredible neatness.

She had other qualities, too. She did not stand in awe of him but she did not look down on him either. She succeeded in making the appellation "Sir" sound almost like a nickname. Later she was to call him "Boysy" to his face and "the little man" affectionately to his friends.

She listened carefully to what he said and when she disagreed with him she did so boldly but charmingly. (When, after he became King and abolished the "San-

dringham time" established by his over-punctual grandfather and set all the clocks back half an hour, she administered one of her reproofs: "I think that was very
naughty of you, Sir," she told him on the telephone.)

It is not surprising that he quickly fell head over heels
in love with her. He had been in love before. At the age
of twenty-one he had wanted to marry a charming and attractive Englishwoman who was, unfortunately for him,
a commoner. King, palace, and ministers combined to op-
pose him. The story is well authenticated but not well
known. For the next decade a procession of foreign princesses was, figuratively, paraded past him like contest-
ants at an Atlantic City beauty-contest. But he had told
his grandmother when he was twenty that he would never
marry except for love, and he meant it. Alexandra probably believed him, for she was fond of fairy tales in which
the handsome prince falls in love and marries the beautiful princess. But nobody else did. In 1928 Queen Mary
had Marlborough House refurnished at a cost of $100,-
000, ostensibly for the occupancy of a Prince and Princess of Wales, but these elaborate preparations were in
vain.

In Wallis Simpson the Prince found what he had been
seeking. She and Ernest Simpson made with him a three-
some which gave rise to the inevitable jest about "the
importance of being Ernest." At first the relationship had
been concealed behind a mask of coincidence. The Prince
and his party would appear at a nightclub and Mrs. Simpson and a party would also happen to be there. An equerry
would walk over and ask Mrs. Simpson, casually, if she
would care to dance with His Royal Highness. Mrs.
Simpson always looked surprised and delighted and said
she would.

But this charade was soon dispensed with and the Prince became a constant visitor at the Simpson flat with the pale chartreuse walls at Bryanston Court. He had a propensity for indulging in brandy, but she swiftly cut him down to a single glass a day. He would come into her drawing-room and pour himself a drink and she would glide in, remove it easily from his hand, smile, and say: "I think you've had yours for today, haven't you, Sir?" She watched his health. He had a weakness for catching a chill and she saw that he was wrapped up properly. On the occasion of his father's funeral it was she who convinced him that he should wear a heavy coat while following the cortège and when he said he didn't have a suitable one she suggested he wear his father's. Indeed, there were times when she seemed to be parent as much as friend. She catered to his nervous stomach. He ate little breakfast and his lunch often consisted of nothing more than an apple, a sandwich, and a glass of Vichy water. It soothed him at the day's end to arrive at her flat and sit down at her mirror-topped table with its pink china tea-service to one of the delicately contrived meals for which she was noted. The brook trout *au beurre,* the roast guinea hen, the *pomme soufflée* and the *crème brulle* seemed chosen especially for him. After the baroque palace everything seemed so neat and fragile: the consommé piping hot in cups of black China lacquer, the salad crisp on crescent-shaped plates of delicate crystal.

By this time he had become her humble and obedient servant. At Biarritz, when she went to have her hair dressed, he followed her and sat with her as it was being dried. At Kitzbühel, in the Austrian Tyrol, in 1934, when he grew out of sorts she simply moved to another table and sat alone. He followed, with apologies. An eyewitness watched them board the train for Vienna on a frosty midnight, the Prince "looking slightly raffish" walking down the platform, Mrs. Simpson just behind him. As they passed, her words came clearly through the crisp Tyrolean air: "For God's sake put your hat on straight and don't forget to take it off when you say good-by to the mayor."

The romance did not go unmarked at Buckingham Palace. The Prince undoubtedly hoped to make Mrs. Simpson acceptable to his family, but in this resolve he did not appreciably progress. He was strictly forbidden to bring her to the ball marking his father's Jubilee. He brought her anyway.

Then a complication terrifying in its potentialities occurred. George V died. The Prince, standing by the bedside, suddenly realized that he was King, when his youngest and favorite brother, George, Duke of Kent, knelt before him in homage and kissed his hand. The gesture startled and embarrassed him. He stumbled from the room, laid his head on Queen Mary's knee and cried out: "Mother, mother, mother!"

He was King. Bathed in the throne's fierce light, his romance and his life now became immensely involved. The high wall of palace protocol began to close in upon him and there was no day on which he was not conscious of it. When he turned the clocks back at Sandringham and told the Beefeaters in the Tower they might shave off their beards, there were murmurs. When he cut short a garden party because of a rainstorm, there were tears. When he announced that he would not give the annual Christmas radio broadcast inaugurated by his father there were protests. The spectacle of a King who dialed numbers and answered phone calls in person, who walked across the Mall in a bowler hat carrying an umbrella when his predecessors had taken the Daimler, did not sit too easily with a parliament that had spent a hundred years perfecting its own conception of what a constitutional monarch should be.

There were more changes. He refused to use the royal "we," part of the Speech from the Throne since time immemorial, and substituted the first person singular. When the occasion came for him to drive in state to open parliament he switched the plans at the last moment, canceled the state coach with its handsome black horses, also part of the ceremony from time immemorial, hopped into a motor car, and drove at a fast clip down Whitehall, to the disappointment of the waiting crowds. This casting aside of the traditions of his fathers in favor of streamlined simplicity reached its peak when he flatly told the Duke of Norfolk that he intended to have as simple and swift a coronation service as possible and that the coronation procession was to be as short as it could possibly be. This pleased nobody. It meant that the press of the crowds squeezed into this shorter distance would be intolerable, and that the price of the now necessarily limited number of seats would go sky-high.

The King's own personality during these difficult months became itself increasingly difficult. He began to discharge old servants and cut the salaries of his aides. At Balmoral he reduced the number of servants' canteens from three to one. It was a bewildering change in a man who had once been noted for his prodigality. It was said of him, as Prince, that people would line up to open the gates for him on the hunting field because he gave each a five-pound note. Now he was personally poring over the palace milkbills, trying to save tuppence per bottle, and reprimanding servants for wasting bath soap. In his own eyes he was a reformer, paring costs as his predecessors had done. In palace eyes he was a meddler, interfering in things that didn't concern him.

The frugality on one hand was accompanied by prodigality in a different quarter. An expensive firm of Paris interior decorators had redone several rooms of Fort Belvedere in modern French décor and now there was talk of their invading the Regency drawing-rooms of the palace itself. This was the same firm that had also done over Mrs. Simpson's flat. Mrs. Simpson had moved out of her flat, alone, into a palace-like mansion on Cumberland Terrace near Hyde Park—a monstrous edifice fronted by Ionic columns with heroic figures of Love, Justice, Wisdom, and Victory upon the roof. (Mr. Simpson had packed up and gone to the Guards' Club.) A private telephone-line linked the palace on Cumberland Terrace with the palace on the Mall. Mrs. Simpson wore jewels which had been bequeathed to the King by Victoria and Alexandra. At Mrs. Simpson's disposal the King now placed pots and pans, champagne, housekeeper, chauffeur, Buick, and bodyguard, all from the royal household. In addition, he sent her each day five pounds' worth of long-stemmed roses.

More and more the two lives he was trying to lead, one as King, the other as a man, became inexorably mixed. His Buick would dart off at all hours to Cumberland Terrace or Fort Belvedere and the King could not be found. The royal standard which by tradition flies over the palace only when the King is in residence ceased to be a faithful indication of his presence. The court circular, the Bible of the monarch's official activities, ceased to be a Bible. Though he did not know it, many important state papers were held from him, for those around him feared his indiscretions. It is hard to blame them. Often he would take the papers to Fort Belvedere to sign and sometimes he did not sign them at all. After he abdicated, a secretary, clearing out his office, discovered a box stuffed with documents which had been sent for his signature and which he had forgotten to return.

And all the while the stage was being set for the drama that was to come. In the summer of his reign the King had leased the $1,350,000 pleasure yacht *Nahlin* from Lady Yule, the so-called "richest widow in Britain," for a Mediterranean cruise. The cargo included a good many cases of champagne and three thousand golf balls. The guest list included Mrs. Simpson. The cruise was widely reported in the foreign press, but hardly a whisper of it leaked out in Britain. The London *Daily Mirror* had in one edition printed the guest list and a photograph which included Mrs. Simpson, but deleted it in the next. Mrs. Simpson's name and photograph had occasionally appeared in the British society columns, but her name had been linked with the King's on only two occasions: both in the court circular printed in *The Times*. On the first occasion the editors of *The Times* had pondered for an hour before reaching a decision to publish the intelligence that Mr. and Mrs. Simpson had been the King's guests at dinner. The second occasion was more significant. Mrs. Simpson was on the guest list but Mr. Simpson was not. It would have been simple enough for the King to have deleted her name on both occasions, but there is no evidence to indicate that he at any time tried to hide from the public the fact that she was his constant companion. Indeed it was generally believed at the time that he made a point of inserting her name in the court circular because he believed she was being snubbed by the press, which had on previous occasions deliberately left her name out of guest lists at social functions.

In Vienna Mrs. Simpson stayed at the same hotel as the King, was seen with him nightly at opera and ballet, and daily in the office of the Viennese specialist who was treating him for an ear ailment. Of this the British public knew nothing. American periodicals reported that the King looked happy for the first time since he had been on the throne and that he had facilitated photographers taking his and Mrs. Simpson's picture when police had tried to prevent it. This intelligence was clipped from the magazines before they went on sale in England.

All that fall the curtain stayed down in Britain. The King and his antagonists were each hoping impossible hopes. The Baldwinites and the palace guard continued to hope wistfully that the King would be content with a secret alliance with Mrs. Simpson, something entirely divorced from his official life, something discreet in the manner of his grandfather Edward VII. There was even talk of marriage to someone else. They did not know their man. His every action, his every utterance had pointed in only one direction: he would be content with no other arrangement than the one enjoyed by the lowliest of his subjects—open and public marriage with the woman he loved. He did not propose to have them hide his romance any more than he would allow them to hide the houses of the unemployed in Wales, or the mutilated soldier in the Belgian hospital.

He, too, dreamed wistful dreams. Somehow he felt that he could prevent the inevitable drama, that he could marry Mrs. Simpson, make her his Queen or at least his wife, and stay on the throne. Yet surely an inner voice of common sense must have whispered to him that it could not be. It took every ounce of his stubborn resolve to have his way with as simple a matter as the direction of his profile on the stamps and coins. When it came to his vacation he had to give ground; he could not go to Italy: it would be undiplomatic at that moment in history. When he had gone again to Wales and made his famous remark that "something will be done," *The Times* had instantly rapped him on the knuckles for this "constitutionally dangerous proceeding." How then could he hope to force the immensely complicated and difficult problem of marriage to a twice-divorced American commoner through the needle's eye of British morality and royal tradition?

In the Midlands, the curtain rose on the first act. The Bishop of Bradford preached a sermon, which he said he had written six weeks before, knowing nothing of Mrs. Simpson, and which ostensibly referred only to the King's negligence in attending church: "(He) needs the grace of God. . . . We hope he is aware of his need! Some of us wish he gave more positive signs of such awareness." This was enough to burst the dam of press censorship. The Yorkshire *Post* and four other provincial papers spoke up gingerly with an identical editorial. In Fleet Street, the Jovian *Times,* which had been forging and reforging a carefully phrased editorial thunderbolt for some days, prepared to cast it. Over the phone that night to the editor, Geoffrey Dawson, came the slow, homey tones of Stanley Baldwin. He was phoning for the King, and not for himself, the Prime Minister said. He was merely a post office passing on information: "He asks if you are going to have a leader on the Bishop of Bradford's sermon, and if so would like advance proofs so that he may suggest any amendments that occur to him that he thinks

might be fitting. That is the end of the King's message."
A pause. Then again Baldwin's slow voice, slightly in-
credulous: "You know, Geoffrey, the little man hasn't the
least *idea* of how this country is governed!"

The drama moved swiftly to its inevitable climax. The
King's whole restless life seems, in retrospect, to have
been moving relentlessly toward the single tragic week
that followed. All his frustrations, his nonconformities,
his rebellions, all the prodding doubts that sprang from
the duplexity of his instincts seemed to be distilled in the
crucible of those seven days.

The decision was never really in doubt. Since the days
of the Reform Bill there could be only one outcome in any
serious dispute between sovereign and prime minister.

The King fretted his brief hour upon the stage. His
gray, preoccupied face, framed in the windows of his
maroon Daimler, merely hinted at his inner turmoil.
Closer observers noted one phenomenon: he nervously
ripped the carnation from his buttonhole every ten minutes and substituted a fresh one. But one night he walked
to his room in Fort Belvedere with his legal adviser, Sir
Walter Monckton. "Well, I'll leave you now, Sir,"
Monckton said. "No, don't go, Walter," the King said.
"Do you mind just sitting here until I fall asleep?" The
King undressed and Monckton sat in silence. Then suddenly the King buried his face in his hands and began to
cry.

After one of these long nights his valet called him in
the morning and remarked that the lights were still burning in his room. The King made a bitter reply. "Isn't that
quite normal for a prisoner in his cell?" he asked.

Wallis Simpson, her face veiled, her slender body en-
veloped in furs, had already left the country and was

speeding across France in a black Buick, pursued by journalists. The pugnacious Churchill and the wizened Beaverbrook had sprung to the King's side, had said their pieces, and retired in defeat. Baldwin's stocky John Bull figure dominated the footlights, quoting from *Hamlet:* "His will is not his own, for he himself is subject to his birth." The tall, brooding figure of Cosmo Lang, Archbishop of Canterbury, with his grave eagle's face, waited in the wings to have the last bitter word.

At long last the King, now no longer a King, spoke. The country listened and sighed. All his life this man who now quarreled with his destiny had been seeking a chance to show what he was made of. Finally, dramatically, the chance had come. Had he taken it? The King undoubtedly thought he had. Most of his countrymen disagreed.

For a week the land had held its breath. Trade suffered a relapse. One book-publisher's sales dropped to a seventh. Unemployment increased. Now, the irrevocable decision taken, the wheels began to turn again. The memorable words faded and the popular songs took their place on the wireless . . . *Here's to Romance* . . . *Love in Bloom* . . . *Those Foolish Things Remind Me of You.*

At five o'clock of a cold morning, the King who was now a Duke slipped into the harbor of Boulogne, with Mrs. Simpson's Cairn terrier under his arm. He had been scheduled to leave England on the Admiralty yacht but at the last moment he was switched to the destroyer *Fury.* It turned out that the yacht's name was *Enchantress.*

Now the restless migrations that had marked his youth began once more: Vienna, Switzerland, Germany, Paris, the Riviera, Spain, America. Still he seemed to be a man trying to accomplish something on his own. There was an

128

interview with Hitler and a proposed tour of the United States under the auspices of that dubious international figure Charles Bedaux, whose "speed-up" system had angered international labor. It was canceled suddenly, a few hours before sailing time, when the mountain of protests got out of hand.

Occasionally, during this interregnum, the Duke made chance remarks to friends that were picked up and quoted in the press. Once he said: "I can do without ceremonies but not without love and self-esteem." And on another occasion: "I always told the idiots not to put me in a gold frame."

In England, the shy, bowler-hatted figure of his brother was picking up the loosened reins of monarchy, initiating the endless small talk, reviewing the numberless troops, shaking the countless hands, and performing the various tasks of varying boredom that are the lot of the sovereign. And yet, of the two brothers it is probable that in the end it was the elder who was the more bored. He kept asking for a job to do, but the best that could be found for him was on an obscure possession in the Caribbean where he too could shake unnumbered hands, but never to quite the same purpose. Fort Belvedere, which had been the seat of his happiness as well as his trials fell slowly into disuse, the red flags rusting on the miniature golf course, the dead leaves floating on the surface of the swimming pool, the weeds blurring the flagstones, and the weather obliterating the name tags on the shrubs and flowers which he and the woman he loved had planted so carefully.

In some future era his story will be told and retold. Plays will be written about the King who gave up his throne; novels, movie scripts, definitive histories, nostalgic romances. Today he is less of a historical figure than a sort of international curiosity roaming restlessly across the Atlantic and back again. His face still appears in the public prints, but he seems to smile less today. He is occasionally seen dancing in a Parisian nightclub or charity ball or airing the Duchess's dogs, whose names, at last census, were Pookie, Preezie, Gremlin, Bundles, and Yackie. Occasionally he has had to deny the published rumors that he and his Duchess are on the brink of divorce. For whatever else may come, these two must stay in love forever.

Now and again he pays a lonely visit to the country over which he reigned so briefly. Here he used to see his mother, Queen Mary, who was always fond of him. Once, when he was King, he said to her: "I am going to marry Mrs. Simpson and when I do you will have to receive her." Whereupon, she replied: "Oh, I shall, shall I? Well, we will see about that." He continued to bring the matter up until she died, but the answer was always a firm "No." The Duke once described one of these interviews to a friend.

"How can you expect me to receive a woman who has two other living husbands?" Queen Mary had said.

"Really, Mother," replied the Duke. "What do you want me to do—bump them both off?"

Her answer is unrecorded. She did not refer to the Duchess by name nor did the rest of the court. But above her mantelpiece she kept a picture of her exiled son. It did not show him as Duke of Windsor or as King Edward VIII, but as he was in those nostalgic days when, as Edward, Prince of Wales, the country was at his feet, the world seemed his for the asking, and romance lay just around the corner.

Chapter 7: *The Younger Brother*

The shadow of the abdicated King hung for a long while over the palace. More than a decade later, when his niece Elizabeth made her memorable twenty-first birthday speech during her family's tour of South Africa, it was still there.

This was the speech in which she made her solemn dedication to duty. "I declare before you all," she told her father's subjects, "that my whole life, whether it be long or short, shall be devoted to your service. . . ." She did not write the speech, nor did she change any of the writer's words, though she cried a little when she read the draft, for the ideas it contained corresponded to her own somewhat mystical feelings for the task.

But Albert Windsor, who, as George VI, had had monarchy thrust upon him, made one deletion. The speech would have had her say that, had she been born a boy, she would undoubtedly have carried the proud title of Prince of Wales. The King struck it out. "I don't want to give any excuse to anyone for dragging in this damn nonsense about my brother," he said.

For the "damn nonsense" had plagued him for most of his reign. He could never escape the fact that he, an untried and nervous man, was following in the footsteps of an elder brother whose whole life had spent preparing for kingship and whose popularity had been so enormous that the other brothers had always been in his shadow. On the eve of Albert's wedding in 1923, *The Times* had remarked that "the public awaited with still deeper interest the marriage of the Duke's brilliant elder brother." When he had returned from his tour of Australia with his Duchess, the cheers had been louder for David, who rode with him in the state homecoming procession, than for himself. When he had made one of his sound but hesitant industrial speeches and opened the newspapers next day he almost invariably found it buried in the back of the paper, while his elder brother's words were reproduced almost verbatim on the front page. This puzzled him sometimes and he occasionally remarked on it.

Now, as he ascended the throne, David was still making the front pages, reading the lesson from a Vienna pulpit, issuing press statements, visiting Hitler, preparing an American tour, hinting that he might write his memoirs. It was some time before the personality of the new King made itself felt among his subjects.

He was very like his father and not at all like his brother. His life moved in the same orderly groove (though he did not collect stamps with the same enthusiasm and had once remarked that he couldn't understand how his father could spend so many hours in the stamp room). He was a man of some humility, who went to church faithfully each Sunday with his family and whose favorite book was *Pilgrim's Progress*. His official life had been spent on industrial tours. He had made an average of eighty of them a year, so many that his family nicknamed him "The Foreman." They contributed to his notable lack of pomposity. During his early navy years when someone insisted on calling him "Your Royal Highness," he had snapped back: "Don't be an ass; I'm just a middy like you, here." When a gardener at Windsor Castle used the same appellation, he had said to him: "You can call me that once a day, and no more. I'm sick of it." He admitted to friends that he was "not palace minded," and he agreed to handle industrial tours only on one condition: that there be "none of that damned red carpet." He respected honesty but could never stand people making up to him. On his industrial visits he enjoyed talking to the workmen in their own language. One of his cronies was George Isaacs, an old-time trade-union leader who became a cabinet minister in Clement Attlee's Labor government. Isaacs and the King used to chat about various union members whom the monarch had met. "How's old so-and-so?" the King would say, referring to one heavy drinker. "Is he on the tea as much as usual?"

His tastes and habits dovetailed neatly with those of his Queen, who, having been born a commoner, had an ease of manner about her which is not usual among royalty. But their personalities were quite disparate. To her, life had always been a broad and gently winding highway down which one could proceed leisurely and gracefully. To her husband it was a cliff up which one struggled with raw and bleeding fingers, never wholly sure of reaching the top.

All his days he struggled. He struggled with his own emotional makeup: with his inherent shyness, with his ungovernable speech blockage, with the irritability of his temper. He struggled with the frailty of his physique: with influenza, dyspepsia, pneumonia, whooping cough, ulcers, appendicitis, arterial sclerosis, Buerger's disease, and the cancer that finally killed him. He struggled with his destiny: with the memory of his brother that haunted the early years of his reign; with the complexities of a job for which he was never prepared; with the responsibilities of kingship in the most difficult decade his realm had ever suffered. But most of all, he struggled with his own fear of failure—and in this he emerged victorious.

If he insisted that his two daughters have a normal upbringing, it was because he himself had not. He was a shy child and his shyness was increased by a lack of boyhood companions and a father who felt that frailty was a weakness. In the presence of the bluff sailor King, young Bertie, as the family called him, became tongue-tied. He was so shy that he would sit alone in the dark by himself rather than ask a servant to light the gas. He was born left-handed but his tutors forced him to use his right. All this combined to give him a stammer that made his every public utterance a painful and embarrassing ordeal. It was noticed in later years that when he did anything with his left hand he did it well. He played left-handed tennis and was the first member of royalty to enter the tourneys at Wimbledon. And though he stammered uncontrollably around the palace, when he got away from these gilded environs and out to sea, he stammered hardly at all.

His own affliction made him tolerant of others' weaknesses and it embarrassed him to witness embarrassment. During his early naval training one of the senior officers took the cadets with him to see some pheasants he had shot. One of the city-bred boys made some comments that showed his ignorance and the others jeered at him. Bertie took him quietly aside and explained what he wished to know.

All his life he was plagued by the frailties of the flesh. At Osborne, where at the age of thirteen he began his early naval training, the twin diseases of influenza and pneumonia were visited upon him. At Dartmouth, where he continued his training, he suffered an attack of whooping cough so serious that he spent his entire vacation recovering from it. Dyspepsia plagued him all his life, making him a bird-like eater and contributing to the pallor of his features, often masked, on official occasions, with a tan makeup.

All through his war service a gastric condition haunted him and during one nine-month period at sea he was tortured by an intense pain that stabbed at him for hours on end. Sent to shore duty for two years, he struggled back to sea again to take part in the great battle of Jutland. He watched the battle from the gun turret, occasionally poking his head up in his excitement until somebody warned him to pull it down. A midshipman popped in and asked him if he might have the silver in his pocket if he was killed and he replied with a brusque negative, offering it instead to a shipmate in the turret with him (who would, of course, have been killed as well). He was known, during this period, as "Mr. Johnston" by the officers and "P.A." (for Prince Albert) by the crew. (His main pursuit on shore was birdsnesting.) His navy career was cut short soon after the battle by his chronic illnesses. He was hospitalized again and for the rest of his life fought his own personal Jutland for his health.

The specter of his nervousness continued to haunt him. During his naval days he had been disconcerted in far-off ports by strangers who asked for his autograph. "I write awfully badly and I have heaps of names," he would say hesitantly. "Do you want them all?"

In 1918 he joined the Royal Air Force and learned to fly. He enjoyed being away from the palace with its restrictions and staying on his own in a small cottage where he could dig quietly in his garden in his off moments. "Oh, I'm loving this freedom," he remarked one day to his gardener. But his fellow trainees thought him stuffy, for he found normal converse difficult.

Years later he marveled at the comparative ease with which his own daughters mixed with people. "I don't know how they do it," he would say. "We were always so terribly self-conscious and shy as children." Watching Elizabeth take the leading role in a Christmas panto-

135

mime, he asked again: "Where does she get her poise? I was always terrified of getting up in public." In his days as Duke of York whenever his car halted he would pull his blind down in case somebody in the crowd might recognize him. "I never get used to it," he would say helplessly.

His stammer consisted of an inability to say certain words, especially those beginning with hard gutturals. At Dartmouth his tutor, not knowing about this defect, had asked him in class to define the half of a half. He found it impossible to say *quarter,* and was, as a result, subjected to a stream of withering abuse. In later years, after his marriage, he would sometimes go into the nursery at his daughters' bedtime only to find that he could not say the words *Good-night* to them. At his Duke of York's camps, where he mixed public school boys with those from the industrial classes, he could laugh and chaff easily. But when the time came to leave he could not get out a *Good-by.* As a result, there were those who thought him rude. "I know that people have said I have a bad manner," he would say, "but it's just that I *couldn't* speak to them." Ironically, two of the words which he had the most difficulty with were *King* and *Queen* and he generally referred to his parents as *Their Majesties.* On formal or public occasions his speech troubles were accentuated. At privy council meetings it would be a near impossibility for him to get out the single word *Approved.* Yet when the council was done he could stand around easily and chat with his ministers. His nervousness always showed through the quivering of a muscle in each cheek, especially during ceremonies of high emotion or when the national anthem was being played. In his early years the problem of his speech plunged him into deep bouts of despair, and after a particularly embarrassing public address he would often sit silently for hours wondering if there was any use continuing. He later described this period of the early 1920's as "struggling through."

He took a great interest in his speech and it did not embarrass him to talk about it objectively. Once he was introduced to a man who had only one vocal chord. "I've got two," said the King, "but they're not much bloody good to me." He once confessed to a high prelate that he never knew how to start a conversation. "That is a less serious problem than your father's, Sir," came the dry answer. "He never knew how to end one."

In the end he managed to win the struggle with his stutter. He began, in 1926, to take voice exercises from Lionel Logue, a speech therapist. Logue was an unknown Australian at the time, and the King, then Duke of York, was his first patient. Logue told the Duke's equerry that his patient must come to his office, for "that imposes an effort on him which is essential for success." The next day the Duke arrived and Logue later described their meeting: "He entered my consulting-room at three o'clock in the afternoon, a slim quiet man with tired eyes and all the outward symptoms of the man upon whom the habitual speech defect had begun to set the sign. When he left, at five o'clock, you could see that there was hope once more in his heart." From then on, for two years, the patient never broke an engagement. Even when out hunting, in the middle of the chase he would leave the field when the time came, hurry back to the city and do an hour's exercises before dinner.

The accession and coronation ceremonies were particularly difficult problems, for none of the words which caused him so much trouble could be changed. With

Logue, the King wrestled out each of his set speeches phrase by phrase until he could say them without hesitation. On each occasion, Logue was present to give him an encouraging glance. He was also with the King when he made his first broadcast after his coronation and it was his voice that could be heard at the beginning whispering "Now take it quietly, sir." The King stood up, as he always did, to make the broadcast. He spoke hesitantly, but there were none of the stoppages that had marked his early public life. In an adjoining room sat his Queen, with tears filling her eyes.

She was his greatest helpmate and it is hard to imagine how he could have got through his fifteen years on the throne without her. This remarkable woman, who, at the age of three, had the self-possession to dance before strangers, and whom the painter Sargent called "the only completely unselfconscious sitter I ever painted," has an inward serenity that is enduring and an outward presence that is dynamic.

Of all the family in the palace, she alone understands the functions of the press. As Queen, she was adept at swiftly posing her husband and daughters into compact and informal groups that delighted photographers. Her husband was stiff when having his picture taken and always tended to look directly at the camera, but she would look away and busy herself so that the effect might be a candid one. If a flash-bulb failed to go off, she always noticed it and repeated the pose.

Her sense of public relations never left her and as a result she has played a vital part in the humanization of the monarchy. Once, in Auckland, during a royal tour, a woman called on her to stop and look at her twin babies. She did so at once, called her husband over, and the two of them peered into the pram at the sleeping infants. Again, in Cape Town, she and the King were about to get into the royal limousine when she noticed a crowd watching from behind a barrier. The Queen swiftly crossed the road and began to talk to the people and it was remarked that she made a special point of talking to the Negroes. In Ontario, when the Dionne quintuplets were presented to her and little Cécile held out her arms, the Queen bent down at once and in a spontaneous gesture kissed her. All her life she has had the happy faculty of being able to maintain upon her face a look of pleased surprise.

She has her mother's character. The Countess of Strathmore was a strong, serene, imperturbable woman completely unmoved by the perpetual family turmoil that went on about her. "If there be a genius for family life, she has it," a friend once said of the Countess. She had ten children and she taught them all to read and write and went on from there to teach them music, dancing, and drawing. In the evenings she played the piano in a fifteenth-century drawing-room lit by candles and at night she tucked them into bed and read them their Bible.

They were all brought up at St. Paul's, Waldenbury and at Glamis Castle where Macbeth lived and Malcolm died. This gloomy fortress, with its hangman's room, its gray lady who walks by night, and its Glamis monster lurking in a remote tower, did not in the least worry the imperturbable family. They laughed the ghosts out of existence. Young Elizabeth used to put dummy ghosts in people's beds and the Countess proudly kept books of press clippings about the spirits.

Glamis was the summer residence. St. Paul's, the family seat in Hertfordshire, was winter quarters. It is a stately Queen Anne mansion of rose-red bricks, surrounded by mossy statues, temples, and fountains, and a wood supposedly enchanted by fairies with long avenues cut through it in the French fashion. Here George VI's Queen spent her childhood.

Despite the opulence of their surroundings, hers was a frugal family, and the Countess's Scottish economy had its effect on her daughter. Years later, when Elizabeth Bowes-Lyon was Queen, a Hartnell emissary brought a new dress to the palace for her approval. Its cost was a hundred and fifty pounds. "Surely that's a great deal," said the Queen. "Perhaps we might bring it down if I took it without the trimmings." She then removed a large bow from the dress and went over to a drawer where she kept a great collection of bows from discarded gowns. "There!" she said triumphantly. "We can make do with one of these." The Hartnell firm dutifully reduced the price of the dress.

But if it was a frugal childhood it was a gay one. After the evening meal two pipers would enter and parade around the table, pipes skirling and kilts swinging. There was considerable practical joking. Water was sometimes poured on arriving guests from the tower. Elizabeth once impersonated a servant, showed a group of visitors around her home, and gravely accepted a tip. It was a musical family and she learned to play the harp and piano well. There were charades, comic speechmaking, and a good deal of dressing up in costume. There was a dancing master named Mr. Neal, who had played the violin for fifty years until his beard was worn away on one side and who used to skip around behind the children as he sawed away on his fiddle.

Elizabeth's favorite brother was David Bowes-Lyon. The two were very close. When David was spanked for a misdemeanor she sat up in bed and sobbed. The two of them would gum feathers to their clothes and play at Red Indian and once, during World War I when Glamis was turned into a convalescent center, Elizabeth dressed David up in cloak, veils, furs, hat, and skirt, introduced him as her lady cousin and took him gravely around the wards.

As a child she was perfectly self-possessed and, in the words of one friend, "responsive as a harp," a wistful, rosy-faced girl with black ringlets, dewy gray eyes, a flower mouth, and a tendency to gurgle when she laughed. She did not care for pompousness and before stuffy luncheon parties used to arrange with a friend to laugh together on signal when one raised her left eyebrow. She had a charm that has stayed with her all her life. When she was seven, her older sisters were consulting together about how to handle a difficult and taciturn guest. "Let's ask Elizabeth," one of them said. "She can talk to *anyone.*"

Today, the serenity of her character is reflected in her tastes. She likes Jane Austen's quiet novels and chamber music by Bach. She likes gentle colors. The famous powder blues and delicate peach shadings of her dresses are matched by the pink and lavender exterior of Royal Lodge, the duck-egg-blue and cream of her own rooms, and the pale hyacinth of the hangings in the dungeons of Windsor. During the war she refused to wear a uniform. She thought it preferable to remain as feminine as possible.

She brought the same serenity to the unexpected tasks of queenship. Following the coronation, she and the King went to Deeside for their vacation. She visited Birkhall, which had been her home as Duchess, to say good-by to her gardener before taking up residence in neighboring Balmoral Castle.

"The last time I saw you was in the pictures, Ma'am," the gardener said.

"Oh, the coronation," sighed the Queen. "An awful ceremony. A terrible ceremony!"

"It's a wonder you and the King stick it out," the gardener said.

"Oh, but when it's your duty, you stick out anything," she answered with a smile.

There had been a time when she was racked by doubts and indecisions regarding the life of duty. Bertie, Duke of York, had proposed twice in his shy, hesitant way and she had refused him, for as she remarked later: "I said to him I was afraid, as royalty, never, never again to be free to think or speak or act as I really feel." But in the end she accepted him. The incident is already becoming wreathed in legend. One story is that he was afraid to propose and sent a friend to do it for him until she insisted that he come on his own. Another is that at the final moment he could not find the words and had to write his proposal on a scrap of paper. There was a brief attempt to keep the news secret in order to ensure privacy, but it leaked out. "The cat is now completely out of the bag," Elizabeth wrote a friend, "and there is no possibility of stuffing him back."

Once committed, she devoted herself wholeheartedly to her husband and his job. In the ten years following World War I, the royal family carried out three thousand public engagements. The Duke and Duchess of York handled eight hundred of these. This meant that once every five days the tiny Duchess (her shoe size is only three and a half) and her shy husband were before the public.

She was almost always by his side. When he began to stammer she would look around brightly at the crowd as if to say: "It's all right; it's nothing to worry about." At one luncheon engagement his hesitancy was more pronounced than usual and he came to a point in his address where everyone feared he could not go on. As he struggled vainly to speak she quietly reached out, grasped his fingers and gave them a little squeeze. Then he was able to continue. She had a habit of wearing sharply contrasting accessories, and when he struggled for a word she would catch his eye, move her purse or gloves slightly, and he would carry on. Close observers would note that she moved her lips with his, trying to say the words for him.

She was his crutch and he leaned heavily on her. Once at a garden party an acquaintance watched them proceeding up the lines of people, greeting those they knew. The King was detained by a bore while the Queen moved ahead. Then she realized that he had been left behind and with a graceful movement, she turned about, floated back, touched him on the elbow, and whispered in his ear: "Shall we twinkle?"

They used to stroll in Hyde Park, or window-shop, hand in hand, along Bond Street. They liked to do things together. During abdication week they went to St. Paul's and prayed together that they should not be called upon to reign. When they realized that the burden of sovereignty was on their shoulders, they took one last walk together in their garden. Later it became necessary for the new Queen to have her ears pierced to safeguard the valuable royal earrings. The King went along with her and held her hand during the operation. And at the end of his days, when he was confined to a motorized wheelchair, the Queen ordered one, too, so that the two of them could drive around the palace gardens side by side as they had always been.

On only one point did they differ, and this had to do with their completely opposite temperaments. The King was a punctilious man. Like all his line he was almost fanatical about manners of dress and deportment. He liked official affairs to proceed with clockwork precision and he was angered when anything went wrong. His high-strung nature insisted on a split-second punctuality.

There is none of this timetable exactitude about the Queen. She is the sort of woman who, in order to see the view properly from the royal train, could absentmindedly pluck a priceless diamond brooch from her dress, to pin back the expensive ninon curtains, and then drift off later leaving the diamonds dangling. She had little sense of time. At the various affairs and ceremonies they attended, she would wander from person to person, conversing amiably while the royal car waited and the King, gazing at his watch, danced with impatience. "Are we a little behind time?" the Queen would ask him pleasantly. As the royal train neared Balmoral, he would pace restlessly up and down the car listening to the voice of his wife in her sitting-room chatting away with her maid. Finally he would pound on the door crying: "Ladies! Ladies! Are you aware that the train is approaching Ballater?" Back would come the Queen's gently reproving voice: "Not at all, Bertie—you must remember the clock's fast."

It maddened him, this casual, leisurely approach to life which he found so difficult to understand. Once he was waiting for her in the great hall of Balmoral. As usual she was late and the King was pacing the red carpet and drumming his fingers on the pale Hungarian ash of the woodwork. Finally, in an excess of impatience, he darted into an anteroom. At this point the Queen floated down the staircase, pulling on her gloves. The King popped out again into the hall to find his wife standing placidly before the great fireplace. "Oh there you are, Bertie," she said sweetly. "I've been waiting for you." "Waiting for *me!*" cried the King, his nose an inch from his wife's face —but he could say no more.

He had always been highly strung. As a child he had an ungovernable temper, so bad that he used to break pieces of furniture. He brought it under control, but even as an adult he sometimes had a tendency to throw things. Later, as illness sapped his strength, the old irritability returned, especially if the even tenor of his day was upset. Then the telltale muscles in his cheeks would signal a warning to his aides. Once, during a visit to Cardiff, a group of enthusiastic schoolchildren broke through police lines and ripped the buttons from his naval uniform. The King was so angry at this lack of discipline that he canceled a reception at the city hall. Once he was sitting with the Queen at a ceremony involving the Lord Mayor of London. The Lord Mayor suggested a change in the seating arrangements so that the microphone would not block the Queen's view. As they got up to make the change, the King's voice could be heard rapping out: "For God's sake, sit in the bloody seats you were told to sit in!"

He often got angry when photographers took too long getting his picture, and sometimes when he was in a rage he would fling a book or other object on the floor as his father had done before him. Periodically, the King used to fire his valet, Thomas Lawrence Jerram. The valet, disturbed, would go to the Queen, who would tell him not to worry—the King didn't really mean it.

For his temper cooled as quickly as it rose. Once he was returning from Aldershot on the royal train in a fury because things had not gone quite right. He was roaring that he couldn't trust a single member of his household—that they were all secretly disaffected to him. In the midst of this outburst he paused and looked out of the window at the name of a station flashing by. It was Runnymede, the name of the island where King John signed the Magna Charta. "My God," cried the King, "that's where it all began!" Everybody laughed and the frayed tempers were forgotten.

His humor, like the rest of his tastes, was of a simple kind. He enjoyed practical jokes—the cutting off of the white flannel trousers of visitors to his boys' camps, and the ducking of the camp chiefs into an improvised pond. He liked the ancient puns and rowdy songs of the British music halls. "How do I like my tea?" the King would ask, and answer himself: "In a cup! Ha-ha!" He liked jazz records and got a good deal of enjoyment out of running films backwards at Royal Lodge. On industrial tours he was always delighted when things wouldn't work. "It's because I'm here," he would say in a voice touched with glee. Once he inspected a "foolproof" envelope-stamping machine. He pressed a button and a sheaf of envelopes promptly shot through unstamped. At Lloyd's, he was shown a system guaranteed to produce the name of any British ship and her captain anywhere in the world. The King mentioned an obscure vessel that had taken him between Australia and New Zealand when he was Duke of York and was delighted to find that they had got the captain's name wrong.

On these industrial visits his sense of the meticulous always showed. He had a mechanical nature and in his younger days had constructed wireless sets at a bench in his home. He liked to see how things worked and he could not be dragged away from anything that caught his eye. On defense tours he made it a point to try out all the new weapons. During the war he had a lathe installed in Windsor Castle so that he might turn out machine-tool parts in his spare moments. One acquaintance noticed this quality under somewhat different circumstances during a family showing of Princess Elizabeth's wedding presents. She had been given several beds as gifts and the King and Queen were going about testing them all, bouncing up and down on them to make sure the springs were solid.

For he was a conscientious monarch. He always carefully read all reports of crimes in which capital punishment was evoked. But he was careful to read them after the sentence had been carried out so that he would not be tempted to interfere unconstitutionally in a matter which is still, in theory, a right of the sovereign. One day he was inspecting a glue factory where the smell was pungent to the point of being overpowering. His escorts tried to keep him out of those departments that smelled the worst. The King would have none of it. "People work here, don't they?" he said. "If they can stand the smell, I can," and he insisted on visiting every section of the plant.

No detail of dress or decoration was too minute to escape his inquisitive scrutiny. He was keen on shoes being shined and belts being polished and he was an admirer of the minutiae of service. He showed Field Marshal William Slim how to salute properly while carrying the baton of his rank, and he ticked off Field Marshal Montgomery for wearing two cap badges. He himself designed the George Cross and he collected the orders of British chivalry and knew the full history of each. He had five hundred suits and his kilts were always superbly tailored. He liked brightly colored shirts and in the Highlands wore a tweed coat in the Scottish fashion and carried a shepherd's crook. It was he who popularized the tartan dinner jacket, an innovation which made Savile Row wince.

Once he visited Stratford-on-Avon to watch Anthony Quayle play the title role in *Henry VIII* in the Shakespeare Memorial Theatre. At the reception afterwards, while the players were being presented, it was noticed that the King's attention was straying. Finally he turned to Quayle, who was still in costume, and said: "You know, you're not wearing my Garter properly." Everything came to a standstill while the King, using the royal shank as a model, gave Quayle a lesson in how to put on the Garter. Quayle took it all in, made what he thought were the proper readjustments, and then the handshaking got under way again. But the King never properly got back into the swing of things. He kept looking at Quayle's leg and shaking his head. Finally he turned to the Queen, shrugged his shoulders, and was heard to remark, *sotto voce:* "The fellow couldn't put it *on!*"

A mind devoted to such outward details did not have the inward capacity for intellectual curiosity. In this George VI resembled his forebears. He did not care for ancient music or modern painting, and he is supposed to have thrown a book at an aide who suggested it would be a good thing if he were seen more often at the opera. For he was an uncomplicated King, devoted to uncomplicated interests—to home movies and jazz records, color photography, birdsnesting, medal-collecting, gardening, the *Times* crossword puzzle, and, above all, grouse-shooting. If he was called into London for business when he was in the Highlands, he would take the night train back so that he might be on the moors again by eleven a.m.

It is a tribute to his courage and his stubbornness that this shy and unassuming man, with his nervous temperament and his tender physique, should turn out in the end to be so strong. All his life he was plagued by the defections of his frail body and in his final months he knew that death was certain and imminent. The hardening of the arteries that had caused his leg operation had not been checked. The cancer that had forced the removal of one lung had spread to the other. But he refused to compromise with his destiny. He continued to go out onto the moors of Sandringham and into the glens of Balmoral on the forays after grouse which he loved so much. At Balmoral his head keeper tried to rearrange the drives to make things easier for the ailing monarch. He would have none of it. He would insist that the party continue to breast the steep hills as they had always done, nor did he want anyone to wait behind for him. "No—no—no! Go on—go on!" he would say testily. "Don't bother about me—I'll get there sometime." They would go on ahead and wait for him on the knoll and look down the incline at the thin figure of their King slowly but surely struggling up the hills as he had indeed been doing all the days of his years.

He struggled to the end. One evening at Sandringham he received, as he always did, the daily report from the House of Commons prepared by the vice-chamberlain. His careful mind studied it minutely, as always, and he found in it a figure which seemed wrong to him. Back to the vice-chamberlain went a prompt query. The vice-chamberlain replied that the monarch was right; a cipher had indeed been misplaced. This done, the King went to bed. It was his last official act. Next morning he was dead and the Queen whom he had so carefully trained to replace him was reigning in his stead.

THE KING IS DEAD

The news spread swiftly by a moccasin telegraph that epitomized the mid century: the two-way radios of taxi-drivers, bowling about London. Long before the newspapers were on the street the people knew from the taxi-men that a reign was ended.

By noon the cinemas had closed their doors, the stock market had shut down, the Lutine Bell in Lloyd's had rung its mournful message, the flags had dropped to half-mast, and even the Windmill Theatre, whose motto is "We Never Close," had closed.

The news did not reach the King's daughter so swiftly, for she was in Africa. A newspaperman got it first, by wire from his London office. He told Martin Charteris, the private secretary, who went white as a ghost. Charteris was wearing a Canadian square-dance costume he thought appropriate for climbing up the tree in which his Princess, who was now his Queen, was staying overnight.

Charteris phoned Michael Parker, the equerry, who was with the new Queen. "I cannot tell the lady," said Parker. "I must have confirmation."

But something had gone wrong. There was no word from the palace. It was as if all converse had ceased now that the man in charge was dead. Parker turned on the BBC news at two p.m. East African time, and there he heard what he was expecting to hear. He told the Duke of Edinburgh and the Duke told the Queen.

When the reports from Africa began to filter into Fleet Street there was no mention of tears. "Hell," said a sub-editor. "She *must* have cried." He put it in the

copy. But she did not cry. For six months, each time the
national anthem sounded, her eyes had filled up, but
now they were dry. She had one hundred and seventy-five
minutes to pack up and catch an airplane home. She
sat down at a desk and began inscribing photos of
herself as mementos for the staff who had served her.

In Durban, South Africa, the Zulus had ceased their mid-
day games.
In Valletta, Malta, the shops were draped in crepe.
In Karachi, Pakistan, a drydock opening was postponed.
In Singapore, Malaya, a reception for an ocean liner was
canceled.
In Hong Kong, the radio stations went off the air.
The Egyptians, who were fighting the British, imposed a
fourteen-day mourning, and the Indians, who had ceased
fighting the British, closed their bazaars for eleven days.

And all along the Tasman Sea, the bells began to toll.

The queue began forming before dawn on February
twelfth. Outside Westminster Hall, the people were waiting in thousands. They stretched back four miles, past
the scaffolding of Victoria Tower, along the north bank,
over Lambeth Bridge, down the Albert Embankment,
and back around Lambeth Palace where the Archbishop
lives. For three days, in the cold, the sleet, the rain, and
the snow, from dawn until two a.m., the Londoners
waited neatly in line, as they had waited during all of
his reign, for ration cards and cinemas and buses and
chocolates.

The city wore black. The music on the BBC was black.
The smart shops on Regent Street and Grosvenor Street

featured black merchandise—black handbags, black gloves, black shoes. Men wore black ties, including one man who had worn a scarlet shirt all his life and still continued to wear it in this mourning period, but with a black tie. In the schoolroom drawing-classes the children drew black pictures of hearses. In the great queue two street peddlers were arrested for hawking copies of funeral music without a license. They were taken off to jail wearing striped trousers and black bowler hats.

Within the cold gray hall of William II, where Charles was sentenced and Hastings tried, the purple catafalque, draped in the yellow and red of the royal standard, glowed like a fire in an unlit room. Upon it, the crown, the orb, and the scepter sparkled like bright embers. Past it, in endless line, shuffled the cobblers and the queens.

On the lawns at Windsor Castle they spread out the tributes in neat floral lines, and as the rain poured down, a new pilgrimage, three miles long, assembled. Here were great crowns done in daffodils, and a huge George Cross all in flowers, and a giant plaque several feet square from the city of Gloucester. And here was a tiny crushed handful of snowdrops from a group of children in Bermondsey, all laid out carefully for the people to see.

At the palace, in a neat black dress, the new Queen was already taking up the burden of her task. There were fifty thousand letters to be attended to, and fifteen thousand telegrams, and on her desk the little leather boxes were beginning to pile up.

And there was still no time for tears.

Chapter 8:
The Girl in the Iron Mask

Elizabeth II, as all the world knows, is a petite, serious-faced girl with a twenty-five-inch waist and golden eyebrows, who can't stand oysters but likes champagne, doesn't smoke in public but keeps cigarettes on her desk, prefers canasta to bridge and horse-racing to boxing, likes her drapery cherry-red and her notepaper bottle-green, enjoys Jane Austen but thinks Dickens rather a bore, is madly in love with her husband and knows how to shake hands at the rate of twelve a minute.

She is also, as these crumbs of personal trivia indicate, the most widely publicized young woman of modern times. Her orbit is as carefully charted as that of the planet Jupiter, and she lives so much within a goldfish bowl that it is difficult to disassociate her private life from her public existence. Yet the two are, in many ways, quite dissimilar. So much is known about her that is superficial: that she enjoys *L'il Abner,* keeps a faithful daily diary, likes to suck on barley sugar, doesn't like the sea. So much less is known about her that strikes deeper. Long after the ink has dried on the acres of newsprint devoted to her person, the question still remains: what is the girl in the palace really like?

What would she be like if she were subject instead of sovereign? A man who has observed her since childhood recently indulged in this game of make-believe. She would, he said, have been a country girl, the kind usually described as "horsy." She would have ridden a lot, always astride, and most of the time she would wear tweedy things. She wouldn't come into the city a great deal and when she did it would be to see a musical comedy or a vaudeville show or a movie. She would be a lively girl, laughing a good deal, not too interested in style or the

154

arts, surrounded by her own kind of unsophisticated, un-intellectual upper-middle-class country folk. She would have a large family and be great fun at a party, where she would dance all the lively dances with bounce and enthusiasm. She would be matronly and she would be wholesome.

This is not the picture of Elizabeth Windsor the public sees. The serious, almost prim figure in the modish suits and frocks reading her careful speeches, the austere, military form in the sidesaddle at the Trooping ceremony, the dazzling, satin-gowned fairy queen at the ballet do not seem to bear much relation to a bouncy country matron in tweeds. It is hard to remember sometimes that this is the same girl who likes to lead a Conga line through the palace, dance eightsome reels all night, and hum Cole Porter's *Night and Day* in her husband's ear; who loves to stalk deer through Scottish forests, angle for trout in mountain streams, or put five pounds on a horse's nose at Goodwood; who has learned how to tap dance well, enjoys cowboy movies, especially those starring Gary Cooper, and likes to lean over a piano of a winter evening singing *Greensleeves* with the gang.

It is almost as if there were two Elizabeths, one public and one private, and this curious double existence was quite apparent to those who traveled with her on the royal train across Canada in 1951. In the privacy of her quarters she was a lively, animated girl who rocked with laughter at small talk and cradled a cocktail glass between her hands. But the train would stop and the laughter would die; the talk would cease, the cocktail would vanish, the smile would fade, the shoulders would stiffen, and Elizabeth would move resolutely toward the rear platform, exactly, in one observer's words, "like a soldier coming to attention." Then, the anthem sung, the greeting accepted, the cheers acknowledged and the speech delivered, she would return again to her private world, sink into a couch and double up with mirth at a remark or an incident or a scene that had tickled her.

"I have been trained since childhood never to show emotion in public," Elizabeth once remarked to a dinner companion, and this is one key to her outward reserve. Infused in the hard metal of her character are those qualities of stoicism and constraint the British prize so highly. They have always been with her. As a child she was particularly enchanted one day by the quick action of a group of marching sailors, one of whose members fainted. The others simply closed in on either side of him and without missing a beat marched the insensible man along with them. At the age of ten she added to her reputation for being able to maintain a poker face when, during a church sermon, a bee settled on the minister's nose. Those around her stuffed handkerchiefs in their mouths to stifle their laughter. But Elizabeth's face retained its composure and only the flowers jiggling on her hat revealed her inner mirth. Years later she was inspecting an honor guard of servicewomen when one girl collapsed almost at her feet. Elizabeth walked on without changing expression. Nor did her expression change, or her voice betray her concern, when during the Empire Youth Festival in 1946 she read her speech to the accompaniment of dozens of children fainting in the hot, stuffy atmosphere of Albert Hall.

The cast of her face is of that mold which always appears serious and even a little sullen in repose. It is very like the cast of her late grandmother's granite features. The brows are heavy and the lips full, imparting to Elizabeth an especially somber look. When she smiles she seems to be a different person, but she has not yet got the facility to smile before crowds which distinguished her mother as Queen, though the smiles now come easier than they did on her Canadian tour when she phoned her mother from Vancouver. "Are you smiling enough, dear?" the elder Elizabeth asked. "Oh, Mother!" came the reply, "I seem to be smiling all the time." But it is not in her nature to smile all the time in public. When she does, the photograph flashes around the world.

Indeed, she sometimes seems to be wearing a mask, and so of necessity she is. It is the family face—the iron mask of royalty that those who came before her have worn on public occasions. It is not that she lacks a woman's emotions. But her whole background has made her chary of revealing them. "I am not a Hollywood movie star," she told her staff at the outset of her Canadian tour, "and I do not propose to act like one." Nor did she.

To some North Americans this was a puzzling side to Elizabeth's personality. There was an incident in Calgary, when the Dosiettes, a group of little orphanage children skilled in square-dancing, put on an exhibition that delighted the royal couple. The plan was that toward the end of the dance two of the smallest children would lead the visitors onto the floor and dance with them. But Elizabeth, when approached about the idea in advance, flatly refused to dance before a crowd. It was reminiscent of an earlier incident in her life when she had been an enthusiastic Girl Guide. She had loved the Guide camp in the daytime, but as night drew on she always had some excuse for returning to the sheltering stone of Windsor Castle. She did not want to undress before the other little girls. Dancing in public is rather like undressing; it belongs to the secret world behind the mask.

There was the time in Toronto in the Sick Children's Hospital when she was to walk past a row of tiny patients laid out for her to see. The photographers reached this vantage point well in advance for here, surely, was an opportunity for a great photograph. The Princess was the mother of two and it was in the cards that she would pick up one of the tiny bodies and cuddle it. The cameras were trained and the crowd waited, but Elizabeth walked down the line as if she were inspecting a rank of guardsmen. For sentiment too is a luxury which must only be indulged in in private.

Beyond the gaze of the public eye her grave look melts away. She laughs and cries easily. She rocks when she laughs, throwing her head back and swinging her clasped hands high above her head and down between her knees. She literally dances when she is excited or interested, balancing on her heels and executing two little steps to the left then two to the right. If things don't go well she can look daggers and tap her foot in fury. Like her forebears she has two swear-words she isn't afraid to use: "damn" and "bloody."

In public she sometimes gives the impression of a woman who understands the treachery of her own emotions and is therefore all the more determined to keep them in check. In Calgary and Toronto, where she was greeted by large numbers of children, those standing close to her noticed her throat muscles tighten, her fingers twist tightly in the straps of her handbag and her eyes cloud up.

There was one moving moment at Government House in Ottawa at the end of the private square-dance party that the Governor-General, Lord Alexander, held for his royal guests. Elizabeth had been dancing gaily all evening when suddenly, at eleven thirty, she prepared to go and the band struck up *God Save the King*. The chatter and the laughter ceased and in the words of one observer, "a sort of emotional wave swept over the guests." One man began to sing the words of the anthem and the others took it up. Somebody stole a look at Elizabeth. The mask had slipped and she was starting to cry.

Her iron control has often stood her in good stead. On her official visit to the Channel Islands, after the war, she became so seasick she almost collapsed. As the ship docked she was asked if she felt fit to go ashore and she could only nod her answer. Philip, who was with her, had to help her down the gangway. But she swallowed two aspirins and a glass of water, stepped into her carriage, and set off on the full tour without a murmur or a change of expression.

The serious mien Elizabeth presents to the world is a direct reflection of her attitude toward her job. Not long ago she commented tartly on the fact that, after she succeeded to the throne, everybody went around saying that she looked twenty years older. But in her moments of seriousness she has always looked older than her years. She is still, in every sense, the good little girl who used to jump out of bed every night to get her shoes exactly straight and her clothes arranged just so, who insisted on wearing her gas mask for a prescribed period every day during the war as the regulations required and cleaning the eyepiece methodically every evening, and who warned her sister that it wasn't polite to rush for the tea table at a royal garden party. Responsibility, the heritage of the Coburgs, has always rested with its full weight upon her shoulders. On the battleship that took them to Africa she and Margaret entertained a group of sailors. A few days later they had occasion to pass the same group again. Elizabeth looked straight ahead of her but Margaret could not resist a smile. "Behave yourself," Elizabeth whispered sternly. Whereupon Margaret made her now famous retort: "You look after your Empire and I'll look after my life."

The contrast between the two sisters is not quite as great as it appears to be. Both are fun-loving young women who like jokes and parties and dances and weddings. But the gap widens in public. One has her Empire; the other her own life.

In a sense Elizabeth has from her childhood days played the role of the little mother, alternately leading or pushing her younger sister down a prescribed pathway; speaking up for her entry into the Girl Guides at an earlier age than normal ("She is very strong you know. And she loves getting dirty, don't you, Margaret?"); worrying about her presence at official ceremonies ("I do hope Margaret won't disgrace us by falling asleep"); reproving her with a stern headshake when she started to smile at Zulus dancing their war dance in South Africa. Before her reign is ended she will undoubtedly be thought of as the mother of her country, a stern, straight figure rather like Queen Mary, speaking up for her people, reproving them when necessary, and always setting her own example.

All of her days her temperament has been leavened by a stubborn resolve to do what is right. Is it right to play, Crawfie, with Grandfather lying dead? Is it right to be too happy with the terrible war raging across the Channel? Surely it is not right for Margaret to dangle her legs

at the solemn moment of Mummy's and Daddy's coronation! And is it really right to play practical jokes on the
gardener? It is fun, of course, but is it *right*? The round
and solemn young face gets quite pink at the thought.

There is more than a trace of Albert of Saxe-Coburg
in all this. The serious prince with his methodical ways
and his high resolve seems to be standing, ghost-like, over
the little girl's shoulder as she carefully sorts out her
pieces of barley sugar into neat piles, each arranged according to size. (Margaret is stuffing hers into her mouth
in great sticky handfuls.) The little girl becomes a big
girl and, to her first military inspection she brings the
same method that she did to the arrangement of the barley sugar. Here is a Grenadier Guardsman with his belt
buckle unpolished! She points it out quite seriously and
there is a great flurry and the guardsman goes red and,
when it is all over, somebody has to tell her, tactfully, that
she doesn't need to be *quite* so meticulous on these occasions.

But Albert's shade pursues her. She is standing on the
bridge of HMCS *Crusader* on the way from Vancouver
to Victoria, talking to the commander. The talk gets
around to British Columbia's official flower, the dogwood.
How far do the roots go down? To everybody's astonishment Elizabeth has the answer. She has looked it up.

For she is a woman who leaves little to chance. In Winnipeg, Canada's windiest city, a Toronto *Star* photographer was assigned to get a photograph of her with her
hat blowing off. He tried in vain. She had taken the pre-
caution of securing it firmly with a pin. Her handbag,
which she carries in to banquets, is fitted with a special
clip so it can be secured to the table within easy reach
and never drop to the floor. Her lady-in-waiting is

equipped with extra shoes and stockings in case of a run or a loose heel.

Elizabeth is a woman who keeps a firm eye on the clock, a royal trait that goes back to the days of Edward VII. In Calgary she suddenly stopped short in the midst of a reception and said firmly: *"Now!* . . . We must go back to the carriage." She set off immediately, leaving her husband chatting with the crowd. "Good heavens!" he cried. "Where's my wife got to?" and off he ran to catch her.

One of the most famous pictures of Elizabeth shows her riding erect in the sidesaddle on the occasion of the Trooping of the Color. This was as studied as her knowledge of the dogwood roots. She practiced for a month in order to do it properly, riding each morning in the royal mews and on weekends at Windsor to build up the thigh muscles which are needed to hold the horse. For though it would have been easier and certainly more pleasant to ride astride, it would not have been the right thing to do.

It would have been pleasant, too, to stay at the radio on the night of the Randy Turpin and Sugar Ray Robinson fight. But again she must do what was right: leave the radio in an early round and welcome her dinner guests on her sick father's behalf and sit pleasantly smiling at the head of the table and wait anxiously until a footman passed her a surreptitious note from her father: "You may relax now. Turpin has won!"

Elizabeth is not a brilliant woman, nor is she required to be, but she can be a stubborn girl, and this quality, which is also an ancient family trait, will stand her in better stead as Queen. It was at her own insistence and over her parents' objections that she finally won her point and was allowed to enter the services during the war. Once, when she was in her teens, learning constitutional history,

Sir Henry Marten, the bald savant from Eton who tutored her, told her that some of the bright boys over at the school could rattle off the names of all the kings of England, together with the dates, in so many seconds. Elizabeth determined to better this record and she did. For she has something of her grandmother's thoroughness. When she got interested in horses as a child she was not satisfied until she had read all the books she could find on the subject of breed. On her first visit to the Bertram Mills circus, she surprised the management by identifying correctly every breed of horse in their stables except one —a pair of rare Frisian blacks. In her early days as Queen she brought the same stubborn concentration to the state papers set before her. She insisted on reading all of them and asking questions about most of them. The questions were often more searching than her late father's and there were some ministers of the crown who felt she was taking the whole thing just a little too seriously. But it is not in her nature to treat such matters sloppily or lightly.

In this context it is intriguing to examine her relationship with her husband. In private the strong-willed Philip is master. It is he who decides, on vacations at Sandringham or Balmoral, what the family will do. It is he who gives the orders to the servants and looks after domestic details. But on all public matters Elizabeth takes charge, and sometimes, when occasion demands it, she overrules him. During the royal tour she was told in Victoria that an Indian Princess had come several hundred miles to see her but couldn't be fitted into the ceremonies. "The Indian Princess stuff is out!" snapped Philip. But Elizabeth told him quite firmly that she intended to see her. Later, in Montreal, the mayor approached the couple to explain that a lot of people wanted to shake hands. Philip said there wasn't any time. Elizabeth turned to him and said: "Philip, I *want* to shake hands." And she did. In Greece, in December 1950, she asked a photographer to come along and record her visit to the Acropolis. Philip, who is not fond of photographers, tried to wave him away, but again Elizabeth intervened. Later she could be heard saying to her husband, a little heatedly: "That may be so, Philip, but it is not *my* way." When the couple's marriage portrait was being painted, the artist had trouble getting Philip to pose. He simply didn't see why he should. Finally Elizabeth put her foot down and told him the portrait had to be done. "You just stand there!" she said to Philip. And he did.

She is just as stubbornly determined never to be a party to any diminution of the ancient dignity of the monarchy. "How is your father, Ma'am?" someone in Canada asked her. Elizabeth replied with an icy look. "Are you referring to His Majesty the King?" she asked, and turned away. There is an even more telling story recounted of her first weeks as Queen. During this period a veteran courtier, leaning casually against a mantelpiece, had engaged the new sovereign in conversation. Suddenly the Queen interrupted him. "Are you tired?" she asked. The courtier, puzzled, said he wasn't. "Are you perhaps ill then?" No, Ma'am, certainly not ill. "Then," said the Queen in a good-humored voice with only a suggestion of mettle, "don't you think you should stand erect when talking to the sovereign?"

In 1952 Elizabeth grew furious at newspaper reports which hinted that she was pregnant. Several members of the cabinet, including Churchill, were meeting at the palace one day and the Queen in a blazing voice discussed the matter and ended with the command: "I expect these rumors to stop!" It was after this incident that the Prime Minister was credited with the much quoted remark: "She may not be pregnant but she is certainly regnant." She was equally unmovable a year or so ago when she discovered to her annoyance that a silver trophy she was to present in Edinburgh had been inscribed simply "Queen Elizabeth" —a reminder that the Scots do not recognize her earlier namesake. Elizabeth had the trophy shipped back and ordered that the numeral "II" be appended.

Yet she is in no sense an arrogant or a domineering Queen. When waiting in the airport to leave for Malta she was quite capable of purchasing a pack of cards and dealing out hands to her staff in a canasta game. She has the ability to think of others, even in moments of high emotion. On the eve of her wedding crowds began to gather outside the palace hoping to see the royal couple, and the BBC sent a mobile unit down to cover the event. Elizabeth, listening to the nine p.m. news broadcast, heard the BBC man cut in to say that everyone was hoping she would appear but so far she hadn't done so. She immediately took her fiancé by the hand and went out onto the balcony so that the broadcasters could describe it before the end of the news.

The personality behind the mask is still that of the shy, nervous little girl who had to suck barley sugar to keep her spirits up on her first official inspection. One man, who knows her well, remembers seeing her with Philip, driving by carriage to some of their first functions together, holding onto one another's hands so tightly that the knuckles were white. "Elizabeth is not only shy," says an acquaintance, "but she's also shy of making other people shy."

For the first fifteen years of her life she led a confined

existence behind the palace walls. She was not known to the public and she did not get to know them. As a result until she married she had only a hazy idea of the world beyond the palace and she still has not got the happy faculty for official small talk that her husband has. Philip can walk into a room without introduction (as he did in Toronto) and breezily say "Hi!" then walk up to the nearest pretty girl and remark (as he also did) : "Golly, this is a much more attractive audience than the one I've just left." Elizabeth cannot project her personality in this way. In the receiving line she often seems to be trying to think of something to say next, and she has a habit of looking away after a gap in the conversation and then turning back and starting in again when a new thought has occurred to her. One man who has watched her continually in official conversations says that she seems to be thinking to herself: "I must say something to this person: now what can I say that won't sound inane that he will be able to answer?" Once, in Malta, during one of these interludes, she said naïvely: "Well . . . I can't think of anything more to say about that," and drifted off.

As the years go by these shortcomings will vanish— and indeed they are vanishing with astonishing speed. It was noted that on her Kenya tour she was much more self-possessed than she had been six months previously, in Canada. She was more relaxed and she smiled more easily. There was one incident that caught everybody's fancy. A small native boy was brought up to her to present her with a bouquet, but at the last moment he grew shy. Elizabeth smiled and gracefully put her hand around his back, where he was hiding the flowers, and took them from him. And in her two busy years on the throne she has already acquired a sureness of manner that is a surprise to some of her ministers. "We thought she'd be stuffy," one of them remarked after her accession. "She's anything but." She crossed the first two hurdles of her reign with ease: the opening of parliament and the royal variety show, both of which took place in the same month of November. They are entirely different ceremonies, one a formal and traditional ceremony before the highest peers in the land; the other a lively evening before bookmakers, publicans, theater people, and press agents. She obviously enjoyed herself at both these functions and they helped to settle her firmly on the throne.

For she is quick to pick up the gambits of her trade, as her equally shy father was before her. In Winnipeg she arrived at the airport and made an opening remark that had a familiar ring to the RCAF commandant who greeted her. "Every time I come to an airport there seems to be a terrible wind," Elizabeth said. It was exactly the same phrase that George VI had used on two similar occasions in the RCAF officer's presence.

Elizabeth cannot yet make extemporaneous speeches and this was again particularly evident during the royal tour of Canada. In the Sunnybrook Hospital for war veterans in Toronto she suddenly realized that she was expected to speak. She did not know what to say until her private secretary, Lieutenant Colonel Martin Charteris, scribbled a few notes on the back of a cigarette package and handed it to her. In Calgary a microphone was set up for her and the citizens had the impression she would say a few words. But there had been a mix-up and no prepared address was ready. Elizabeth declined to say as much as "Hello." Similarly in Montreal she was supposed to make a few remarks to a group of children announcing a half holiday. Somehow the speech was missing from her purse. Somebody suggested she just tell the children anyway, in French. But Elizabeth found she simply could not do it. On the other hand she reads a prepared speech clearly, if in a rather stilted fashion. She braces herself, looks at her husband, swallows, moistens her lips, and plunges ahead. Again one is reminded of the good little girl chosen to read the valedictory speech at the high-school graduation.

Her speeches are written for her and she does not make many changes in them, for she is not a woman who initiates ideas. Once she and Philip visited the London Palladium to watch Danny Kaye, then the idol of England. After the show Philip suggested they go back stage and congratulate Kaye. Elizabeth was quite startled at the suggestion, which she was happy to comply with. It simply had not occurred to her. In her personal tastes she has shown a similar passivity. As a Princess she had no strong ideas about furnishing or decorating her room, as her sister had. She was quite happy to settle down in surroundings arranged by someone else. Nor, until her marriage, was she in any sense clothes-conscious. A year or so ago she sat for her portrait and the artist, who was to complete the work in her studio, borrowed some of Elizabeth's clothing to fit onto a dummy. This included a special petticoat with slits down the sides which the Queen wears for greater freedom when she has considerable walking to do on official occasions. The artist had only got started on her job when a hurried call came from the palace: "The Queen is going out of town tonight and must have her petticoat back. It's the only one she has!" Elizabeth has never had any desire to be a fashion leader and although her general attire has become much smarter than it used to be, some stylists still shudder at her accessories.

In November 1952, Elizabeth attended a fashion show at Claridge's, looked at the new dresses and commented: "They frighten me!"

For she is not a woman whose nature is marked by the extremes of taste and inclination, nor is it proper that she should be. She does not pluck her eyebrows or wear bright varnish on her nails. She would rather foxtrot than rumba. She knows her Kipling but has no affinity for Gertrude Stein. She can understand horses but she does not pretend to understand Picasso. Exotic foods leave her unmoved: she would rather have roast lamb and green peas. Her disposition is generally pliable and undogmatic. She has few fanaticisms, always excepting the crowning fanaticism with which she approaches her job. In this she is resolute and unswerving. She might prefer the infinitely simpler role of a horsy young woman in country tweeds, but she knows that this is not to be. She knows that in the political climate of her time monarchs who take their duties lightly have been notably unsuccessful. The fat Farouk lost his throne through philandering. The solemn Baudouin weakened his by lying on the beach when the floods racked his country. Even her own father was criticized when by an unfortunate coincidence he chose the bitterly cold winter of 1947 to visit sunny Africa. Elizabeth has no intention of falling into such pitfalls. The road she must take runs straight as a red carpet without curves or forks. Before its end is reached Elizabeth II may occupy the last throne in the world. But if her will be done she will not be the last Queen of England.

Chapter 9: *The Schoolroom*

Elizabeth II followed her father to the throne better equipped than any British sovereign in more than a century. Since the days of the Hanoverian Georges it had become almost axiomatic that the heir to the crown be so out of step with one or both of his parents that his character and personality were affected. But although Elizabeth still has some of the shyness and nervous tension that is characteristic of her family, and although she is only now beginning to shed those traces of naïveté that are the inevitable result of a confined childhood, her own temperament has a tranquillity that was never the most notable attribute of her predecessors.

It is no accident. Part of it springs from the fact that George VI, as a second son, was able to choose a commoner for a wife who had a serenity about her not usually found in the inner circles of royalty. Some of this serenity Elizabeth has acquired. Part of it comes from the fact that before he ascended the throne, George VI was able to rear his children in their earlier formative years in a manner considerably closer to normal than is usual with royal offspring. Part of it comes from a set determination on the part of both parents to make their children equal partners in the family circle.

Some, though not all of the personality of the parents rubbed off on Elizabeth. She gained her mother's composure, though not her effervescence. She acquired all of her father's stubborn devotion to the job but less of his equally stubborn temper. And she gained as well a sense of duty which both of them sought to instill in her as much by example as by word.

"Take care of the children," George VI once said, "and the country will take care of itself." Some of this feeling can be seen glowing brightly between the rather stilted lines of some of Elizabeth's early speeches as a Princess. She told a Mothers' Union: "I do not think you can perform any finer service than to help maintain the Christian doctrine that the relationship of husband and wife is a permanent one not to be broken because of difficulties and quarrels." To a Church of England Youth Council she said: "For better or for worse the roots of our daily lives are planted in our homes. . . ." She told a welfare association meeting: "The need of every child to be surrounded by love and security is now well known." And to a medical group, she referred to "the happiness of home and family life on which the true worth of a nation depends."

It was the home life of her own family that secured the crown after its greatest trial. The public got occasional rewarding glimpses of it. One day a traveler in the Highlands came upon the whole family picnicking at Loch Muir shortly after the King's accession to the throne. The King, in khaki shorts and open shirt, and the two Princesses in their little kilts were out in the water looking for pebbles. The Queen was seated on the shore doing some needlework. It was a minute or two before the witness to this domestic scene realized that this was indeed royalty relaxing.

For the royal parents were proud of their children. They always took their holidays together as a group. Each morning at nine there would be an hour's romp in the bedroom. Neither the King nor Queen believed in sending children off to boarding school, with the result that both girls saw their parents almost every day except when they were away on their 1925 tour of the Antipodes and later of Canada. Neither parent had any compunction about getting down on all fours and playing bears with the children. Their elder daughter's first remark, when she was told that she was to have a new sister, was: "Now there will be four bears instead of three."

The bond between the King and his elder daughter had always been close and intimate. He talked to her as an equal and when he returned from his 1939 Canadian tour he could hardly take his eyes from her. Margaret he tended to spoil, for she was not destined to be Queen. But the standards set for Elizabeth were high. No matter how late the night before had been, the elder Princess always had to rise early next morning to fulfill her duties, which increased slowly as she grew to womanhood. Margaret was often allowed to plead a cold and stay in bed. The King was unruffled by criticisms of his younger daughter's dusk-to-dawn parties. "You're only young once," he would say to her, "have a good time." For he himself had not always had a good time as a boy.

Occasionally the informality of private life brought public embarrassments. The little girls were not required to treat their parents as King and Queen, as the previous generation had done in George V's day. During one discussion, when George VI was entertaining guests, Margaret impulsively broke into a conversation with the words: "Oh, don't be a fool, Daddy!" The King's face froze. A few minutes later Margaret, her features white with embarrassment, made an excuse and left the room. She had forgotten for a moment that her father was also the monarch.

It was a family whose tastes and recreations were simple. They liked to play canasta in the evenings, or a simpler card game called "racing-demon" that involved a lot of running about the table. They preferred the simplicity of Royal Lodge, with its pink stucco and its plain unpolished oak furniture to the musty regality of neighboring Windsor Castle. Here, on weekends, where there were no state servants in livery, Elizabeth's mother would don an apron and cook the evening meal. They preferred the isolation of Birkhall, a whitewashed seventeenth-century building, shaded by birch trees, to the tartans and turrets of nearby Balmoral. To Birkhall would come Miss Annie Shande, a folk-dance expert from Aberdeen, to play the piano while the Princesses and their parents danced. A visitor to one of these gatherings remembers the King, who was then Duke of York, and his brother, the Duke of Gloucester, their coats off, their faces flushed, dancing like madmen until they could dance no more, then slumping onto the floor with their children, exhausted.

Elizabeth's early childhood was spent for the most part at her parents' home at 145 Piccadilly, near Hyde Park. It was a house notable for its lack of ostentation, not differing greatly from other upper middle-class homes in London with its carpets and walls of brown moleskin, its pale green pillars, sofas in deerhound chintz, and peach-colored curtains. One of the few concessions to the royal background were the Brussels tapestries along the staircase down which Elizabeth used to throw her toys onto the heads of the people below. There was a nursery presided over by Mrs. Clara Cooper Knight, better known as "Alah," who had been in the family service since Elizabeth's mother was a child. She had a passion for neatness, made the children brush their own clothes and fold them carefully before going to bed, and provided them with toy mops and dustpans. Each morning there would be a cleaning session in which for an hour or so the little girls would seriously sweep the Persian rug. The chief article of furniture in the nursery was a large mahogany cabinet full of special toys which were too delicate to survive the rough-and-tumble of everyday play or which had been sent as special gifts to the Princesses on official occasions. Alah's services were shortly augmented by those of a governess, Miss Marion Crawford, the famous "Crawfie," who was later to tell in detail of her years with the royal family. She was selected partly because of her youth. George VI had always had unhappy memories of the elderly savants who surrounded him when he was a child.

Elizabeth provided several contrasts with her younger sister which later were to become more marked. She was shyer and quieter, more inclined to think of others, less interested in clothes or appearance, not as talented musically or histrionically, less apt to make friends, more apt to keep them, and concerned at all times about the rights and wrongs of her own conduct. She had more tendency to temper than Margaret, but also more ability to control it. And she had an inborn streak of stubbornness that has never quite left her. She once got so bored during a French lesson that she took an ornamental silver inkpot and emptied its contents over her head, thus dyeing her face and her hair a bright blue. On another occasion she absolutely refused to have her teeth brushed and sat in her bed with her lips clamped shut. Alah and another nurse stood on either side of her, one holding a toothbrush, the other a tumbler of water, coaxing, pleading, threatening. The child remained adamant until her father was called. "Elizabeth," he said, "how does Father do his voice exercises?" She opened her mouth to say "Ah" and Alah promptly inserted the toothbrush.

But she inspired few anecdotes, unlike her younger sister, who startled her maternal grandmother at the age of eleven months by humming the *Merry Widow* waltz. Margaret was forever playing jokes on her more serious elder sister, putting tapioca in her bath water and salt in her tea, and during art lessons, while Elizabeth seriously concentrated on her draftsmanship, Margaret was inventing a character called Pinko Ponko, who lived in the air and ate caterpillar sandwiches and green jam. Elizabeth was never clothes-conscious but Margaret had a ribbon on her hair as soon as she learned to tie a knot. When she was four years old she was already crawling under the table at dull luncheons tickling the grownups' feet. When she was ten she was remarking how "frightfully handsome" the footmen were, and when she was fourteen she was caught sampling the palace cellars. All her childhood was spent trying to keep up with Elizabeth—insisting on a train equally long at the coronation, insisting on mascara and lipstick as soon as Elizabeth was allowed it, insisting on turning up at teas for young guards officers which Elizabeth gave during the war. Early in life Margaret was exhibiting the Hanover charm, the Hanover tendency to bright and extreme clothing, the Hanover propensity for practical jokes, gay living, and easy conversation. Elizabeth, on the other hand, had the Coburg reserve, the Coburg dedication to duty, and the Coburg sense of inward discipline. She was also inhibited in a way that Margaret never was: as soon as her family moved into the palace, she was the heiress to the throne, and this was something she was never allowed to forget.

Her parents' treatment of her was exactly the opposite of Albert's attitude toward his son, who was always made to feel that he was different from and superior to his fellow men. Elizabeth was brought up with the glitter of the palace around her, and indeed on one occasion, she reached out for Queen Mary, who was dressed in state, seized the Koh-i-noor diamond and demanded it as a toy. But all her early training was designed to teach her the lesson that she was the servant and not the mistress of the people. One day she was reading a book of fairy tales about beautiful, wealthy, and omnipotent princesses and she suddenly looked up and remarked upon the realization that she was a princess, too. But her mother sat her on her knee and explained quietly that princesses in real life were considerably different from princesses in fairy books.

One day when she was five years old, she was rude to her governess and was punished in the English manner by being "sent to Coventry," which meant that nobody would speak to her. When she tried to say "Good morning," Crawfie refused to answer. Finally, after several tries, Elizabeth in a burst of petulance cried imperiously: "You *must* answer. It's royalty speaking!" For this she was given a smart dressing-down from her mother and a warning never to use the phrase again.

On another occasion she was taken to a concert in Queen's Hall by Queen Mary. About halfway through she began to squirm in her seat and the old Queen asked if she would like to go home. "No," said Elizabeth, a little vainly. "We can't leave before the end. Think of all the people waiting to see us outside." Without a moment's hesitation the Queen turned to her lady-in-waiting and told her to pack the Princess out by a back entrance and send her home by taxi.

Her early training was handled by her mother in much the same manner that the Countess of Strathmore had trained her children. The elder Elizabeth enjoyed the company of her girls and it was sometimes her habit to amuse them before bedtime with train imitations, complete with a trip through a tunnel, the engine whistle, and the arrival at the station near Glamis Castle. She taught Elizabeth her alphabet by the time she was five and had her reading when she was six. Like most English children, the future Queen started out on Beatrix Potter's tiny, shiny little books with their watercolor illustrations of Peter Rabbit, Benjamin Bunny, and Jemima Puddle-Duck, and on Barrie's *Peter Pan*. Elizabeth soon learned to read the comics—the English favorite *Pip, Squeak and Wilfred* and the American *L'il Abner*. One fall evening in 1937 when the family were preparing to leave for Balmoral, the Princesses were put to bed early in the royal train. The railway policeman engaged to guard the premises was astonished late in the evening to hear a steady tapping on the window of the Princesses' compartment. He investigated and saw that the blind was drawn back and the round little face of Elizabeth was pressed against the pane. She was brandishing a shilling in her hand and saying: "Please, policeman, go and buy us a comic paper to read."

Later there were more classics: Lamb's *Tales from Shakespeare, Dr. Doolittle,* and *Pinocchio.* She did not care for *Alice in Wonderland,* but read *Black Beauty* so often the volume began to fall to pieces. For since her baby days she has been crazy about horses. She used to pretend to ride horses in her crib and instead of dolls she had toy horses on wheels, thirty of them, each a foot or so high, with miniature saddles and bridles which she carefully cleaned and polished each day. As soon as she was old enough she learned to ride and in her adult years horse-racing has been her greatest extracurricular interest. She attends most of the major races and seldom misses placing a bet.

She was a favorite of her grandparents. George V used to get down on his knees and play horse with her, and she was recommended to him as tonic when he was recovering from his 1928 illness. Queen Mary was very fond of her. During her parents' tour of New Zealand, Elizabeth stayed at Buckingham Palace, and she used to be brought down to tea with her grandparents every afternoon. "Here comes the bambino!" Queen Mary would cry with delight. When Elizabeth made her first radio broadcast and spontaneously asked her little sister to say good-night to the children of the world tears came into the old Queen's eyes.

As the child's education progressed, the firm if tactful voice of her grandmother began to be heard asserting itself through the skillful little notes that her lady-in-waiting sent to Marion Crawford. Some of these notes are reproduced in Miss Crawford's book *The Little Princesses* and they are minor masterpieces of the iron-hand-in-velvet-glove technique. They cover everything from the children's style of handwriting to their hours of going to bed. Historical dates are very vulgar and old-fashioned, but perhaps they may be useful at some time. Surely some arithmetic lessons can be dropped to make a place for more history. ("But perhaps not!" writes the lady-in-waiting, tactfully.) And of course geography is hopelessly old-fashioned, and so is learning poetry by heart, and in-door-teaching games sound awfully priggish, but one never knows; one must remember Elizabeth's future career. After all she should have a detailed knowledge of the Dominions, and poetry can be rather wonderful for memory training, and perhaps it might be a good thing to have the occasional alternative to racing-demon. And Miss Crawford will understand that none of this is to be taken as criticism. Miss Crawford saw to it that the schedules were revised accordingly.

As Elizabeth developed, Sir Clarence Henry Kennett Marten, the vice-provost of Eton, was brought in twice a week to lecture to the little girls on weightier academic matters. He chewed the end of his handkerchief, sucked sugar lumps, taught them constitutional history, and occasionally addressed them as "Gentlemen! Gentlemen!" in the absent-minded belief that they were Etonian scholars. As a result, Elizabeth got an academic background considerably sounder than that enjoyed by the average well-born Englishwoman. She read Muzzey's history of the United States and Fisher's history of Europe. She read Chaucer, Shakespeare, Keats, Browning, Coleridge, Tennyson, Dickens, Scott, Trollope, Stevenson, Conan Doyle, and John Buchan. She studied French until she could speak it almost without accent and read Racine, Corneille, Rostand, Anatole France, Maupassant, and Daudet, in the original. She read the English poets and the Russian novelists. She studied music, took weekly piano lessons, and learned to enjoy Sibelius, Brahms, Chopin, Beethoven, Haydn, Handel, and the Andrews sisters. Her favorite pieces of music included the *Pastoral Symphony, Valse Triste, Le Fiacre,* and *Let's Fall in Love.*

There were more lessons. There were swimming lessons, and she managed to earn a lifesaving certificate before she became heiress to the throne and the crowds threatened to get too big around the pool. There were elocution lessons, and she was taught to act out parts in dramas to learn self-possession and to take part in pantomimes in Windsor Castle, including one called *Old Mother Red Riding Boots* which the Princesses wrote themselves. There were dancing lessons under a Miss

Vacani, who used to teach the children of King Alfonso of Spain while he was still King. There were singing lessons, and the high soprano voice of the Princess could be heard in the elevators and hallways of the palace going to and from her rooms, and around the piano singing *Blow, Blow, Thou Winter Wind* in the madrigal groups which she and her sister organized at Windsor Castle.

In fact there were lessons in almost everything imaginable every morning from nine fifteen to twelve thirty and the Princess learned almost everything there was to know except for one thing: she did not learn much about the world. She was in every sense the antithesis of her great-grandfather, Edward VII, who, as Gladstone said, "knew everything except what was in books." Elizabeth knew everything that was in books but she did not know much more. She joined the Girl Guides and learned to cook over an open fire, but she never spent a night under canvas or took a walking trip across the moors. She joined the wartime Auxiliary Territorial Service for women, at her own insistence, and learned the mechanics of motor-trucks, but she never drove an automobile alone through the country lanes of Surrey or in the traffic of the Strand. She was hostess to young guards' officers at tea in Windsor Castle, but she was never able to hold hands with one of them across a nightclub table. Of the people who lived beyond the walls of the royal residences she knew next to nothing, and when the servants at the palace struck for a wage increase she saw it only as an act of disloyalty to her father. As a result she came into her twenties with a naïveté and a lack of presence that were her greatest weaknesses.

Her parents were reluctant to see her grow into adulthood, and they tried to keep her a child as long as possible.

They were aided in this resolve by the fact that she had a sister four years younger. The sisters dressed in similar clothes with the result that the younger sister wore clothes that always seemed too advanced, while the elder sister wore clothes that never seemed advanced enough. She always appeared younger than she was, and this feeling carried over into her manner so that even in her early twenties she had about her some of the awkwardness of the teens. Only in her attitudes was she adult; here she always had a self-discipline and a sense of propriety that were well beyond her years.

For her first fourteen years she was kept by her family in complete seclusion from the public. This was an attitude that nothing could shake. The King did not want his daughter to become the property of his subjects until it was absolutely necessary. It was as if he was reluctant to share this favorite possession with others. But it was more than this. He was a man who never got used to the white incandescence of the public spotlight. He found it a torture and he did not care to torture his children any sooner than he felt he had to. The veil began to be lifted slowly in the middle war years. There were a few public appearances and these became more numerous as the years went by. But even on the 1947 tour of South Africa (where Elizabeth complained that she met only elderly people and hardly anybody her own age) she was given very little to do on her own. When she was married the next year her early days as a bride were spent telephoning her mother to ask for advice on the smallest matters: her choice of clothes, what engagements she should accept, how to handle her household. This annoyed her husband and before long the calls ceased. Only after he took her with him to Malta did she begin to gain a certain aplomb.

Here she lived in much the manner of any naval officer's wife, wandering around town with a scarf tied about her head, getting her hair done by the local hairdresser, and dancing in the public rooms of the hotel on weekends. When she returned she slowly began to absorb some of the official royal tasks. The King made certain that she saw the secret foreign-office telegrams (which she read conscientiously but found heavy going). In the final year of his reign she carried out no less than thirty of the forty-eight official engagements which the royal family undertook. Now she was swiftly learning the mechanics of her craft. There remained only one further item on her curriculum of training—a royal tour of her own. This she undertook in the fall of 1951 when, for six weeks, she toured Canada and made a swift side-trip to the United States. It served as a sort of final examination for a girl whose whole life had been spent on the uncompromising schoolroom of queenship.

BLUE MONDAY

Monday, October 22, 1951, is a day which Captain R. A. Pennington, a tall, spare ex-naval man, in Victoria, British Columbia, is not likely to forget for some years to come. For six weeks, from dawn until two a.m., Captain Pennington's time had been occupied solely with plans for the morning of this particular day. Captain Pennington represents the province of British Columbia and this was the day the province was to play host to the Princess of England and her husband.

The first of Captain Pennington's many problems was weather. There were charts and tables to show that the odds overwhelmingly favored a bright day, but unfortunately the tour was postponed at the last moment because the King was being operated on. When the charts and tables came out again the odds were six to four for rain. Everything had to be changed, but it was fortunate that the changes were made. True to the weatherman's promise, Victoria had one of the worst days in its history on the blue Monday on which the Princess toured the city.

Then there was the problem of food. What should the province serve its Princess at the official luncheon in her honor? Captain Pennington did some research into royal eating habits and found she was fond of lamb. Then he checked with the Vancouver menu to see what the neighboring city would be serving. Vancouver was serving chicken, so Captain Pennington decided on lamb and green peas. To his chagrin, Vancouver switched to lamb at the last moment.

Captain Pennington tried to get some information about his Princess from the Federal Government at Ottawa but none was forthcoming. Fortunately her secretary, Lieu-

183

tenant Colonel Martin Charteris, had come through on a
scouting trip some weeks earlier and had been most helpful. Colonel Charteris told Captain Pennington that
neither Prince nor Princess smoked in public. Well, then,
how would the luncheon guests know when *they* could
smoke? The Princess's husband would produce a dummy
cigarette-case and wave it and that would be the signal,
the Colonel said.

The Colonel also remarked that the Princess was fond of
champagne, so Captain Pennington dutifully added champagne to the menu. And she also liked orange juice. Accordingly an entire jug of freshly squeezed orange juice
was placed in the hotel suite which she occupied for twenty
minutes in Victoria. There is no record that she drank any
of it.

Captain Pennington discovered in his researches that his
Princess's personal standard must fly wherever she happened at the moment to be. Unfortunately there were no
copies of her personal standard in Canada. Captain Pennington got the details and had six flags made, but even
then he realized there wouldn't be enough. So he drew up
a plan whereby, as soon as the Princess moved from one
spot to another, a naval team would pull down the standard and rush ahead with it to a new point.

There were some other matters. Suppose the Princess
wanted to go sailing at the Royal Victoria Yacht Club?
An unlikely situation, but just in case, a royal pennant was
provided for the eventuality.

Suppose the Princess didn't bring a slicker? Slickers must
be arranged for at every point. (But the Princess did
bring a slicker, after all, in a becoming blue.)

As the crucial day grew nearer Captain Pennington decided on a series of rehearsals to make sure everything went off correctly. Everybody who had anything to do with the tour attended these, from Premier Byron Johnson right on down. It was a good thing that everybody did rehearse. During the first tryout, when the pseudo-royal car drove up to the Legislative Buildings, it was found to the horror of all that the door wouldn't open. It was catching on the stone of the first step. Careful chalk marks were made in the road so the driver would know exactly where his front wheel was to come to rest.

On the day before The Day, a casual observer might have noticed a curious drama being enacted in the Legislative Buildings. A royal reception was taking place, attended by everybody from Premier to flower girl. All the citizens who were to be presented on the following day were solemnly going through the entire business in advance. Everybody was on hand, and standing in for them, gravely accepting the bows and curtsies of Victoria society, were Captain and Mrs. Pennington.

On the following morning, with the rain beating down outside his window, a harassed Captain Pennington reached his office at seven thirty. During the next two hours the switchboard clocked one hundred and fifteen calls for him. Someone had lost his pass: What should he do? Someone had forgotten the time of the reception: Where should she go? Captain Pennington noted dryly that most of the calls were from women. What should one wear? What colors were best? How far should a frock be from the ground?

One man phoned to say that his wife was four-months pregnant and insisted on being presented in a Persian-lamb coat. If she couldn't wear a Persian-lamb coat over her dress, then she simply wasn't going to go at all. Well —*could* she wear a Persian-lamb coat? Captain Pennington rolled his eyes heavenward in supplication. He would be happy when this gray, wet, complicated, yet strangely rewarding day was over.

But no happier than the two for whom the fuss was all about.

Chapter 10: *The Test*

On an October day in 1951 a crowd of fifteen thousand Canadians stood silently at Dorval airport, outside Montreal, Quebec, and watched a pale young Princess in a short mink coat and teal-blue dress step hesitantly down the gangway of an aircraft. It was observed that the small black handbag on her left arm was trembling and that as she greeted her welcomers she continually moistened her dry lips. Only an iron self-control hid her overwhelming nervousness. Thus, under the worst of conditions, did Canadians catch their first glimpse of Elizabeth of England.

Five weeks later, under rather different circumstances, they bade her good-by, a laughing, relaxed figure with a scarf tossed over her hair, smiling into the teeth of a Newfoundland gale. She boarded a lighter, waved farewell, and headed out over the choppy sea to a waiting ship. Almost everybody else was seasick, but not the Princess. She swung aboard in good fettle announcing that she was famished. Then, with the most exacting job of her young career behind her, she relaxed with a copy of *Kon-Tiki* and headed home to England.

In between these two incidents she had traveled close to ten thousand miles by aircraft, train, limousine, and destroyer; inspected twenty-four guards of honor, signed twenty-one golden books, and shaken hands with fifty-three Canadian mayors, their wives, and their associates. She had eaten Laurentian trout, Cape Breton partridge, Winnipeg Goldeye, and a bewildering variety of banquet dishes that ranged from fiddleheads in New Brunswick to sowbelly in Alberta. She had been given rubies, diamonds, and emeralds, gold, silver, and platinum, and such lesser gifts as a stuffed lion cub and a Cowichan Indian sweater. She had accepted twenty-three official bouquets from little girls in gossamer gowns, and thirteen illuminated addresses all beginning with the words: "May it please Your Royal Highness." She had pumped official hands at the rate of thirty thousand a week, had heard the National Anthem played one hundred and fifty times, and had jumped quite noticeably as each twenty-one-gun salute thundered in her ears.

She had, as expected, survived her first overseas tour, which, next to a coronation, is the most arduous and complicated piece of pageantry that royalty has to face. On the royal family's tour of Africa in 1947 all were sometimes ill from exhaustion, and George VI lost fourteen pounds.

The Canadian tour was Elizabeth's test by fire. Some of those close to her suggest that she almost suffered a nervous breakdown during the opening days of the long trek across the continent. The tour was in a sense a preview of queenship, at once terrifying and inspiring. For the first time in her life, the girl of twenty-six from the cloisters of Windsor, found herself completely on her own. All the public decisions were hers to make. Though she had the advice of her husband and her aides, hers was the final responsibility.

Worries beset her. She worried about her father, ill from a critical operation; about her own appearance (she felt she was too heavy in the bosom); about the strange new country, which she did not fully comprehend; about the landing in Quebec, whose people, she had been told, didn't like the English. More, she worried about herself and her ability to do the job. She could not sleep on the flight across from England, so she rolled dice with Philip in the bar of the aircraft. He tried to teach her a game called "liar dice," involving the purposeful telling of untruths, but she could not concentrate on it. "You'll never make a good liar with that Empire on your shoulders," he said, and they went to bed.

The wave of silence that greeted her arrival at the airport was the first of many surprises. In England she had been used to cheers; here, she could not know that the crowd was as awed and uncertain as she. Her husband patted her arm and she gave him a grateful look, but the uncertainty persisted until the following morning when, as she stepped from the royal train, he turned to her and said: "Darling, you look simply smashing!" At this calculated compliment she brightened.

But in Toronto there was a second surprise. She was to be received by the mayor and she expected the familiar, cosy English ceremony: the knot of respectful officials, the fumed-oak chamber, the inevitable dry sherry, the careful small talk. Instead she got a bunting-draped platform, glaring floodlights, and a crowd that choked the streets.

She was nervous about her speeches and could eat little at the state dinners. Only as the tour progressed did she begin to relax. This was due to Philip's ease. He kept her smiling and relaxed as they drove through each city. "I've seen that woman before," he would say, pointing into the crowd. "I remember her by her teeth," and the Princess would brighten up. Philip made sure there was a radio in the royal limousine tuned to the local broadcast of the tour and it became a game to spot each commentator. "Bet you half a crown I can find out where he is before you do," the Duke would say and the Princess would smile and answer: "You're on!" Whenever they spotted their man they would wave directly at him and then giggle as the voice on the air said, in excitement: "I believe the Princess just waved at me." On foot, the Princess played another game. "I always smiled directly at the announcers," she told a friend later, "because I knew it would put them off."

The two quickly learned to converse without moving their lips. The Duke would incline toward his wife and say something. Her mouth would twitch. Then he would catch her hand and squeeze it. Sometimes, at official banquets, he would tease her to make her smile and she would give him a kind of bat with her hand under the table.

In Calgary, one observer insists she heard this *sotto voce* conversation:

PHILIP: This is Doukhobor country, you know.

ELIZABETH: Really?

PHILIP: Yes, if you look over on the edge of the crowd, I think you'll see one of them.

ELIZABETH: Naked?

Thus the two became a team, complementing each other in small ways and with tiny signals of the hand or eye. Small things unnoticed by Elizabeth—a bouqet-throwing child in Winnipeg, an aging veteran in Saint John—were spotted and acknowledged by an observant Philip. Small errors by Philip—he almost turned his back on the Ottawa Cenotaph and almost sat down too soon at the Winnipeg ballet—were caught and corrected by a vigilant Elizabeth.

Most of the time the royal entourage lived aboard the train. Elizabeth and Philip rarely got to bed before midnight. In between appearances they listened to rebroadcasts of tour commentaries, read *The Times* of London and the local papers, or saw movies such as *The Duchess of Idaho*.

Throughout it all, the Princess never forgot the tour's main purpose: to display the heiress presumptive to the people. In chilly Ottawa she refused to wear a coat during a river trip because she feared the public would not spot her if her bright red suit were covered. In Toronto she kept the car to four miles an hour, though the itinerary called for speeds up to twenty-five. It was here that she and Philip asked that spotlights be placed in the open car —and it was here that the curiously effective Plexiglass top was born from a chance remark by Philip, who said something about the bubbles on destroyers. The words were hardly out of his mouth before a transport officer was speeding out to the De Havilland aircraft plant. The company literally dropped everything and, working non-stop, produced the transparent top in thirty-six hours. The result was dropped into Winnipeg just as the delighted royal pair arrived. They were, in the words of an army officer, "like a couple of kids with a new toy." The fish-bowl effect disturbed the Princess at first. "Michael, Michael—how do I look?" she called back to Parker, the equerry, over the intercom. "Like an orchid wrapped in cellophane," he replied, and she relaxed.

The problem of being seen properly continued to occupy them. Philip was often outspoken about the security measures, which he sometimes felt to be too strict. In Winnipeg he remarked to Elizabeth that he hoped the crowd would break through the police lines, and was delighted when they did. In Vancouver the security arrangements occasionally approached the level of farce. There was the football game at which Philip was asked to autograph the ball. Before he could do so it was seized by a security officer. A covey of these watchdogs then retreated around the corner of a building, where they were observed to solemnly deflate the football, examine it carefully, and reinflate it. After this the autographing was allowed to proceed. Later that evening Philip planned to slip away to an informal naval party. To his disgust, he found himself being escorted by seventeen policemen on motorcycles. It was then, according to one fairly knowledgeable source, that Philip decided to take matters into his own hands. After the naval party he picked up his wife and drove her himself over to Sentinel Hill to look at the lights of the city below them.

By this time the western papers were commenting that the Princess looked very tired and that the tour was too grueling. She had seemed nervous at the civic banquet and Philip, noticing this, had leaned across the mayor and said quietly: "Come on, Betty, let's go home." She seemed more relaxed at church next day. The Dean later reported that when she left with her presentation prayer-book she whispered to him out of the corner of her mouth: "Looks like I'm pinching a book from the church, doesn't it?"

It poured rain all next day in Victoria and the couple were both obviously relieved to begin a three-day vacation. At the day's end Philip tossed his naval cap over the balcony at Government House, danced a little jig, and cried: "Thank God *that's* over." They spent the evening in their rooms listening to the British election news on the radio. The following afternoon they drove to Eaglecrest, the luxury resort on Vancouver Island that was reserved for them.

But if a royal tour is an exacting ordeal for the principal actors, it is almost equally trying for the stagehands. For weeks the entire nation had geared much of its energy to making sure the royal welcome went off without a hitch. In Vancouver, one newspaper held its own royal rehearsal three days in advance and covered it as though it were the real thing. In Calgary, cowboys stayed up all night shoveling frozen earth to soften the rodeo ring so the stam-

pede arranged for the royal couple could go on. The Prince
Arthur Hotel in Port Arthur, where the royal party rested
overnight, spent ten thousand dollars renovating one
suite. Furniture, china, chef, and elevator operator were
all flown in, and a window was raised three feet to keep
out the public gaze. In Kapuskasing, Ontario, a chef kept
making tea every fifteen minutes between seven and nine
thirty a.m. so that whenever the royal couple awoke it
could be sent fresh to their room. In Halifax, plans were
laid to keep the Princess away from the well-baby clinic
at the naval center there, to forestall any rumors that she
was pregnant. And on HMCS *Ontario,* which bore her
to Newfoundland, the crew was issued with rubber sneak-
ers to cut down noise on the steel decks.

Elizabeth was not aware until well along in the tour
that the cars she rode in were not the same in each city.
It took a full gross of Cadillacs, Lincolns, and Chryslers
to see the tour through. The cars were spotted in sets of
twelve in each of the twelve major centers. The plastic
tops (there were three—one for each make of car) took
a minimum of eight minutes to adjust. The moment the
train came to a stop a decision had to be made on the basis
of the local weather whether the top would be needed.
Then Elizabeth and Philip had to step off the train and
hold up proceedings for eight minutes while army mechanics struggled with it. The royal couple soon grew
adept at these delaying tactics.

The excitement occasioned by the tour was so great that
the slightest incident made headlines. There was, for example, the business of the Vancouver *Sun's* Ottawa cor-
respondent's tie. When the royal couple officially met the
press, the *Sun's* man turned up wearing a lively tie and
Philip remarked on this in passing. The reporter did not

bother to record the item, but he was immediately besieged by his colleagues, who wanted to know what the Duke had said to him. He gave a faithful account of the Duke's very matter-of-fact remark. The story grew in the retelling and appeared on the news wires in this fashion:

THE DUKE: What newspaper are you from?

REPORTER: From the Vancouver *Sun*, sir.

THE DUKE: You seem to be wearing the Vancouver sun on your tie!

This witticism was front-paged by the *Sun*, picked up by British correspondents, wired to London, picked up by a *Sun* man in London from the British press, and wired back to Vancouver, where it again appeared on the front page. Meanwhile, the tie in question was rushed to Vancouver by air and displayed to large crowds in a department-store window.

Elizabeth could have only a small inkling of all this backstage clamor. Royalty arrives on the scene at the last, perfect moment to find the clockwork running smoothly, the gears carefully concealed behind the sheltering curtain of the flag. Yet she, more than most royal scions, is aware that there are gears at work. In the Auxiliary Territorial Service, where she trained in wartime motor-vehicle work, she got a fleeting glimpse at the complicated mechanism of the royal machine. One day she found herself caught up in a frantic polishing and shining bee and when she asked the reason was told that the King and Queen were coming the following day. Only then did it occur to her for the first time that all royal movements are attended by an inevitable hubbub.

Probably the most elaborate preparations of all were those made at Eaglecrest, the private lodge on Vancouver Island where Elizabeth and Philip spent a three-day holi-

day. Eaglecrest is one of the largest and most expensive
log buildings in the world—built by a multimillionaire
Canadian senator, who hired a hundred men for a year
to put it together. After the senator's death it was turned
into a luxury lodge for paying guests. The owners were
simply called one day by the lieutenant-governor of British Columbia and asked to entertain the royal couple.
They received no other instructions and were completely
on their own, but they spared no expense to prepare a lav-
ish welcome. Flowers were imported to garnish the royal
suite. Orchids were chosen to match the exact shade of
blond oak on the royal dressing-table. Lilies of the valley
scented the royal bathroom, where the toilet and facial
tissues were powder blue. Chartreuse chrysanthemums
were mingled with green grapes to deck the royal table.
New radios were placed in every room and sterling-silver
lighters and cigarette-cases were purchased for the royal
household.

The royal entourage was preceded by sixty-five members of the R.C.M.P., whose job it was to search Eaglecrest for hidden bombs and other infernal machines. This
laudable security measure was frustrated at the last moment when the lodge was alerted that Philip and Elizabeth would be arriving half a day early. The Mounties
were put to work moving furniture and when the familiar
procession of black limousines, with their three tons of
baggage, arrived, everything was ready, though staff and
police were all panting slightly.

Here the royal pair swiftly recovered from their fatigue. Indeed, they seemed eager for exertion. They went
hunting for grouse, called for saddle horses, and arranged
a fishing-expedition. It was late October and every boat on
the coast was beached for the winter, but they managed to

collar a Nor-Craft and in this cockleshell they ventured out to sea with two aides.

The spectacle of the heiress to the British throne and her husband adrift in a tiny single-engined boat in strange waters and heavy seas, with a gale blowing up, drove the security officers to a near frenzy. Officials raced up and down the coastline, vainly trying to commandeer rescue craft. Finally they stood in a forlorn knot on the beach, waiting for the worst. Nothing happened. The wind died, the sun appeared, and the party landed eight grilse.

Philip and Elizabeth returned to the big log lodge, played some Bing Crosby and square-dance records, looked at a cowboy movie, and filled in the time pasting clippings about the tour into a scrapbook. Meanwhile a Canso aircraft was flying the six silver police-motorcycles to Vancouver so that the next leg of the tour might commence.

The royal entourage, complete with Plexiglass tops, moved swiftly back across the prairies. The couple's worst day came on Monday, October 29. It began at nine a.m. with a tour of Port Arthur at the head of the Great Lakes and ended at eleven p.m. with a hockey game in Montreal, a thousand miles away. Four times the royal couple went through the stylized movements of a civic tour: the address of welcome, the bouquet presentation, the inspection of the guard, the signing of the book, the drive through the town, the pumping of scores of official hands. The following day was almost as arduous: a seven-hour, seventy-eight-mile drive through Montreal with 477 more hands to shake at the end. On these two days the blurred, waving wheatfield of faces was seldom out of their gaze. Photographers and dignitaries riding with them had to close their eyes to stave off dizziness. But the two young people in the leading car must always be smiling and waving.

There was a brief interlude in Washington, which delighted and puzzled Elizabeth. The press reception at the Statler Hotel was something she had never encountered before. Here, in a great ballroom jammed with newspaper, radio, television, and film men, she found herself paraded about almost like a champion dog at a show. The U. S. photographers called her "Princess" and occasionally "Liz," shouted "Hey!" at her, got her to pose with the bandleader, asked her to "hold it for just one more," told her to stand still, walk about, move closer and smile, smile, smile. She took it all in good part. This was the only occasion during the entire five weeks in which she found there was someone else to look to to make all the decisions. From the moment when Harry Truman put a fatherly arm around her, she seemed to relax.

Back in Canada there was a second holiday near the little village of Ste. Agathe in the Laurentian Mountains. Here the Princess indulged in her hobby of movie-making. A visitor watched her one morning whip the camera to her eye and in a nasal American voice cry out to her husband: "Hey! You there! Hey, Dook! Look this way a sec! Dat's it! Thanks a lot!"

By the time the tour moved on to the Maritimes she seemed completely at home. In the drawing-room of the Premier of Nova Scotia she sat on the edge of an armchair and cheerfully dangled her legs. One day at the end of a city tour Philip got the limousine driver to turn on some square-dance music and the two of them stamped their feet and whistled. On Prince Edward Island, Elizabeth gave out with a cheery "Whoops" as a presentation trophy came apart in her hands. She seemed a different person from the nervous girl of a month before. In the Charlottetown Hotel, as they were going down to dinner, Philip spotted a spectator peeking between a mountie's legs. "Good Lord," he said, stopping dead in his tracks. "A dwarf!" Elizabeth laughed so hard the elevator had to be held. At dinner that night she kept grinning at Premier Walter Jones, "trying to get a rise out of me" as he later told friends. It was here that Elizabeth said she wouldn't mind doing the whole tour over again.

She had arrived with only the vaguest idea about this oldest member of her Commonwealth. She was leaving with the dossier of her country sealed within the filing-cabinets of her memory. The greatest surprise of all was the vastness of the continent. She remarked on it again and again when she returned home: "It's simply impossible to understand how big it is until you've seen it! Really!"

If the tour was occasionally tedious for her she did not indicate it, though there were some baffling contretemps, as the following conversation between her husband and secretary, overheard on a railway platform, suggests:

PHILIP: Well, what's on the program today?

CHARTERIS: We're going to an experimental farm.

PHILIP: Good. A day on a farm. We should see some nice stock.

CHARTERIS (a little grimly): You are going to see a bunch of Boy Scouts, Girl Guides, and veterans.

PHILIP: What? At an experimental farm?

Finally, the long tour came to an end; the last hand was shaken; the last scroll accepted; the last appreciation murmured. The Princess worked with her secretary for a full week on her farewell speech. She wanted to make absolutely certain it sounded sincere.

This done, her ninety-seven pieces of baggage were loaded on the ship. Womanlike, she stood on the dock and watched it go aboard. One could almost hear her counting each piece, and when the last trunk had gone she gave an audible little sigh of relief. The test was over. The job was done.

Chapter 11:
One Day in November

It is seven o'clock of a dull, drizzling, terribly English morning in November in the first year of the new reign, and London is hardly yet awake. In Lyons Corner House near Charing Cross a few early risers are gulping morning coffee with their kippers but few other restaurants are open. The commuters' trains are not yet disgorging their human cargoes into the streets and most of the city's white-collar workers are still slumbering in suburban villas. But in a baroque bedchamber, at the end of the Mall, a chime is sounding and one executive is already throwing back the monogrammed sheets. The Queen is preparing to meet her day.

She is sipping tea from a delicate porcelain cup brought to her by her red-headed and taciturn Scots maid, Margaret MacDonald, and she is listening to another MacDonald from the Scots Guards playing the pipes outside her window. By eight o'clock she is ready for the morning ritual of the BBC news, for the mail which comes in on a tray, and for the papers marked for her in advance.

But she reads more than the marked sections. Her own photograph smiles from most of the front pages this morning, for she has been to a fashion show and almost all the papers have devoted half of a page of rationed newsprint to it. The Queen, says the *Telegraph,* showed "an intense interest" in the designs; the Queen, says the *Mail,* "asked detailed questions as to the manufacturing and weaving."

There are further royal items. The amount of daily newspaper space devoted to royalty is a measure of its popularity in this first year of the new Queen's reign: another artist has been commissioned to paint the Queen's picture; the Queen's husband has taken his first flying lesson; the Queen's mother has visited the Middle Temple. The Queen's name or picture is on every page.

By now the Queen is ready for her own coffee and kippers and porridge salted in the Scottish manner. She takes her mail into the dining-room where she meets her husband. She gets about seventy letters a day (plus some sixty packages) and she cannot read them all, but she opens and reads those which are marked in such a way that she knows them to be personal.

The clock on the white marble Regency mantelpiece has already chimed nine and it is time for the children to greet their parents. They come in, led by their nurse, Helen Lightbody, a Scotswoman of even temperament and twenty-four years' experience, who believes strongly in routine for babies (bed at the same hour each evening, no eating between meals, no cuddling in the middle of the night). Charles bows to his mother, and runs to his father. The Queen picks up her daughter Anne, a sunny, fair-haired child with a certain explosiveness of temperament. For the next hour the two parents play with their children. Then the day begins.

The Queen takes leave of her family (her husband has his own day ahead) and her high heels click-click briefly across the parquet floors to be muffled quickly in the emerald-green rug of the sitting-room she uses as an office. Here, at a massive, cluttered Chippendale desk, she begins her work. From around the walls the eleven members of the family of George III, painted on copper, stare down at her, a slight girl in a business suit who is their lineal descendant.

There now enters a tall, stooped, slightly Edwardian figure in the narrow trousers of an earlier day. This is Sir Alan Lascelles, the Queen's private secretary, who has served the crown for thirty-two of his sixty-five years and whom the President of France once called "the most discreet man in Europe." For ten years no major palace decision has been made without consulting this eagle-faced courtier with the piercing brown eyes and the steel-rimmed glasses. He is a power not only within the palace, but outside it, for it was he who persuaded Clement Attlee to change his mind and appoint Ernest Bevin to the foreign office, rather than Hugh Dalton, in the first days of the Labour government. Soon he will retire with a peerage as his reward. But now, in his quiet, deferential way he is talking to his Queen, and she settles back in her armchair and smiles and calls him by his nickname: "Tommy."

With Lascelles, the Queen goes over her diary of future engagements, signs a sheaf of documents, and discusses the day's news, the cabinet minutes, and the latest foreign-office dispatches.

Lascelles leaves and an assistant-private-secretary enters. This morning it is Lieutenant Colonel the Hon. Martin Charteris, a deceptively casual courtier whose makeup and background are so typically British upper-class that he seems like something out of a Bulldog Drummond novel. Charteris is the son of a peer, the brother of a peer, and is married to a peer's daughter. His background is Eton and Sandhurst, his hobby is wildfowling. It is hard to realize that this mild, dyspeptic, and sometimes absent-minded man once roamed the alleyways of Jerusalem in a tarboosh disguised as an Arab, was torpedoed and cast adrift on a raft to be rescued at the point of death, and took part in some of the earliest and bitterest desert fighting of the war. His manners are quite impeccable: it is recorded that while tossing on the raft he carefully apologized to all and sundry for being sick.

Now this onetime adventurer, who may someday become as powerful as Lascelles, must deal with less adventurous matters. He has some photographs for the Queen to sign. Each regiment, air force station, and naval vessel is entitled to one. The Queen, who signs her name fifty times a day, signs it again. This done, she goes over the details of some forthcoming engagements with Charteris, who as a former Intelligence officer, briefs her succinctly on the background of the people she is to meet. Occasionally he has been known to secrete reminders on little slips of paper in the pocket of her dress or the edge of her handbag. Today she is to lay a cornerstone at the bomb-damaged Inner Temple and Charteris reminds her that the Clerk of the Works was present when her father opened another damaged portion.

Charteris takes his leave, not backing toward the door as his predecessors did in Victoria's day, but simply saying: "Thank you, Ma'am," and walking out. A few minutes later Sir Piers Legh, the Master of the Household, makes his entrance. The fabric of this man's life is woven out of the same aristocratic fiber as the two who preceded him into this Regency drawing-room with its green curtains and silk damask sofas. Like Charteris, he is the second son of a peer. The playing fields of Eton, the parade ground of the Grenadiers, the trenches of World War I, and twenty-three years at court have shaped his life. He looks the part of an Old Etonian and a retired guards' officer: bald, spruce, red faced, toothy, and correct; his mustache slightly abristle, the tiniest suggestion of a handkerchief peeping from his pocket. The Queen, like almost everybody else, calls him "Joey."

Now this old army man is marshal of a domestic army of valets, housemaids, footmen, porters, and pages. He is majordomo of the largest home in the realm and he is here to discuss its problems with its mistress. (An old servant has reached retiring age, the cellar needs stocking, a footman has given notice.)

Domestic details dealt with, the Queen turns to more personal matters. She chats briefly on the phone with her sister, then calls in one of her acting women of the bed-chamber, Lady Alice Egerton. Lady Alice fits neatly into the jig-saw puzzle of palace hierarchy. Her sister, who was lady-in-waiting to the Queen when she was Princess, is married to a Colville who was once secretary to the Princess and who is in turn related to another Colville whose wife is the daughter of Sir Piers Legh. Lady Alice herself fulfills one of the requisites of a lady in attendance on the Queen: she blends quietly with the tapestries and the woodwork. At twenty-nine she is neither quite pretty nor quite plain. She wears quiet suits in quiet colors with a quiet string of pearls, and her hair is perfectly but quietly coiffured. She presents a wholesome, well-bred English appearance and her features, once remarked, are difficult to recall. One feels that she might make an admirable member of the Secret Service, for when she is with the Queen on official occasions her presence is scarcely heeded.

The two transact their business: appointments with dressmakers and portraitists to be made, thank-you notes, invitations, and letters ("Her Majesty, The Queen commands me . . .") to be written.

Faintly now through the French windows come the familiar notes of the royal salute blown on a bugle by the trumpeter of the Queen's Life Guards at the head of twenty-two mounted troopers down Constitution Hill toward Whitehall, where they will mount the Long Guard as they have done daily for three hundred years. On the top floor, little Prince Charles presses his face against the nursery window and watches the troopers ride by in their scarlet tunics and white breeches with their shining cuirasses and breastplates and plumed helmets.

The Queen is pausing for coffee, white, without sugar. She would like a chocolate biscuit, of which she is very fond, but she is dieting. All about her the great unseen hive of the palace is buzzing. Sir John Wilson, a cheerful and burly Scot, is for the millionth time hinging new stamps in one of the volumes of the royal philatelic collection. Sir Dermot McMorrough Kavanagh, the crown equerry, is attending to the refurbishing of the gold coach for the Coronation. In the press office, Lieutenant-Commander Richard Colville is tactfully warding off the insistent questions of an American reporter who wants to know what the Queen eats for breakfast. Elsewhere, in offices that look more like drawing-rooms, secretaries are dictating to their secretaries and servants are serving other servants. The Yeoman of the Silver Pantry and his assistants are busy polishing five tons of gold plate. The Vermin-man is looking for rats. The clock-man is winding the palace's three hundred clocks. Twelve men are cleaning windows. The table decker is filling all the flower vases and in the Royal Mews two men are polishing all the brass on all the harness which is so seldom used but is always on view in its glass cases. And when the clocks are all wound, the plate all polished, the vases all filled, the windows all washed, and the harness all shined, they will all need winding, polishing, filling, washing, and shining again.

Into the Mews now clip-clops a little single horse brougham, bearing the dispatch boxes from Whitehall. Now the Queen's day has reached the point of its greatest meaning, for in these boxes of black, red, and maroon leather, embossed with the royal arms, are locked the very vitals of the monarchy. They are the vessels that transport to the palace the oceans of paper without which the Empire cannot function, and through them, twice daily, the Queen's fingers can reach out and lightly brush against the shifting panorama of her realm. The appointment of a bishop, judge, governor-general, poet laureate, or astronomer-royal cannot be effected without the ritual of these boxes. Within their steel and leather casing lie the bones of history: minutes of cabinet meetings, reports from governors-general, ministerial letters, ambassadorial notes, secret documents and public memoranda, programs of future events and accounts of past ones, suggestions, ideas, appeals, and protests flowing into the palace in an unending stream from the Empire, the Commonwealth, and the world.

The Queen, who must read everything and sign or initial most of it, attacks the red boxes first, for they contain the most important and secret documents, intended only for her eyes. Attached to each is a slip of paper "From the Prime Minister." The Queen takes a solid gold cylindrical key from a chain and unlocks a box. She reads and signs each document, blotting her signature on the black paper which is provided and which is destroyed daily to prevent any secrets escaping. This done, she turns the route slip over, fits it back, and snaps the box shut. On the other side is written: "From H.M. The Queen." Soon the little brougham is jogging off again and the business of the realm moves on.

Now it is time for her audiences, a morning ritual which is almost as rigid as the boxes. For these she walks through a little anteroom and into the Forty-Four room, named because of its occupancy in 1844 by the Emperor

Nicholas of Russia. His painted face, imprisoned in its
heavy gilt frame, stares down on the Queen with those of
Louis Philippe of France and Leopold I of the Belgians,
both of whom once occupied these quarters. Like almost
every room in the palace the Forty-Four room is a miniature museum, with its cabinets of Sèvres china, its
Louis XIV writing-tables, its Ch'ien Lung jar of *famille*
rose porcelain, and its cream-and-gold Regency chairs up-
holstered in scarlet silk. Over the red-carpeted threshold
and into this exquisite little showpiece of a room the tides
of Empire wash daily. Sooner or later every important official of the crown will come to this or to a similar room
to meet his Queen: field marshals to receive their batons,
prime ministers to report on their corners of the Commonwealth, colonial governors fresh from the coconut palms
of the West Indies or the blue jacarandas of Fiji, high
commissioners, foreign-office men, first sea lords, career
diplomats.

Today there will be four audiences of about fifteen min-
utes each, granted to a cross-section of the realm: to the
Earl of Birkenhead, chairman of the Royal Society of
Literature, to the Rt. Hon. Sir Arthur Salter, Minister of
State for Economic Affairs, to Mr. Henry Studholme,
M.P., vice-chamberlain of the household, and to the Rt.
Hon. William Jordan, a New Zealand elder statesman
who is to be knighted.

Each visitor arrives at the Privy-Purse door at his appointed moment, and is conducted by a page down the long
hallways, past the white busts of former kings, the
French-Empire clocks, the Winterhalter paintings of Albert and Victoria, and the Carrara pillars of the Marble
Hall, into the presence of his Queen.

Here is William Joseph Jordan, a former London policeman, round and florid in his morning coat, being dubbed a Knight Commander of the Most Distinguished Order of St. Michael and St. George. The Queen taps him lightly on the shoulder with the flat of a ceremonial sword, then swings it flashing in a wide arc above his head and taps him again on the other shoulder, and the accolade is conferred. Jordan is, in a sense, a symbol of the realm— a tradesman's son from Ramsgate who left the old country for New Zealand and climbed slowly but stubbornly up the ladder of Labour politics until he returned to his homeland to serve as High Commissioner for fifteen years. Now, under the white-and-gold ceiling and the double Corinthian pillars he is reaping his reward. A tiny clock which forms one of the eyes of a black Negress's head on the mantelpiece ticks off the minutes while the old man at the end of his career talks to the young Queen on the threshold of hers. Then Bill Jordan, now Sir William, leaves his sovereign's presence, soon to slip out of his morning clothes and back into the blue single-breasted suit with the hard collar and high waistcoat that has been his uniform for a generation.

It is twelve forty-five and the palace is at lunch. Down in the servants' hall the platoons of housemaids are chattering like busy sparrows as they break their bread, and in the stewards' room which is one step higher, the pages, footmen, yeomen, and valets are eating. Above stairs, the lady clerks, the Queen's police officer, the chief accountant, and their like are taking their meal in the official mess, and in the household dining-room, which is again higher up the ladder, the assistant secretaries, equerries, and aides are lunching in carefully graded equality. Sir Alan Lascelles is slipping into his velvet-collared coat and preparing to take his only exercise—a brisk walk down Pall Mall to the Travellers' Club. And in the Carnarvon room, where George VI and Churchill used to serve each other with cold buffet (for their talk was so secret that no servant must hear it), the Queen is sitting down to a simple three-course meal of fruit, meat, and ice cream, in the silent painted company of Philip II of Spain, Rudolph II of Austria, Louis XIII of France, and Cardinal Richelieu.

After the meal, she can rest briefly, then spend some time in the nursery. An ornate wrought-iron bird cage of an elevator takes her to the top floor, then down another red-carpeted hall she goes, past the endless varieties of palace bric-a-brac which fills every space and cranny: the marble-topped tables and Chinese vases, the lutes tucked away in alcoves, the busts of former servants, the paintings of royal race-horses and ancient naval battles—everything that has ever been presented to or collected by royalty.

The painted horses soon give way to hobby-horses and other toys lining the hallway: a scale-model Austin and a baby's pram. The Queen enters the green-walled nursery playroom, whose chintz-curtained windows overlook the Mall. On a chair by the window a teddy-bear sprawls—Charles's constant bedfellow. Charles himself is a small package of quicksilver, darting about the room and hiding in closets, pursued by his small Corgi, Sugar. For tomorrow is his birthday and he can hardly contain his excitement. The Queen discusses the party preparations with him and with his two nurses. There are to be fourteen guests, a cake shaped like a galleon, and the usual games. Anne is being taught to say "Happy Birthday, Charles," when they awake the following morning.

The play ends; the work begins again. The Queen returns to the Belgian suite on the ground floor, which she is occupying temporarily until her mother and sister move out of the royal apartments and into Clarence House. Here, where most of the crowned heads of Europe have rested, she changes into an afternoon frock, dons a holly-red coat trimmed with black, a red, matching off-the-face hat with a half veil, a pair of black gloves, and black "peep-toe" shoes, which, though they have gone somewhat out of fashion, she still clings to. Now with Lady Alice she walks a few yards down the corridor to the garden entrance royalty always uses. There is a servant on duty here, dwarfed by the great suits of Indian armor, the elephant tusks hanging on the dark green walls, and the great perfume-burners guarding the doorway. He is wearing the palace uniform of smooth royal-blue battle-dress with gold monogram and buttons, designed by George VI to save palace laundry bills. He earns a little less than twenty dollars a week, but he gets his board and keep at the palace and a pension when he retires. At the moment he is surreptitiously chewing tea-leaves, for he has been across to the Bag O' Nails for a pint of bitters and this is the accepted palace method of cleansing the breath. The palace resists change, and chlorophyll has yet to invade its precincts.

The red-and-maroon Daimler is waiting, with Chivers, the tall, impassive chauffeur who has a boy fighting in Korea, at the wheel. The detective-inspector who guards the Queen leaps out and opens the car door for her. His associates at Scotland Yard joke about this and call him "the footman inspector," but he will have the last laugh when his palace days are done and he gets his MVO and superintendentship.

The Daimler moves away with the lady-in-waiting on the jump-seat, and the Queen, a single, lone figure in the back. It moves across the red gravel forecourt and out through the wrought-iron gates and the crowd that always seems to be here sends up a cheer. The Queen acknowledges it with a smile and a slight upright motion of her gloved hand in which she is clutching a tiny folded handkerchief.

The car moves like a shiny, flat beetle down the broad avenue of the Mall toward the Temple, seat of British justice. Since the night of May 10, 1941, the Inner Temple has lain a mass of rubble. Now it is to be rebuilt, and the stiff little ceremony that follows is as necessary to that rebuilding as bricks and mortar.

The Daimler stops alongside the excavation that marks the site of the bombed building. The Queen walks up five steps to a dark red carpet protected by a striped canvas marquee. Here she is greeted by the youngest of a group of sage and venerable jurists, Lord Justice Singleton, aged sixty-eight. He leads her down the red pathway to a larger marquee where the others are presented to her: Lord Simonds, aged seventy-one; Lord Goddard, aged seventy-six, and Viscount Simon, aged eighty. They hover around the tiny bright-coated Queen like lean, black hawks, these legal old men, bowed over by the twin burdens of age and wisdom: Singleton who was in parliament in her grandfather's day and Simon who was in parliament in her great-grandfather's day and Goddard, and Simonds whose memories, like those of the others, go clearly back to Victoria's Jubilee.

At the end of the marquee there stands a piece of furniture as curiously out of place among all the brick and rubble of the excavation as the old men in their wing collars and cutaway coats. It is a Chippendale table, and here the Queen takes her seat and picks up the quill pen in her gloved hand and signs the visitor's book. This done, two more ancient figures are presented to her: Sir Hubert Worthington, the architect, who is almost seventy, and Sir Guy Lawrence, the contractor, who is almost eighty. The Queen remarks that the series of brick foundations for the new structure seem very like the foundations which remain of the old one, and the old men nod and agree that this is so. For the Temple, like the monarchy, must endure as before and it is possible that these men, whose careers are the link between two Temples and two Queens, are privately remarking that this new Queen has some of the foundation qualities of her predecessor.

There are other dignitaries to meet. The Queen does not forget to speak to the Clerk of the Works, whom Charteris recalled to her. Then she proceeds to lay the eighteen-hundred-pound stone. She daubs a corner with a trowel of mortar, taps it twice with a mallet, and her work is done. Mallet and trowel will be carefully preserved at the Inns of Court as relics of this day.

The Queen walks back across the grounds with the old men to the Treasurer's chambers for tea, waving and smiling at the cheering crowd as she goes. She takes a piece of brown bread and butter and a slice of plain cake with her tea and remarks how pleased her father was to serve as Treasurer of the Inner Temple. Then, as the band of the Irish Guards plays a march, the Daimler threads its way back to the Mall through crowds of her subjects seeking their own respite in afternoon tea. The inevitable crowd is waiting at the palace to cheer and wave and be waved back at in return. It will always be there whenever she comes and goes, and it will be there, watching and waiting, on the day she dies.

Within the great gray palace she picks up once more the

loose threads of her day. There is some private correspondence to attend to and the next day's menus to choose.
They come up handwritten in French from the chef, a
burly, round-faced Yorkshireman named Ronald Aubrey,
who came to the palace fourteen years ago from the
Savoy. She pauses briefly over the evening papers, and
again there is news of personal interest: All the papers
announce special feature-articles coming up the next day
about Prince Charles.

For another hour she reverts to her role as mother
and plays with her children. While this is going on, Mr.
Henry Studholme, M.P., is doing his duty by his Queen.
As vice-chamberlain it is his daily task to prepare "the
telegram"—a written report of the day's session of parliament. Mr. Studholme is a country gentleman by profes-
sion and a Conservative member of parliament by choice.
Like almost everyone connected with the palace he looks
the part to an uncanny degree—a reed-thin, aristocratic
figure with an aquiline face and a clipped mustache of
iron gray. His report runs to about four hundred words
and he writes it carefully in longhand, making it, as he
says, "respectful but readable" and trying his best to be
"a faithful mirror reflecting the atmosphere and high-
lights of the day."

Her playtime ended, the Queen learns something of
the atmosphere of the afternoon in Mr. Studholme's
respectful but readable prose. (Mr. Churchill has provoked laughter with a wisecrack and the Queen laughs
with him.) But she will not be satisfied with the four
hundred words of the telegram, which is really only telegraphed when she is out of London. Later she will read
all of Hansard.

It is time to dress for dinner. Two thousand electric

lights have been switched on and an army of fifty house-maids has suddenly appeared to draw all the curtains. The Queen bathes and selects a semi-formal gown from two laid out by Miss MacDonald, who hovers in attend-ance over her. This discreet Scotswoman is as close to the Queen as any subject can be, so close indeed that she sometimes talks of herself and the Queen as if they were a single person. "We got engaged," she told a friend when the Queen's betrothal was announced.

The Duke of Edinburgh, back from an official visit to Cambridge, comes into the sitting-room in his dinner jacket and together they listen to the six p.m. BBC news, which reports what they already know: that the Duke has been to Cambridge to receive an honorary LL.D. and that the Queen has driven to the Inner Temple to lay a cornerstone. Then the two go up to the nursery to watch Charles and Anne put to bed. The children sleep on firm, hard mattresses and their pillows are stuffed with hair so that they will not sink their faces into them and smother. There are no night-lights in their room, but there are microphones above their beds so that if they cry the sound will be communicated at once to their nurses.

The Queen reads the children a story and helps with prayers, then she and her husband return to their quar-ters for a pre-dinner drink, Tio Pepe sherry for Eliza-beth, pink gin for Philip.

Sharp at eight thirty the two sit down by candlelight at a polished mahogany table to a dinner of Consommé Brunoise, Suprême de Turbot Bonne Femme, Perdreau en Casserole, Salade, Crème au Caramel, and Sablés au Fromage. After dinner Philip orders some nuts, which he cracks between his teeth, as he once did in the navy.

After dinner the inevitable boxes are waiting again and

there are more documents to sign, Hansard to read, and magazines to digest. Only in the last hour of her day can the Queen relax. There is a canasta game with her husband, mother, and sister. The Duke sips a scotch and soda, the Queen a liqueur. Both of them are looking forward to the weekend, which is one day distant, when they can flee the city for Royal Lodge, where there are no servants in livery, where the furniture is chewed by pet dogs, and where, except for the inevitable boxes, one's time is one's own.

As the canasta game draws to its end, the palace and the city begin to run down slowly like an unwound clock. The theaters in Leicester Square disgorge their crowds and the crowds disperse. The restaurants close their doors and the buses slow their schedules. At the end of the Mall, the lights wink out slowly one by one. The crowd in front of the railings has finally gone. Now the only movement is the sentry mechanically walking his beat and the three lions *passant gardant* rippling in the cold night breeze above the dark bulk of the Queen's home. The long day is done and the Queen and her household are asleep.

Chapter 12:
The Man in the Background

There are times when Philip, Duke of Edinburgh, must feel that in his position as consort to Queen Elizabeth II he is teetering on a gossamer strand. For only a slack-wire artist knows the sense of precarious poise that is the lot of the husband of a British Queen. On one hand he must never give the impression that he is trying to run the show. On the other he must never let his countrymen think he is tied to a woman's apron strings.

In a country where the male is still recognized as supreme, he alone must take orders gracefully from his wife. In an age in which each man's task is defined with pigeon-hole efficiency, his is vague and nebulous. Constitutionally he is a nobody. Historically he is a freak. Politically he is a cipher.

The last consort, Albert, was a man of Job-like patience and consummate tact, whose whole upbringing had been a preparation for the task. Philip on the other hand can be both impatient and tactless and his own upbringing has been the exact opposite of Albert's. Yet at the outset of his career he is already more popular than Albert was at the end of his.

Even if he were an ordinary young Englishman, Philip's background would seem unconventional. He is Danish and German by blood, Greek by birth, and British by breeding. His father was an exile; his mother is a nun. Until his marriage he had never known a real home of his own. His uncle, who brought him up, is one of the most unorthodox and strongest-willed members of the British peerage. The school to which he went is in many ways the antithesis of all the other public schools in Britain for it places the accent on the individual rather than on the team. From childhood Philip has been reared to think and act for himself. Now he finds himself in the one job where it is difficult to do either.

Outwardly this does not seem to bother Philip of Edinburgh, late of Schleswig-Holstein-Sonderburg-Glücksburg. He climbs amiably down mine shafts, saunters cheerfully through bazaars and exhibitions, makes his breezy, offhand speeches, and keeps a pace or two behind his Queen. His extemporaneous witticisms have been widely circulated. In Washington, D. C., a young woman about to be introduced to him murmurs: "Mmm!" Philip looks her over and responds: "Mmmm-*mmmm!*" On the Canadian prairies a woman calls out: "I've got a life-size picture of you!" Philip calls back: "How ghastly!" In Niagara Falls a photographer mistakes him for a colleague and asks: "What did you get?" Philip replies: "I got bloody wet!" In the West End he is sitting in a theater box watching a musician in the orchestra pit puzzling out a crossword question. Philip drops the answer on the drum. In Paris, as the crowds cheer, he turns to a French cabinet minister and says: "Too bad you sent your royal family to the guillotine." In London, during a garden party, he winks at a lady reporter and asks, *sotto voce:* "When do we get to the gin?" In Windsor, Ontario, at the railway station, a dog makes straight for him during a ceremony. The crowd stands petrified while a soldier does his best to lure the offending animal away. Only those closest to Philip notice that while he is staring innocently at the sky he is also snapping his fingers to attract the dog's attention.

This is all very unconventional, coming from the midst of a royal family noted for its public reserve, and it has helped make Philip the delight of the masses. But it is not the only unconventional thing about him. Behind the outer garment of amiability, behind the pliable grin and the jaunty air, there is a harder core of alloy much less pliable. Of all the members of the family in the palace (always excepting the Duke of Windsor), Philip alone has thoroughly rubbed his shoulders against the world. The country is full of men who have brushed past him at school, in the navy, on the playing fields, in a club. Yet few know him well enough to tell what he is really thinking or exactly what makes him tick. At school he knew everybody and everybody liked him, but he had no confidants and he had no nicknames. In the bull-sessions he was careful to express no opinions. One of his former classmates puts it this way: "Philip had a great deal of superficial charm, but underneath that charm there was a constant wall of reserve, and beyond that barrier you simply could not go."

The barrier is still there. This tall young man with the long German neck, the straight profile, the quizzical look, and the penetrating blue eyes is still an unknown quantity on the British scene. Before his career is over, the smiling Duke could change the nature of the monarchy. For he is a man who likes to do things for himself and it sometimes irks him when he finds he can't. "I really feel I should decide for myself where to go," he remarked fairly recently to a friend, regarding the various ceremonies arranged for him. "That's the best way of putting over this idea of the monarchy."

He prefers to run the palace lifts on his own and open doors for himself. "I'm not bloody helpless," he sometimes remarks. He likes to mix his own pink gin, rather than have the butler do it, and he has on occasion prowled into the cavernous yellow-walled palace kitchens to do his own cooking.

His approach tends to be frontal. Rather than call an aide to get a job done he will often send an order directly to the man involved. Rather than send for his head stalker, as George VI would have done, he whistles for his dog and goes off to find him. Rather than call a chauffeur, he prefers to pack his family into his pastel-green Ford Zephyr and drive along the Scottish roads for a picnic.

He would prefer to answer the phone himself. Once, after a minor accident in which he was involved, a reporter phoned Clarence House, where he lived with Elizabeth before her accession, and asked for details. Philip took the call himself, told the reporter what he wanted to know, and rang off without revealing his identity. One London morning paper got a two-day scoop on his engagement to Elizabeth. It heard there was an announcement coming and phoned Philip, who confirmed it.

In matters mechanical, from the running of a movie projector to the driving of a car, he likes to have his way. When he took his first flying lessons the RCAF remarked on the fact that he did not seem to be doing any landing practice on the field. He simply flew off with his instructor and wasn't seen again until the lesson was over. It turned out that Philip had decided to do his landings and take-offs on the grounds of Windsor Castle, a good many miles away.

He likes to drive the royal vehicles himself and is impatient of average speeds. During his Canadian holiday he clocked ninety-two mph up the twisting Vancover Island Highway. On one excursion to open a Scottish hydro project he popped the chauffeur into the back seat, took the wheel himself, and reached the scene before the official welcoming party. Early in the new reign he packed chauffeur and detectives aboard a train and drove the Queen from London to Windsor on his own—an incident that caused Scotland Yard to complain that the sovereign's life was being endangered.

He brings the same breezy independence to his speeches and is proud of the fact that many are his own work. Before giving a major speech he records it on his tape recorder and plays it back, to iron out poor-sounding phrases. He has no trouble speaking extemporaneously and his speeches usually have both point and wit. To the British Automobile Association he talked about the need for better rear lights on cars, and to the National Playing Fields Association he insisted that the important thing was not to have beautiful fields but enough room to play on. He drew both laughter and raised eyebrows in Edinburgh when in the course of a speech he recalled that the last time he had been in the city the train was "six drinks late." In Charlottetown, Prince Edward Island, a teetotaling Canadian province, he was asked by the premier to say a few extemporaneous words after the official dinner. Philip rose and said: "I've been told that half the people of Prince Edward Island don't know the taste of liquor. Obviously that half is not represented at this function."

For a royal personage, he is remarkably outspoken. The speeches are directed usually along his pet line—that Britain is badly in need of an industrial renaissance, that scientific progress must be put to immediate practical use by industry. In most of his speeches, this word "practical" appears. "It is all very well to understand the problems which face this country and to have glib theories for their solution," he told technical-college students in the late fall of 1952. "It is quite another matter to have the foresight and courage to embark upon a scheme to do something practical about it." In Montreal he thanked automobile company officials for the free use of cars on the royal tour, but couldn't resist adding: "Why don't you people make a car a fellow can get into without hitting his head?"

It is not surprising in the light of all this that the personality of this stubborn and independent-minded young man can be seen at work behind the gray Portland stone of the palace. Even before his marriage Philip had brought an air of informality to Elizabeth's rather stiff sitting-room by switching the furniture about so that the sofas were pulled up in front of the fireplace for comfort. Before long he had changed his wife's dress and waistline. The Queen's figure slimmed; her clothes became more modish. One day he dropped in on a sitting the Queen was giving to the woman who made the design of her head for coins. Philip criticized the drawing. "I'm quite familiar with the line of my wife's neck and shoulders and you've got it all wrong," he said. It was revised twice.

Everything from the shade of his wife's hats to the furniture in Clarence House came under his influence. The Office of Works, charged with renovating the bridal home, wanted to handle all interior decoration, but Philip demurred. He insisted on choosing his own decorator and initiating his own ideas. He planned it all very carefully, using models and scale plans and lists of wedding presents to help him. ("What do you do with two tons of mahogany?" Elizabeth once asked, looking over the wedding list. Philip had some of it made up into doors; the rest was sold to buy more useful things.)

He had shelves made to fit his own clothes exactly, for he likes to be independent of a valet and to find things in a hurry. His own room had none of the rococo elegance usually associated with royalty. He had it fitted out like a ship's cabin with concealed lighting, built-in cupboards, and sycamore-lined walls. Every piece of furniture was made to his specifications. When workmen were discussing moving and arranging all the new furniture Philip appeared and said casually: "Don't take any notice of that. I like to arrange my own things." Whereupon he took his coat off and worked with them.

In the palace the spectacle of a Prince who acts so independently has caused a certain dismay and it has been less easy for him to have his own way. He was appalled to find the palace kitchens a full half-mile away from the royal dining-room, but the Office of Works refused to approve any costly changes. Philip had to content himself with installing modern concealed lighting in the royal suite and an intercom system along naval lines to replace old-fashioned page boys.

This modern approach to ancient problems is Philip's heritage from Lord Mountbatten, the blooded aristocrat who is himself an unconventional member of his species and whose influence on his nephew has been important and lasting. Philip worships his uncle. Just before his marriage a journalist friend offered to give him some advice on newspaper matters. Philip thanked him politely but added: "I must tell you that there is only one man who can give me advice or help me in any way and that is Lord Louis Mountbatten."

Philip has been under Mountbatten's aegis since the age of seven when he was put in an English prep school after his father, Prince Andrew, had been exiled from Greece. It is generally believed that the Prince commended

Philip to the elder Mountbatten's care after the latter had, as the Greek papers put it, promised the boy "a glittering future." Philip soon became a Mountbatten to his fingertips.

There are times today when he seems to be a carbon copy of his uncle. Both have the same kind of slide-rule mind, the same thorough and methodical German outlook, the same fierce determination to excel in any test. Mountbatten's inventive brain has produced everything from elastic shoelaces and new polo mallets to the imaginative "Pipe Line under the Ocean" of World War II. Philip, who thought up the plastic-topped car, has contributed a good many of his own ideas to the special Rolls-Royce built for the Queen. It contains such devices as a concealed runningboard that automatically lights up when the rear door opens, and a seat for the Queen on the offside which is so constructed that she can be easily seen by the crowd.

Both men delight in modern gadgets and modern modes of living. The Mountbattens had the first penthouse in Britain in the early thirties, crammed with tubular furniture, with built-in cupboards, a bright décor, and a maze of buzzers. Philip has the same bent. The palace intercom, the pushbutton wardrobe, and the tape recorder which he uses to send his wife "letters" on, and which he also uses to record her radio speeches so she can hear herself, all have the Mountbatten touch.

The Mountbatten thinking is as modern as the Mountbatten décor. Britain's aristocrats will not soon forget that as last Viceroy of India under a Labour government he presided over the twilight days of the British Raj. He has been called a Red, though actually he is a mild Liberal. Philip thinks on similar lines and he is the first non-conformist in a hundred years to invade a dynasty always publicly non-partisan and privately Tory.

Philip has acquired another Mountbatten characteristic: the capacity for taking great pains to produce a striking effect. His uncle used to astonish subordinates by boarding various ships under his command and showing a minute knowledge of such trifles as the bosun's broken leg. His officers didn't know that he kept a card index of all ships and men under his command, which he carefully consulted before making an inspection.

Philip similarly astonished four thousand members of the British Association for the Advancement of Science with a speech of considerable virtuosity in which he glibly rolled off references to such items as Kipping's silicon chemistry, Lanchester's Vortex theory and the X-ray spectrum. What the scientists didn't know was that Philip had had boxes of scientific papers shipped to Malta which he carefully absorbed. He had then had the draft checked for accuracy before memorizing it. When he gave it he seemed to be consulting nothing more than a few scribbled notes on paper from HMS *Magpie's* wardroom.

It was quite natural that Philip should have followed Mountbatten into the navy and onto the polo field, where his great ambition is to become as good a player as his champion uncle. But it is still too early to tell whether he has inherited another Mountbatten characteristic: his tremendous personal drive and ambition.

In the roaring twenties Dickie Mountbatten was a deceptive playboy, driving his Rolls-Royce with its silver ornaments and its monogrammed initials at breakneck speeds. He moved so swiftly in the fast, tight social clique which centered around the former Prince of Wales that he was snubbed by the Royal Yacht Squadron and was refused membership. Certainly there was nothing Victorian about him.

But behind the handsome, smiling Mountbatten features burned the hot flame of ambition. His father, Prince Louis of Battenberg, had been First Lord of the Admiralty during World War I, but his German name had caused a wave of national resentment that forced his resignation. All his life Mountbatten's goal has been to reach the position his father had to relinquish. When his friends lay abed after late parties, Mountbatten was at his desk in the Admiralty working his way slowly up the gangway of promotion. Ambition has made him a perfectionist, and he has succeeded in almost everything he has set out to do. He taught himself to play polo by watching slow motion pictures of experts and practicing for hours on a wooden horse. As a result he became one of the world's best players and a textbook authority on the game. "It is a little weakness in me to think I can do anything," he once told Churchill, and this has been the key to his character.

If a polo stick can be shaped to perfection so can a growing boy, and this was Mountbatten's approach to his ward. Philip must be the best dancer in the class, the best swimmer on the team. He must be above average in cricket and hockey and he must be the leading boy at school. And he must acquire that little weakness of believing he could do anything. He must not be told that the King had, and would use, the power to nominate him for the navy. He must go to school like everyone else and sweat like everyone else at academic work and take the naval examinations all on his own.

All this came to pass at Gordonstoun, the school on the

Moray Firth he attended in the years before the war. Here Philip came under the influence of another dedicated and unorthodox man—a graying German with a bloodhound's face and a passionate belief in self-achievement. This was Kurt Hahn, the principal, who had first established a progressive school in Salem, Germany, whence he had fled when Hitler came to power.

Philip had spent a few months at Hahn's Salem school at the invitation of a sister in Germany, but was packed back to England with almost breakneck speed when it was discovered that he continually guffawed at the Nazi salute. "We thought it better for him," his sister said, explaining the sudden switch of plans; and she added: "And better for us."

In Morayshire, Scotland, Philip took his schooling under circumstances considerably different from those enjoyed or suffered by the vast bulk of well-to-do English youths. Faggings and canings are foreign to Hahn's teaching. In other schools a boy is taught to compete against his fellows; in Gordonstoun he learns to compete against himself. Hahn's system stresses such individual sports as javelin throwing and high jumping, less for their own sake than for the sense of achievement they instill in the boys. Each is encouraged to better his own record and, as life is itself something of a high jump, there is more to it than mere physical well-being.

Another aspect of the Hahn system is the emphasis it places on boys doing things for themselves. When Philip became a senior boy he kept his own training record, like the others, and no master bothered to look at it. On it he recorded all the things which he was supposed to do— the two hot washes and the two cold washes a day, the five pushups, the sixty rope-skips. If he neglected any aspect of his training he recorded that, too. If he was punished he carried out his own punishment on his own and recorded the fact that he carried it out.

All this, in retrospect, seems an unlikely sort of background for a future royal consort. But Philip could not read the future. His fellow classmates used sometimes to whisper that he would grow up to marry Princess Elizabeth, but they never said it to his face. As for Philip, Hahn has written that he was occasionally "impatient of . . . the royalty business." It annoyed him when strangers asked him for his autograph. His qualities of leadership were noticeable but they were "marred at times by impatience or intolerance." He had a reputation for cycling at breakneck speeds through the village of Elgin, occasionally threatening to overturn perambulators, but always apologizing so charmingly that he was forgiven.

The charming, dashing, and impatient schoolboy profited by Hahn's training in self-reliance and his record began to show some of that little weakness for perfection that is a Mountbatten trait. The high-jump bar rose higher, the javelin traveled farther under his efforts. He captained the hockey and cricket teams and became head of the school.

He went to Royal Naval College at Dartmouth to learn to be a sailor and here one day he met Elizabeth, Princess of England. He caught her eye by leaping over the tennis nets to show how high he could jump. When the royal yacht departed, all the cadets followed in rowboats until the King ordered them back. But Philip rowed doggedly on, far ahead of the others. "The young fool!" said George VI.

The young fool stayed far ahead of his fellow cadets. He passed his naval examinations and emerged as the best all-round boy of the year. As a naval lieutenant in the war that followed he served aboard eight vessels and took part in a series of actions which began with a bombardment on the Libyan coast in 1940 and ended five years later at the surrender of the Japanese Fleet in Tokyo Bay.

In the navy he continued to get things done by himself. One day he grew angry because the cook had served a saddle of mutton without gravy, so he promptly popped into the galley and made gravy on his own, using everything from sherry to herbs. When he gave orders for his destroyer to be painted he took brush in hand and painted the bridge himself. When Chinese stokers went on strike he blistered his hands shoveling coal until he couldn't hold a fork.

He was known as a good officer but a stern one, and had something of the reputation of a disciplinarian. His language was tough and blistering, but he brought a sense of perfection to his job. As gunnery officer on HMS *Whelp* he knew his equipment down to the last bolt. For his efficiency in action, he was mentioned in dispatches.

His fellow officers observed that he held his liquor well, liked gunroom songs and bawdy stories, and drove his car at top speed on shore duty. (At one shore establishment he held the record to London: ninety-eight miles in one hundred minutes.) He was as high spirited as the next man and enjoyed a wardroom game called "Dive Bomber," which consisted of turning out all the lights, making sounds like airplanes, punctuated by loud explosions, and kicking the furniture about. He ate a staggering amount of food, tucking away great quantities of ham and marmalade sandwiches, and liked when on shore to drop into local pubs for a beer-and-cheese supper. He took his leaves at Sandringham and Windsor, and always referred scrupulously to King George VI as "the Monarch." He liked to sit up late jawing with his fellows, but when any contentious subject came up he seemed to fade inconspicuously into the woodwork. And when at last he and his cronies came to a parting of the ways it was with the realization that they did not know him very much better than when he had joined the ship. He had poured out his soul to no one, this zealous young officer who mixed so well and said so little.

All this time his rapport with Elizabeth had been ripening. Philip's breezy self-possession was found somewhat startling in royal circles. On his first visit to Balmoral in 1946, he was persuaded only with difficulty to wear the sacred kilt, and when he came pirouetting down the staircase crying: "Don't I look beautiful?" it did not sit too well with George VI. Once he was reprimanded by the Queen Mother for remarking that there seemed to be more servants than diners at a family meal. When he became involved in an accident at Hyde Park Corner the King asked him not to drive Elizabeth about any more, but he managed to continue the practice anyway. Finally he asked for her hand in marriage and the King demurred. He thought it better if everything was held up for six months. Off the royal family went to South Africa without Philip. But the affair did not cool in this cooling-off period. Elizabeth hung his picture on her desk in the royal train and when she returned they held hands in the forests of Balmoral, hummed *People Will Say We're in Love* in the halls of Windsor Castle, and went dancing at Ciro's and Quaglino's in London. The secret was out long before the official announcement. For the first time the world began to look curiously at the blond young man in the naval uniform.

After his marriage the blond young man continued to act much as he had before he became the husband of a Princess. He drove his tiny M.G. sports car himself, visited pubs, and turned up at the luncheon meetings of the Thursday Club in Soho, where he consumed great quantities of oysters and sole, sherry and port, and occasionally tossed ripe olives out of the third-floor window of Wheeler's restaurant onto passers-by in Old Compton Street. When the afternoon waned, he remarked casually: "I have to go to the King's house now," and off he went. He did not forget his closest cronies. One, a handsome Australian named Michael Parker, became his equerry. Another, a society photographer named Baron Nahum, began to get commissions for royal sittings. On his wedding day Philip insisted, not without opposition, that all his naval friends from bosun to captain be invited to the Abbey, and he saw that they got seats well forward on the groom's side of the aisle. The more blue-blooded guests on the bride's side noted with some curiosity that the naval men seemed to be giving an inordinate amount of attention to the giant programs which they constantly consulted throughout the ceremony. Those in the gallery spotted the reason: small flasks of rum were being passed about under cover of the sheltering wall of paper.

Each morning after his marriage Philip drove himself to work at the Admiralty, just another naval lieutenant who happened also to be Baron Greenwich, Earl of Merioneth and Duke of Edinburgh. Once, on a tour of Greenwich Naval College, Philip discovered that both he and the captain of the college were calling each other "sir," a situation as confusing as it was ludicrous. Philip took the matter into his own hands. "This is your wardroom and I'm a sailor," he said, "so I'll call *you* sir, sir!"

Philip had his final fling at navy life in Malta, where he was transferred in 1949. Here, as commander of HMS *Magpie,* he was nicknamed "Dukey" by his men, stroked a boat crew to victory on Regatta Day, and once did his best to steal the ship's cat from a neighboring vessel. Elizabeth visited him. He took her aboard ship to show her some radar equipment, which failed to function. Philip swore a great oath that embarrassed the bosun but fazed Elizabeth not at all.

But the free and easy existence became less free and less easy as the shadow of the throne lengthened toward the future Queen. Philip returned to England and bade the navy good-by forever. Soon his usually hatless figure began to appear in the press, carrying out the day-to-day functions of inspection, review, and ceremonial, the hands characteristically clasped behind the back, the head thrust forward quizzically, the face set in the look of serious pre-occupation which the British people have come to associate with royal personages doing their duty. After his wife's accession the Duke no longer appeared among the lively crowd of journalists, actors, and bon vivants who make up the company of the Thursday Club, and old acquaintances began to tell one another that he was growing a bit stuffy. For the gap between Philip and the world he had known was widening as inevitably as the gap between his rowboat and the others that day at Dartmouth when he first saw his future wife.

The new world—the world of red carpets, bowing mayors, secretaries in black morning-coats, footmen in blue livery, plain-clothes detectives in hard hats—brought its own irritations. Philip, who hates any headgear except a naval officer's, now found himself forced to wear everything from Homburgs to gray toppers. The white carnation became a part of his uniform. Every aspect of his dress became a matter of public concern. "I dress comfortably, not to be in fashion," he said and there were murmurs from Savile Row—about his dinner jacket (black suede), his trousers (no suspenders), his collar (too low), his shoulders (too padded), his lapels (too rounded).

The qualities of intolerance and impatience which his headmaster had remarked began to exhibit themselves. After the obscurity of the navy Philip has never yet quite reconciled himself to the fierce glare of flashbulbs which beats upon the throne. He once became so angered at photographers that he took their names as if they were naval ratings and sent them to their employers with a protest.

It is on these occasions that his lack of training for the royal task shows most. In Canada, Philip was very popular with the press at the outset; Elizabeth less so, for she seemed reserved and nervous while Philip was breezy and affable. But by the end of the tour, positions were reversed. The newspapermen had cooled markedly to Philip, who became testy with them, and warmed to Elizabeth, who never showed temperament. "She wears well," one reporter said. "He doesn't."

His most notable brush with the press took place in Montreal. Here it was intended that the royal couple should say good-by to those of the press corps who were leaving the royal train before the tour went on to the Maritimes. Through a mixup the entire corps was assembled. When Philip arrived he instantly spotted that something had gone wrong and that he would be required to shake hands all over again with a group of men and women he had already met officially. "This is a bloody waste of time," he said, and kept his hands in his pockets. But Elizabeth, who has been trained to accept official mixups with resignation, patiently went through the lengthy business of again greeting each of the assembled journalists.

Such incidents represent the fairly human reactions of a man who has not yet got used to the fact that he is required to be on public view. It is a new experience for him and there are times when he fails to hide his own rather forceful feelings. Once, during the royal tour, he was inspecting a steel mill in Sydney, Nova Scotia, and in his quizzical way was asking the usual questions about the plant's operation. "Say," somebody said, "the Duke is really interested in all this." Just then the Duke turned to a man he thought was his equerry. "Let's get the hell out of here," he said and only then discovered he had made the remark to a photographer.

It is not in the cards that this outspoken and self-sufficient consort will follow the advice laid down by his predecessor Albert for the husbands of future Queens: that he "should entirely sink his own individual existence in that of his wife." Philip is not the type. He prizes his own individual existence highly. He is a man who likes to compete and when he competes he likes to excel. It is a matter of chagrin to him that he is still an indifferent shot in a family notable for its marksmen. When he first attended a Highland dance in Edinburgh he had to sit on the sidelines while Elizabeth danced eightsome reels with other partners. He spent the next two days learning the art and at the next ball kept up with the Scots. Lord Mountbatten once taunted him that he could change uniforms in a minute and a half. Philip at once learned to do it in a flat minute.

It is not surprising then that he should already be giving some form to the nebulous job whose attributes and functions have been described as "purely decorative" and "exclusively procreative." In the half-dozen organizations where he holds active chairmanships he takes his job seriously. As chairman of the Automobile Association he allows no major decision to go through without his approval. "Gentlemen," he once said, banging his gavel during an impasse. "I am not moving from this table until a decision has been reached."

It is in his impact upon the Queen that he will make himself felt to the greatest degree. These two, who seem so outwardly different, are in fact quite similar. Their tastes are middle rather than upper class and they both revel in a lack of ostentation. They prefer steak and chips to goose liver, and musical comedy to opera. When they holidayed in British Columbia, they were provided with a complete selection of classical records, but they chose Bing Crosby by joint preference. Their recreation centers on outdoor sport, and their reading runs to magazines and popular best-sellers. It is in their disparities that they complement each other. The tactful Elizabeth can teach her husband something about the delicate craft to which she was born. The outspoken Philip can teach his wife something about the outside world which she has never known.

Philip runs his home—though not his life—in the traditional manner of the British husband. One observer recalls a private dinner which the royal couple gave when Elizabeth was still Princess. The menu was handed to her first, but Philip took it from her, saying: "Come on, dear, let me have this. They all wait for you and they all feel they have to order as you do. I feel like scallops. Does anybody else feel like scallops?" He ordered all round, then handed the menu back to his wife. "All right, dear," he said, "you order the dessert. I don't want any." It is he who decides that Charles has enough toys and will be allowed no more until next Christmas, and when the boy misbehaves Elizabeth always threatens to tell his father. Charles is already taking after Philip, whom he worships. He is self-sufficient, talkative, and insatiably curious. He has the same way of walking with his head thrust inquisitively forward and his hands clasped behind his back, and it is noticed that he, too, dislikes to wear a hat. His tastes in toys and games follow his father's bent. He likes to build things with toy bricks and he and Philip are often on their knees over his mechanical train. He likes to stalk in the forests of Balmoral with a toy telescope and a toy gun. He has a cowboy suit which he likes to try to square-dance in and he and his small sister sometimes play at "dressing-up" as their parents on a state occasion. Philip is already teaching him to swim in the palace pool (using a fishing-pole device of his own invention), for he, like Kurt Hahn, believes that boys should be able to strike out on their own.

When King Charles III finally attains the throne it will almost certainly be a considerably changed monarchy from the one that Britain knows today. This will be due in good part to his father. It is not generally realized how much the royal idea has already been transformed in the past century, yet many features of it would be quite unrecognizable to the young Victoria. It is not so much that the Queen flies across continents or inspects troops from a cream-colored jeep. It is that royalty's attitude has changed toward the people and the people's toward royalty.

Victoria never knew or understood her great middle class (let alone her lower class) and it is doubtful if her son, Edward VII, did either. They lived in an age of easy opulence and they moved in the tight social circle of their own kind. As a man of Philip's age, Edward lived in a house containing three hundred vases which occupied the talents of two men keeping them filled with fresh flowers. His christening party cost a million dollars and the cake was eight feet in circumference. As King, his idea of traveling incognito was to enter Naples harbor escorted by eight battleships, four cruisers, four destroyers, and a dispatch vessel. He and his mother conversed with the monarchs of Europe and in those days a king could transact state business by a friendly call to an uncle or a cousin on a foreign throne. Those days are gone, and so are the thrones. "Being a king nowadays is rather like owning a golf course and having nobody to play with," George VI once remarked wanly.

The British King has lost all vestige of political power and partisanship and this, too, has been accomplished in less than a century. Before Victoria's time, kings appointed ministers and took political sides. George III actually canvassed Windsor in a general election. Even Victoria, a century ago, felt that she had the right to dismiss her foreign secretary, Lord Palmerston, and indeed, helped to force his eventual resignation. Elizabeth would not consider this for a moment today nor would she give any hint of her own political color, as Victoria did until her dying day.

But what the British monarchy has lost in wealth and power it has gained in popularity. The new dragon-class sailing yacht that Philip has purchased may be only one-tenth the size of George V's great J-class *Britannia,* and

the palace meals may have dropped from fourteen courses
to four, but in 1953 the people see their sovereign as they
never did in 1900. As late as George V's reign, the flash-
camera was hardly known and the people knew their king
only through his portrait on coins and stamps. When the
camera came in, George V never let a photographer within
twenty-five feet of him. Today the Queen's picture appears almost daily in the press. Queen Mary was the first
royal personage to draw closer to the people in a different
way: she began to enter the shops, something that had
hitherto not been done. Before this everything was sent
to the palace for royal approval. Elizabeth's marriage
was marked by another change. She was allowed to keep
the wedding gifts sent to her by strangers.

It would never have occurred to George V to move
about the bombed areas of London in World War I (as
his son did in World War II), nor would Edward VII
have countenanced going down a mine shaft or through
a steel mill. Victoria once made a ceremonial visit to a
Yorkshire steel works. The announcement was made days
in advance and a perfect frenzy of preparation went on
at the plant. The interior of the factory was transformed
into a fairyland. The steel was entirely covered in turf,
artificial banks were built and trees planted therein until
the place resembled a park. The Queen finally arrived,
entered the yard in a state landau drawn by four bays,
waited for a few minutes beside the mill and then departed
abruptly. The contrast with her great-grandson, George
VI, who arrived at hundreds of factories on the shortest
possible notice and then went through them thoroughly, is
considerable.

On the other hand, no British papers would editorialize
today upon the monarch as they once did. *The Times*

marked the death of George IV with these words: "There never was an individual less regretted by his fellow creatures than this diseased King. What eye has wept for him? What heart has heaved one sob of unmercenary sorrow?" The *Spectator*, which was pro-George IV, still listed all his mistresses on his death. And the same paper, on William IV's death, referred to him as a "weak, ignorant and commonplace sort of person." He was the last monarch to receive this treatment. From Victoria onward, royal death has been accompanied by complete eulogy.

Nobody hisses Elizabeth today as they hissed Victoria at Ascot, and Albert Edward, her son, at Epsom. A century ago, London crowds rushed to the Tower to gloat because they had read in the papers (wrongly, as it turned out) that the consort and possibly the Queen, too, were being conveyed there for treason during the Crimean War. As late as 1871 mass meetings to attack the royal family were held in Trafalgar Square. And even in 1912 there were rude jingles and ruder stories about George V. Today, in many people's minds, the monarchy is sacrosanct. But it would not remain so if it did not move with the times.

The Dutch and the Scandinavians have pushed their monarchy a step farther along the highway of change than the British. Their kings ride bicycles, answer the phone themselves and send their children to state schools. (Sometimes the children hitchhike home.) It is doubtful if the British monarchy will go this far, but if Philip has his way it will certainly go in this direction. Every one of his actions thus far has borne this out. "I'll be back in London in time to have tea with the kids," he amiably remarked to the crowd that saw him off from Malta. No previous member of the family in the palace has been this informal with the public. Before his days are over this firm-minded and sometimes tactless young man, who dislikes bowler hats and striped trousers, who feels fettered by too many servants and detectives, who would rather roll skittles in a pub than sit in a state box in an opera, will have stamped the oldest of British institutions with his own personality. King Charles III may not be a king on a bicycle. But if his father has his way he will never on any account be a king on a pedestal either.

HEAVY DATE

You are taking your girl to the theater, but actually you do not take her at all, except in a manner of speaking. She takes you.

You do not bother with your car for she will not ride in it anyway. You take a taxi and you drive to her place. A policeman stops you at the gate and asks you who you are. You tell him and he lets you go on.

You go in the door and walk up three red-carpeted steps and a footman stops you and asks you who you are and you tell him and he takes you into an elevator, which is about ten yards away, and you go together to the second floor.

You are greeted by a lady on the second floor who takes you down the hall to your girl. You bow and call her "ma'am." There is a servant in livery and a glass of sherry and some canapés on a silver tray. There are some other guests. You all make conversation.

You go down in the elevator again and into a shiny car with a chauffeur, you and your girl and also, of course, her lady-in-waiting. At the theater everybody looks at you and your girl almost as much as they look at the stage. You and your girl and the others, including your girl's detective, all leave first. The car and the chauffeur are waiting. There is never a parking problem.

You go on to the Café de Paris. The headwaiter who knows all about you takes you to a table which is secluded and covered with flowers.

You and your girl and her lady-in-waiting and her escort all sit down at the table. The detective sits quietly at the next table and never takes his eyes off you. Neither does anybody else.

The lady-in-waiting orders some champagne and you drink it and dance a little with your girl, not forgetting to call her "ma'am" and trying to act as if she were an ordinary girl. When she says it is time to go home you do not argue. You get up to go.

Nobody brings you a bill and you do not leave a tip. Your girl will take care of all that through her lady-in-waiting the following day. She will take care of getting home, too. You say good-by to her at the door of the nightclub, not forgetting to call her "ma'am." You do not kiss her good-night, but you might shake hands.

Then you go home to your flat and the Princess Margaret goes home to her palace.

Chapter 13:
The Strange Rites of Monarchy

Since all human institutions, like the men who devise them, are mortal, the time will come when the anthropologists of some future era will be able to gaze upon the British crown with a detachment not entirely possible in our own day. When they come to study this impossible, unbelievable, obviously unworkable, more than slightly magical phenomenon, they are likely to come up with some queer observations.

They will have to note, for example: That in mid-twentieth-century Britain, a twenty-six-year-old girl, chosen only by the roulette wheel of birth, was given powers so great that she could, on paper, commit murder without punishment or disband the armies of her country without other authority;

That she never actually invoked any of these powers except occasionally to accept as her right a white rose from the Duke of Atholl or a snowball from the Munros of Foulis;

That on certain occasions, she and those around her dressed up in the costumes of their ancestors to take part in rites that had been ancient before those same ancestors were born;

That in the age of the motor car she was to be seen driving about in a horse-drawn coach that had been built two hundred years before and had been obsolete for at least fifty;

That on one occasion in her lifetime two million of her countrymen paid out the better part of a week's wages simply to watch her drive past them wearing a four-pound jeweled headpiece and holding a jeweled stick in one hand and a jeweled ball in the other;

That although she was subjected to a veneration only

slightly less awe-inspiring than that accorded to the Deity, though she was occasionally credited with certain magical powers such as healing the sick or changing the weather, though a special language had to be used when addressing her, she herself was a virtual prisoner in her country, forced to labor at her task until the very moment of her death;

That her life was planned for her, almost to the very minute, weeks and months in advance, and her person surrounded by a thicket of taboos that governed her days as surely as the sun shone on her planet.

A woman, she could not dress like other women. She could never be seen in a bathing suit, and when her younger sister was once caught in one she was submitted to a national persecution. She could not wear the low-heeled shoes which every other working girl in the realm was allowed for comfort. She could not appear in any sort of headdress that covered either the eyes or any portion of her features. In an age when every other woman wore trousers, she could not be seen in slacks or shorts. Once, on a visit to Kenya in Africa, she donned brown slacks in order to climb to the top of a tree. On the way she was scheduled to inspect a group of schoolchildren. She had to carry out the inspection from the car so that the children could not see the offending garment.

She could never have a hair out of place. As a little girl she would grow pale with half-suffocation inside the royal limousines because the windows could not be opened for fear a breeze might disturb her coiffure. Once, on the HMCS *Ontario,* traveling between Halifax and St. John's, a photographer came upon her on deck, munching a date square, a bandanna loosely wrapped around her head. She swiftly whipped off the headdress and re-

243

moved the confection. For she must never be photographed eating.

All her life she was treated as a porcelain figure. Once, when she toured Canada, she would have liked to have visited New York City, the mecca of her age, to see a musical comedy and take in a nightclub; but she could not do so. As a child, her greatest thrill was a subway ride followed by coffee out of thick cups in a YWCA canteen. But when the crowd gathered she was whisked away never to drink out of thick cups or ride the subway again. Her father once tried to, when his car broke down and he wanted to make connections with the royal train. But the manager of the subway, who was one of his loyal and obedient subjects, flatly refused to permit it, for he feared that panic would result.

When this young girl went to the pantomime, she, of all the people there, could see only half the stage; for she had to sit in the royal box, at a discreet distance from her subjects. She had never ridden a bus. Indeed she had not even seen a bus close at hand until one day in Scotland her future husband took her for a drive in his tiny sports car. Later she wrote to a friend to remark in some surprise at the height of the great double-decker that trundled past them.

Her official life was walled away in a musty palace where the light switches were two feet outside the doors, and in a thousand-year-old castle with eight-foot-thick walls and no central heating. And she herself, her life, and even her expression, were cast in the inflexible mold of her ancestors. If her grandfather kept a stamp collection, then she must keep one, too. If her great-grandfather had purchased a Daimler, then she must ride in a Daimler, and there was a hue and cry when her husband ordered a

Rolls-Royce. ("I'd like a car of my own," she once told a friend, "but there's so damn much family talk about which make I must have that I don't think I'll ever get one.") Nor must her features exhibit any of the range of human emotions except to register cheerful amusement. When she greeted her young son after a two-month absence in Canada she could not bend and kiss him, or pick him up and cuddle him. "We are not supposed to be human," her mother had said on *her* Coronation Day. She had been riding for two hours in a golden coach which swayed so badly she was near seasickness and her brow was aching and bowed with the weight of her crown. "I'm so tired I can hardly hold my head up," she said.

For the burden of the crown was always felt by those privileged to wear it in mid twentieth-century Britain.

Now, having said all this, our future anthropologists will have to make a further observation. They will have to note that this curious, unwieldy, time-encrusted, creaky royal machine somehow seemed to work; that it served to remind an island people of their continuing traditions and institutions; that by a strange imitative process it promoted business and stimulated trade; that through a mystical bond nobody could explain it maintained under a common symbol a loose collection of totally disparate peoples, black, brown, yellow, and white; Moslem, Christian, Buddhist, and Jew; Zulu, witchdoctor, prince, and Hottentot.

They will have to note that all these peoples, on given occasions and sometimes several times a day, in churches, music halls, fraternity houses, and tents, were in the habit of jumping to their feet, standing stiffly rigid, fixing their eyes on a distant point, and chanting a prayer for the shy little woman chosen as their fetish. For the taboos erected around her applied also, in varying degrees, to objects, human or inanimate, that were connected with her: to a piece of bunting called a "flag," to officers in the army who held her commission, and relatives who bore her name, and to this anthem that asked God to save her.

In this connection they may come across the incident of Miss Tree, a musical mind-reader who toured England in the mid thirties. Her peculiar abilities consisted of being able to play any tune immediately it was thought of by a member of the audience. One evening the Duke of Portland invited Their Majesties to an evening's entertainment which featured Miss Tree. Miss Tree turned first to Queen Mary, who thought of an obscure English ballad which Miss Tree played at once. King George's turn came next and he thought of a sea chanty and Miss Tree played it. Now Miss Tree turned to her host. The Duke of Portland couldn't think of anything for a long time. Finally he thought of the national anthem. The idea was no sooner in his mind than Miss Tree played it on the piano. The audience immediately sprang rigidly to attention. Miss Tree finished and everybody began to file out. The evening had only begun but, the national anthem having been played, the entertainment was obviously over and the bewildered monarch and his wife, who had only just arrived, had to go home.

These things will all be noted, together with the fact that as long as all these different peoples kept singing together they seemed to get along better, for the most part, than those who didn't.

Such queer goings-on will not surprise the anthropologists, who are used to this sort of thing, but they will certainly astonish and fascinate the laymen of the future, as

indeed they astonish and fascinate some of the laymen today.

It will intrigue them to learn, for example, that some
people in the twentieth century felt a certain magical
thrill in touching the person of their monarch. The Duke
of Windsor, in his memoirs, mentions this curious "touching phenomenon" which followed him all across Canada.
He was never free from hands plucking at him like
branches in a forest. His brother, when Duke of York,
once had to make a speech in Jamaica, which he rehearsed
carefully because of his stutter. As he got through the
difficult words he could feel his ankles and thighs being
prodded by the people beneath the speaker's dais, and at
one point he heard a girl at his heels whisper: "Say, have
you touched the Prince?" and another reply: "Yes, three
times." In Australia he came upon the phenomenon again,
for here were people who believed that "virtue" would
flow from his garments and those of his Duchess if they
were touched. At one point the crowd pressed so close and
stroked the Duchess's coat so repeatedly that the mild
voice of the Duke was heard to murmur: "Please don't
touch the exhibits!" Later he had an even more curious
experience when he held his camp for boys at Southwold.
Each year members of the crowd would push forward
hoping they might touch him and thus be cured of sick-
ness. Indeed, during the last years of his father's reign,
a Scottish cleric wrote to the newspapers suggesting that
a crippled boy who had learned to walk without crutches
might have been cured by "the royal touch." Linked to
this is the equally strange belief in the "King's weather";
a feeling that on great days of royal pageantry—and this
was most noticeable on George V's Jubilee and again on
his funeral day—the weather will always be fine.

None of this curiosa will astonish the anthropologists. For they have seen it all before at some period in history. They know that in Korea the ancient kings were supposed to influence the rain, and in Mexico the kings swore to make the sun shine, and that from the southern Celebes to Homeric Greece, a good king (that is, one who followed in the path of his ancestors) could make the earth rich and the crops grow. They know that in ancient Ireland it was popularly supposed that if the monarch obeyed the customs of his ancestors the weather would be mild; that in the Middle Ages, Waldemar I of Denmark touched the children brought to him to make them thrive, and that Elizabeth I of England touched her subjects to heal them of scrofula. In primitive times, kings and queens often started out as magicians and ended up as gods and goddesses.

There are other points of similarity between the kings of the past and the Queen of today. It may be that in the future the anthropologists will come to the conclusion that the British constitutional monarchy, the supposedly modern development of an inventive nation, is, in reality, as old as the Hellespont.

In the past decade or so it has come as something of a shock to the British peoples to realize that the task of a king or queen is not the enviable one envisioned in fairy tales, where an ermined monarch puts up his daughter as first prize in the dragon-slaying competition. Marion Crawford, the present Queen's governess, has given a picture of what it meant to one man to become King of England: a wan picture of a saddened man laboriously practicing his new signature at his desk; a gray picture of a new Queen saying quietly: "We must take what is coming and make the best of it"; a wistful picture of two small children looking up in horror when they find they must move from a home to a palace.

But the picture does not differ greatly from primitive times, from Cambodia, where it was often necessary to force the kingships of Fire and Water on the reluctant successors to the throne, or Savage Island, where the monarchy actually came to an end because nobody could be persuaded to take the job, or from various parts of West Africa, where a prospective king has to be seized, bound, and kept a prisoner until he is induced to accept the crown.

We may not kill our kings outright, as the Zulus did, or the Shilluk of the upper Nile, but we allow them to kill themselves as surely as the King of Calicut on the Malabar coast of India, who was required to slit his own throat. The entire British world watched its last King die by inches, knowing from the press that the job was destroying him, but never lifting a finger to lessen the more arduous aspects of his task. Indeed, the fact that he committed suicide by doing his duty has been commented on favorably on all sides, as it was in the days when the King of Quilacare in India stood on a specially built platform and hacked himself to death in front of his subjects. Already George VI is being spoken of as George the Good, because of his sacrifices. The last member of the royal line to receive this appellation was Albert of Saxe-Coburg, who also quite literally killed himself from overwork.

"We permanent officials never have a real holiday," King Edward VII once remarked to a fellow civil servant. "We have to be at it all the time." His son, George V, in the final year of World War I remarked that of all his subjects, he alone never knew what a day of rest was like. For always there is the endless signing . . . signing . . .

249

signing. The English monarch signs his name between thirty and sixty thousand times a year. It plagues him until he dies—indeed a reference to it forms the last item in Queen Victoria's diary. But it is the least of the sovereign's tasks.

Every year of her life the new Queen must shake hands with upwards of five thousand people and receive the bows or curtsies of twenty thousand more. She will spend a thousand hours granting interviews and receive up to five hundred bouquets a year. If she visited every one of the 280,000 establishments anxious to receive the royal benediction she would have no time for anything else for the next fifty years. If a new war comes, one of her duties will be to award decorations personally. Her grandfather pinned fifty thousand ribbons on fifty thousand breasts. The time can easily come when her hand is so limp from shaking other hands that she will have to wear it in a sling, or when her voice becomes so husky from speech-making that she cannot talk above a whisper: the last Prince of Wales suffered both these afflictions. "It is absolutely staggering how much they expect us to do and go on doing for so long at a stretch," she wrote her governess after seeing the program for the 1947 African tour. "I hope we shall survive, that's all!" Little wonder then that Bernard Shaw, who did not much care for royalty, was moved to suggest, when George VI ascended the throne, that the country set up a society for the protection of royal personages.

Yet these are not the real reasons why one royal personage accepts the throne with misgivings and another steps down from it with alacrity.

On Mount Agu in Togoland, on the very highest peak, there dwells a powerful but unfortunate man. He is King

of all the land and worshipped as such. But he is doomed
for life to stay on his mountain. He may come down once
a year to make purchases but even then he may not enter
the homes of his subjects and must return the same day to
the heights to which his destiny has banished him.

There is more than a passing similarity between Mount
Agu and the summit upon which the English sovereign
finds herself. Tennyson saw it and, on taking leave of the
aging Victoria, put it into words: "You are so alone on
that terrible height," he said. For the great Queen could
never come down from her mountain. Once, when she had
tasted a little haggis in the cottage of one of the humblest
of her subjects, she remarked sadly that food in small
houses always seemed to taste better than her own. On
another occasion she remarked wistfully that she had
never seen a British railway ticket and was surprised to
learn they were made of pasteboard instead of thin pieces
of paper.

Now a new Queen sits upon the royal mountaintop on
whose steep slopes are implanted the thick forests of
taboo. Future generations may see her task as a Dutch
traveler saw that of the heir to the throne of Loango in
West Africa in the mid seventeenth century. He reported
that his upbringing was so fettered by increasing ceremony
that "at the moment he ascends the throne he is lost in an
ocean of rites and taboos."

Queen Elizabeth II might think it strange that the
King of Loango could never be seen at his meals by any
of his subjects or that the King of the Baganda could
never leave his home on foot but must ride astride a special carrier. Yet she herself has never been photographed
in the act of eating a meal nor can she leave her own
palace on foot: she must take a limousine or a state coach.

If the King of Monomotapa could wear no foreign clothing for fear it might be poisoned, neither can the Queen of England for fear that the action may poison British trade. She must "Buy British" and she must be careful what she buys for she must not favor one manufacturer to the exclusion of all others.

The King of the Matabele would never receive strangers until they had been rendered fit for his presence by being sprinkled with a green sticky substance applied by a cow's tail. But in Britain, no woman can be received at an evening court without three ostrich feathers in her hair.

And if it seems strange that the King of the Ashanti must always appear with sandals on his feet, it is no stranger than the rule which forbids the Queen of the British to appear before schoolchildren in slacks.

It is odd to think that, in common with a great many other peoples, the British use a special language to address the Queen, but one has only to look at the royal proclamations or illuminated addresses with their: "May it please Your Majesty," or their: "Gracious Sovereign Lady Queen Elizabeth," to realize that this is true. In Burma, the monarch on his accession was known only by his title: his name was taboo. Similarly, within Buckingham Palace nobody refers to the sovereign as "Elizabeth." She is "the Queen" or "Her Majesty."

There is one other similarity between the British crown and ancient kingships which is striking. And this, too, the anthropologists of the future must remark: the Queen today is like the monarch of Ponape, one of the Caroline Islands, who was apparently all-powerful and who did indeed know by heart all the sacred prayers and liturgy but whose government was in the hands of a grand vizier or prime minister.

For modern queens, like ancient kings, far from being absolute rulers, are themselves absolutely ruled. They can be bundled into a car, as George V was, and rushed to Westminster Abbey to take part in a thanksgiving service for his recovery, with an open wound still in his back. They can have a four-pound crown clapped on their heads and speeches thrust in their hands, and they must read them as their own, though everyone who hears them understands the fiction and half of those who hear them know in advance what they contain. This so angered George IV that he went to the lengths of inserting the words *Baa-Baa Blacksheep* in the middle of a speech from the throne as a protest. But it did no good, for only one man noticed.

The sovereign must always conform to the mores of the masses. Stockmar, when he was helping to reshape the monarchy, understood the absolute necessity for this. "The English machine works smoothly and well only when the Sovereign is upright and truthful," he wrote prophetically. "When he has been insincere, mendacious and wicked, it has creaked and fouled and jolted to within an ace of coming to a deadlock."

George VI, when he was Duke of York, once came under censure because his subjects believed he had shot at a rampaging rhinoceros on Sunday. It did not matter that he was supposed to have done it to save his own life. (The incident occurred on a weekday, actually, and it was not the King who shot at the attacking beast.) It was enough that he had broken a taboo.

It is difficult for outsiders, then, to understand why

kings and queens are not only suffered but venerated in the age of the atom. For they are worshipped throughout the British realm with a fervor that could hardly have been equaled by the aborigines of old. The cancellation of George VI's royal tour to Australia and New Zealand was a body blow to those countries almost impossible to understand until its implications are understood. For it represented a staggering monetary loss. One Sydney store had purchased a thousand pounds' worth of pocket-knives with the King's picture. Another had laid out one hundred and fifty thousand pounds for clothing of British design. A third had ordered the world's largest Union Jack, five thousand square feet in size. One hundred miles of bunting had been purchased in Sydney, and the city council had ordered one hundred thousand extra plants for its public parks. The Melbourne council had set aside forty-two thousand pounds for a state ball, the Lord Mayor was learning to dance "Strip the Willow" and one wealthy homeowner had re-landscaped his entire front garden to spell out the word *Welcome* in thousands of flowers. In New Zealand the populace was whipped into a similar fervor. Every building in the public square in Christchurch was to be cleaned. The main street in Timaru was to be paved, the race track painted, a hotel equipped with plumbing. The entire country was about to undergo a face-lifting when the tour was canceled.

Why, the stranger asks, should this be so? Why should the monarch be venerated to the point where, when one makes an abdication speech on the radio, the entire nation stands stiffly at attention, including the very husband of the woman for whom he gave up the throne?

The answer, as Sir Winston Churchill has suggested, lies somewhere in the realm of magic, as the ancient kingships did. In a way, the British Queen is looked on as part goddess by a substantial number of her subjects and in this sense she is as powerful in the British world as the spirit of Mohammed in the Moslem. The coronation service, which is a thousand years old, has about it faint whispers of the ancient priest-kings, for its central figure is an archbishop and its signal moment is not the crowning but the anointing—the one item in the ritual which was not televised.

Like a god, the monarch, in abstract at least, is immortal. After his mother's demise, Edward VII spotted a flag flying at half-mast on the royal yacht and immediately sent to know why. "The Queen is dead," came the reply. "But the King lives!" cried Edward and ordered the flag run up again.

Like a goddess, a queen can be nothing less than perfect. Her appearance must be above reproach and a lady-in-waiting must attend her with an extra pair of stockings and an extra pair of shoes to guard against a run in the royal silk or a faulty heel on the royal pumps. Her actions and her appearance must be supra-human and this is why she cannot be shown munching an apple or lying on a beach or riding in the subway. But, more important, her inner being must be godlike: she herself must be pure in heart, she must conform to the accepted standards of her day, and she must follow faithfully in the footsteps of her ancestors as the ancient Irish kings had to do. For if she does not—if she neglects her business, or walks about the streets like a mortal, or seeks to marry a divorcee—the crops of Empire will fail and the fruits of Commonwealth will wither on their vine.

To assist her in this patently impossible duty, she has the backing of press, parliament, and public. Her person is sacrosanct. Her adviser may be upbraided; she never. The "palace" can be attacked but not the sovereign. The strength of this taboo was never more apparent than during the abdication crisis when, for months, an entire nation was kept in the dark about its King's indiscretions so that even the pages of American newsmagazines reporting this national incident were clipped before being placed on the newsstands. The taboo applied alike to the venerable *Times* and the Communist *Worker*. From the British press there pours a daily Niagara of trivia about the sovereign. All of it is innocuous, all of it adulatory. Indeed it is doubtful if a newspaper or member of parliament could long survive the wave of public disapproval that would result from any criticism of the person of the crown. This cushioning of the sovereign from personal publicity has certain weaknesses. It has produced some of the most fantastic rumors and untruths about various members of the family in the palace. As a child, Princess Margaret was popularly supposed to be deaf and dumb, though she was obviously neither. Recently, Prince Charles has been rumored to have a club foot, though he can be seen occasionally in St. James Park walking about quite normally. The very secrecy surrounding the monarchy makes for dark whispers about it.

The veil of secrecy is by no means accidental. It is studied. Palace servants are screened as carefully as members of the U. S. State Department. No one who has business at the palace enters it without being warned of the penalties for speaking about the sovereign in public. Servants who do so are dismissed, their pensions canceled, and a notice detailing their crime posted in all servants' quarters in all the royal homes. Tradesmen who are indiscreet lose their custom. A guardsman once happened to mention

that George V had greeted him one day with the words:
"Good morning. How's your health?" For this disclosure
he was dismissed. Thomas Lawrence Jerram, the late
King's valet, was recently asked to write his memoirs.
Though he lives on only a small pension, he replied that
he would not do so for fifty thousand pounds.

Newspapers that break the taboo, in the mildest way,
find their reporters no longer get entrée to royal affairs.
When a press conference was held to launch an expensive
limited edition of a book about the royal philatelic collection, all papers got invitations except the weekly *Observer,* the dean of the Sunday press. And a man from the
palace was posted at the press conference to make sure
that no one from the *Observer,* under some other guise,
got into the affair. No one knew exactly what the paper
had done to incur this treatment, but no one wanted to find
himself in a similar position.

The palace grapevine is sensitive enough. When a report about the same stamp book appeared in the Toronto
Globe and Mail some hours before it was supposed to be
released, the press officer at Buckingham Palace had a
copy of the paper on his desk within a day and was making
inquiries to find out how the breach had occurred.

But gods and goddesses have their practical uses and
there is little doubt that the British monarchy is worth
every sixpence spent on it.

First, there is the necessary business of trade. The
sovereign is imitated by her realm. When Queen Alexandra developed a slight limp, members of her court
limped with her. When Edward VII left a button of his
waistcoat undone, buttons popped around the Empire.
When the Prince of Wales appeared in a sailor suit, the
streets were white with little boys similarly attired. When

Elizabeth, as Princess, carried out her first inspection of the Grenadier Guards, she wore a flat, brimless hat of green felt, peaked in front on the lines of a military "Broderick." The result was not particularly becoming, but within a few hours Mayfair milliners were flooded with demands for copies and soon women all over Britain were wearing them. This very real power, which the Queen wields, is useful when a nation's business is sagging. Queen Mary's pastel lace dresses promoted the Nottingham lace trade. Queen Elizabeth's purchases at the British Industries Fair have like results.

Then there is the practical business of social leadership. Some modern states without kings have found it necessary to invent a substitute. France needs a president as well as a premier. And New York City found that the mayor's practical duties were becoming so heavy that it needed another man to handle his social tasks: hence Grover Whalen with his white carnation and perpetual smile. The president of the United States, burdened by his considerable duties, must still find time to greet and entertain the representatives of foreign powers. Much of this burden is lifted from the British prime minister's shoulders by his sovereign. Nor has the American president anyone to turn to in moments of despair or indecision—for there is no high and continuing link between the past and the future. In the days following Roosevelt's death, Harry Truman might have welcomed the reassuring presence of a monarch.

There is, again, the mystical business of tradition. The silver trowels in their morocco cases, the golden keys to nonexistent doorways, the silver spades for turning initial sods, the vellum scrolls with their careful illuminations —all these have their place. The presence of the sovereign, moving down the endless lines of troops, attending ancient churches, and taking her part in each of the hoary ceremonies that are her lot, year after year, reminds the English people of their common past and inspires their faith in a common future. In war and disaster the sovereign's presence on the scene offers a comfort at once more practical and more mystical than that of the royal touch for scrofula.

Finally, there is the magical business of the Commonwealth. In the great public pageants it inspires, the British monarchy provides for a common wave of emotion to sweep through the United Kingdom and the scattered lands across the seas; and it is this group sentiment, felt by all, superseding ties, antagonisms, schisms, and disparities, that binds the British world together. Indeed, it is all that is left to do the binding. The marriage of a princess, the funeral of a king, the birth of an heir, the coronation of a queen—these, with the tours of the realm, are the real *raison d'être* of the monarchy. A cynic has called it, with a certain truth, "the national soap opera—complete with commercials."

The illness of a prince—Albert Edward of Wales—once saved the throne. The Jubilee of a queen—Victoria—raised it from its nadir to its peak. A royal pageant sets off a chain reaction of incidents, some great, some tiny, about the globe. A king takes ill and a little girl appears at the gates of the palace with a bunch of violets for him. A princess is engaged and two sentimental young English spinsters making toast together are so moved they wrap up the pieces and send them to her as a wedding gift. She is married and fragments of her wedding cake are passed from hand to hand, like reliquiæ, on the Fijian Islands. A thimbleful goes from Fiji to a girl in New Zealand where it is divided among sixteen classmates. One of these fragments is sent to Australia where it is put on display. Another crumb goes to Pitcairn Island and a third is auctioned off on Guadalcanal. A king's death can cause the cancellation of bridge parties from Moose Jaw to Melbourne. A Jubilee can stop London traffic dead for days. It was Kingsley Martin, editor of the *New Statesman and Nation,* who noticed that, during George V's Jubilee, children over fourteen were allowed, as a treat, to see films usually marked for adults only—a relief similar to earlier tribal festivals when the usually forbidden becomes permissible.

Of all the royal pageants, the transcendent is the coronation. It dwarfs all others by its size, its splendor and its complexity. It takes thousands of men almost a full year to prepare it, though it lasts only a few hours. As early as November 1952, guardsmen were pacing the streets and state coaches were out practicing the turns for the pageantry of the following June. In the model-room of the Ministry of Works, men were carefully constructing a scale model of the route from Palace to Abbey, down to the last tree. In the royal mews, behind the palace, horses were being frightened with gramophone records, trumpets, and dummies in red coats, so they would learn to be calm by the time the day arrived. In Westminster Abbey, closed for five months for complete renovation, peers' robes were placed on dummies and photographed to test the lighting, and toilets were flushed repeatedly to make sure the sound would never carry over the microphones. The great arches through which the procession passed were marked with chalk so that the coaches might go through exactly in the center. The route to the Abbey was timed and re-timed so that the Queen might arrive exactly as Big Ben struck eleven. The guests, some of whom were required to be on hand as early as six a.m., were given exact routes to take through the city from their homes, so that traffic would not be jumbled. The British have always believed that if a pageant is worth doing at all, it is worth doing well and they are ready to submit at all times to as much rehearsal as is necessary to make the machine run smoothly. George V and his Queen actually pinned imitation robes on their shoulders and practiced entering and leaving their carriage and their whole manner of sitting on the dais, at the Indian Durbar of 1911. For nobody in Britain, including the monarch, ever leaves the monarchy to chance.

No other country has a coronation. Britain has had fewer than forty. The fanfare attendant upon the festival is such that when Edward VII's was postponed, the great hotelier César Ritz suffered a collapse from which he never fully recovered. For a coronation occupies the energies and the minds of the nation to the point where all else seems to stand still. The coronation of Elizabeth II caused the circulation of three hundred million dollars in Britain; but more important perhaps was the mystic way in which it took its hold upon her subjects.

To justify it, she must be a good queen, in the anthropological as well as the ethical sense, for no other form of sovereign has satisfied the British since Victoria came to the throne. In this connection, it may be germane to quote the following passage:

The idea that . . . kingdoms are despotisms in which the people exist only for the sovereign is wholly inapplicable. . . . On the contrary, the sovereign in them exists only as he discharges the duties of his position by or-

dering the course of nature for his people's benefit. So soon as he fails to do so, the care, the devotion, the religious homage which they had hitherto lavished on him cease and are changed into hatred and contempt; he is dismissed ignominiously. . . . Worshipped as a god one day, he is . . . a criminal the next. But in this changed behaviour of the people there is nothing capricious or inconsistent. On the contrary, their conduct is entirely of a piece. If their king is their god, he is or should also be their preserver; and if he will not preserve them, he must make room for another who will. So long, however, as he answers their expectations, there is no limit to the care which they take of him, and which they compel him to take of himself. A king of this sort lives hedged in by a ceremonious etiquette, a network of prohibitions and observances, of which the intention is not to contribute to his dignity, much less to his comfort, but to restrain him from conduct which . . . might involve himself, his people and the universe in one common catastrophe. Far from adding to his comfort, these observances, by trammeling his every act, annihilate his freedom and often render the very life, which it is their object to preserve, a burden and sorrow to him.

These words were not written to describe the British monarchy in the days of Edward VIII, George VI, or Elizabeth II. They were written by Sir James Frazer, the anthropologist, discussing the primitive kingdoms of old. But they may, with very little revision, be used again when some future anthropologist casts a searching light upon the monarchy of our times.

A NOTE ON SOURCES

The material for this book was gathered in the course of travels that took me from Vancouver Island in British Columbia to the little town of Elgin near the tip of Scotland, and through a series of reference rooms running all the way from the noisy and cluttered morgue of the *Vancouver Sun* to the silent, domed library of the British Museum. A little more than a third of the information in this book was gathered through interviews with a wide variety of people—from the Canadian Army staff sergeant who drove Elizabeth and Philip through the streets of Halifax, Nova Scotia, to a former private secretary of a reigning monarch. The remainder of the material came from newspaper and magazine files and from other men's books. These, too, cover a wide range, for they run the gamut from *James Michener's* RETURN TO PARADISE (Random House, New York, 1951)—he reported on the final disposition of a fragment of Queen Elizabeth's wedding cake on the island of Fiji—to *Blanche Patch's* THIRTY YEARS WITH G. B. S. (Dodd, Mead & Co., New York, 1951)—she reports Shaw's suggestion for the establishment of a society for the prevention of cruelty to monarchs.

It is possible these days for an energetic reporter to interview almost anybody in the world with one exception. The exception of course is the British sovereign. Other queens (such as Juliana of the Netherlands) have talked to the press, but no British monarch has ever given an interview, and if one did, it is doubtful whether he or she would be able to say very much for publication. Thus, anyone who sets out to report on royalty must be prepared to get all of his information from other than primary sources.

Wherever possible in this book I have tried to use only

material that has been confirmed by several sources or that comes directly from an eyewitness or from someone with special knowledge. For example, the Queen's remark that "I have been trained from childhood to show no emotion in public" came from a man who sat next to her at dinner when she made the statement; the fact that she listened to and laughed at the Charlie McCarthy program during her Canadian tour comes from the serviceman who drove her car on this occasion; the material about Philip in the navy comes from officers who served with him; and the story about George VI and his Queen testing the wedding-present beds comes from a man who witnessed the incident. In those cases where the material is not specifically from eyewitnesses, it comes from an obviously authentic source. For instance, the story about George V and the chef who retrieved his favorite potatoes from the pigs comes from a highly placed palace servant who, if he did not witness the incident, was in a position to know all about it. The story about George VI climbing slowly up the moors in his final days at Balmoral comes from the postmaster at Crathie, Scotland, just outside the castle grounds. There is not much that occurs during the hunting season there that he does not know. Occasionally, when I felt my source to be authentic, but could not check the information, I have reproduced it but labeled it as hearsay. Many stories I have rejected because I did not believe them, or could not substantiate them. The English are notably reverent about the royal family in their press, but there are a surprising number of scandalous and untrue legends continually in circulation about them in private. These stories (the myth that Prince Charles has a clubfoot is one) are avidly passed about and expand in the telling.

264

In spite of this, however, most people in Britain who have access to the palace or to the family within it are reticent about talking to journalists. It is a palace rule that tradesmen and professional men talk to the press at the risk of losing the palace custom. Private secretaries are charming but discreet; press secretaries are clamlike. In my researches on the royal tour in Canada, which took me four thousand miles across my own country, I encountered very little of this reticence. I called on lieutenant-governors (who are the Queen's representatives in each province), on mayors, army and air force commanders, hotel managers, ministers, and railway personnel—anybody and everybody who had brushed shoulders with the royal couple—and few of them refused to see me or talk to me. But in Britain—though my Fleet Street colleagues told me that a Canadian would do better on this sort of job than an Englishman—I found many doors closed to me. Baron Nahum, the society photographer, who is a close friend of the Duke of Edinburgh, refused to see me. Lady Patricia Brabourne, the Duke's cousin, was agreeable to seeing me provided the Queen's press secretary, Lieutenant-Commander Richard Colville, would give his permission. Lieutenant-Commander Colville, who spent many years in the silent service before qualifying for his present position, firmly refused. "I am not what you North Americans would call a public-relations officer," he explained to me at our first meeting, and in this he was correct. When I asked him if I might be shown through the public rooms and corridors of Buckingham Palace, he winced imperceptibly and replied that the palace was a private home, which nobody ever saw. A few days later I called Sir John Wilson, the keeper of the Royal Philatelic Collection and asked him if I might view the royal stamp albums. He cheerfully gave me permission, and as a result I saw a good deal of the palace, for the stamp room is many corridors distant from the Privy Purse entrance.

Those people whom I did see were helpful and friendly, and I should like to thank them here collectively (for they would not want me to name them individually). They were a fairly good cross-section of Britain, from the palace servant whom I drank ale with in the Phoenix public house to the society editor who talked to me over port in the Savage Club; from the schoolmaster in his study at Gordonstoun on the Moray Firth to the graying peer before his fireplace in his country seat in Kent. When my investigations were done, it occurred to me that perhaps the palace press secretary could teach North American public-relations men a few tricks. His curtain of silence so maddens the journalists of three countries that they contrive to dig out and publish more information about the British royal house than about any other comparable institution in the world.

For the reader who is interested in delving further into the subject of the House of Windsor, there are an astonishing number of good books available on the library shelves, as well as an astonishing number of bad ones. The most prolific author of all was the founder of the dynasty, Queen Victoria herself, whose voluminous letters and diaries (two volumes of which were best-sellers during her lifetime) form the greatest literary treasure trove about her reign. Disraeli may have been flattering her (and himself) when he made a passing reference to "we authors," but, all the same, Victoria had one great asset that any writer will envy: an ability to record minute detail. The general reader may not wish to plow through her papers or those of Thomas Creevey or Charles Greville, the diarists of the age, but there are others who have done the plowing and produced first-rate books about her life and times. The most notable, of course, is *Lytton Strachey's* QUEEN VICTORIA (Harcourt, Brace & Co., New York, 1921), a work of great insight and wit, which reads like a novel. Some later biographers, however, were able to make use of later volumes of the Queen's journals which had not been published when Strachey undertook his study. These more recent books include *Arthur Ponsonby's* brief but pithy QUEEN VICTORIA (Macmillan Company, New York, 1933), *E. F. Benson's* comprehensive and searching QUEEN VICTORIA (Longmans, Green & Co., New York, 1935), and *Edith Sitwell's* more emotional VICTORIA OF ENGLAND (Houghton Mifflin Company, Boston, 1936). The most recent addition to Victoriana is *Dormer Creston's* very readable and scholarly book THE YOUTHFUL QUEEN VICTORIA (G. P. Putnam's Sons, New York, 1952). The official biography by *Sir Sidney Lee,* QUEEN VICTORIA (Smith, Elder & Co., London, 1902), is scholarly and complete, but pretty dull for modern audiences attuned to Strachey.

The background of the early days of the Victorian age can be found in *Roger Fulford's* excellent THE ROYAL DUKES (Macmillan Company, New York, 1933) and his GEORGE IV (Macmillan Company, 1949). Both these books give a clear and balanced picture of the lusty Hanoverians, and Fulford is a man who is fair to his subject without being blindly partisan. *Edmund d'Auvergne's* THE COBURGS (Stanley Paul & Co., London) traces the other side of the Windsor heritage fairly completely, as

does *Pierre Crabites'* study of Baron Stockmar, VIC-
TORIA'S GUARDIAN ANGEL (E. P. Dutton & Co., New
York, 1938).

Few readers will want to face up to Sir Theodore
Martin's ten-volume biography of the Prince Consort, or
to the other official volumes of speeches and letters, most
of which were published by the express wish of his royal
widow. But there are first-rate accounts of his life, works,
and character in both *Roger Fulford's* THE PRINCE CON-
SORT (Macmillan Company, 1949) and *Hector Bolitho's*
VICTORIA AND ALBERT (Cobden-Sanderson, London,
1938), a volume that replaces two earlier books on the
same subject by Mr. Bolitho, a man who has written
prolifically about the British royal family, but never quite
so well as he does here. Mr.Bolitho's FURTHER LETTERS
OF QUEEN VICTORIA (Thorton Butterworth Ltd., London, 1938) was also useful.

There are scores of books that capture the feeling and
flavor of the Victorian and Edwardian ages, with special
reference to those royal personages from whom the times
take their name. I can only mention here those I found
most useful to me, which I think will be most entertaining
to the reader. *E. F. Benson's* AS WE WERE: A VICTORIAN
PEEP SHOW (Longmans, Green & Co., New York, 1930)
is very readable and includes a good account of Edward
VII's part in the Tranby-Croft affair. *Sir Frederick Ponsonby's* RECOLLECTIONS FROM THREE REIGNS (E. P. Dutton & Co., New York, 1952) manages to be gossipy yet
discreet. The author, an old-time palace aide, gives good
pictures of Victoria and Edward VII. The best account
of *Lily Langtry's* capture of London is in her autobiography, THE DAYS I KNEW (George H. Doran Co., New
York, 1925). The same general period is covered chattily,

268

but with discretion, by *Margot Oxford* in her autobiographical MORE OR LESS ABOUT MYSELF (E. P. Dutton & Co., New York, 1934). Lady Oxford was the wife of Henry Asquith, the Liberal Prime Minister of the period following World War I. THE EDWARDIAN ERA, by *André Maurois* (D. Appleton-Century Co., New York, 1933), is witty, colorful, and anecdotal. Another picture of the era from a different and more personal point of view can be found in *Consuelo Vanderbilt Balsan's* autobiography, THE GLITTER AND THE GOLD (Harper & Brothers, New York, 1952). THE LIPTON STORY, by *Alec Waugh* (Doubleday, New York, 1950), is the biography of one of Edward VII's sailing companions, and CÉSAR RITZ—HOST TO THE WORLD, by *Marie Louise Ritz* (J. B. Lippincott Company, Philadelphia, 1938), is the biography of the great Edwardian hotelier, by his widow.

The published work on Edward VII is equally voluminous, and again I can only mention here those books which I found useful and which the reader may enjoy. The official two-volume biography by Sir Sidney Lee is definitive, and within the limits of its terms of reference remarkably objective, but most readers will find it too long and too heavy for casual enjoyment. *H. E. Wortham* does a crisper and more readable job in EDWARD VII— MAN AND KING (Little, Brown & Co., Boston, 1931), and so does *E. F. Benson,* that indefatiguable chronicler of those times, in his KING EDWARD VII (Longmans, Green & Co., New York, 1934). Two useful books that deal more with King Edward's upbringing are VICTORIA'S HEIR—THE EDUCATION OF A PRINCE, by *George Dangerfield* (Harcourt, Brace & Co., New York, 1941), and THE TRAGEDY OF KING EDWARD, A PSYCHOLOGICAL STUDY, translated from the German, by *W. H. Edwards* (used with permission of Dodd, Mead & Co., New York, 1938). There is a telling portrait of the King contained in *Christopher Sykes's* FOUR STUDIES IN LOYALTY (William Sloane, Associates, New York, 1950), which gives an account of the practical jokes played on Sykes's uncle and namesake. Two contemporary works, while low in literary quality, contain a good deal of personal trivia about the King. These are THE PRIVATE LIFE OF EDWARD VII by a member of the royal household (D. Appleton & Co., New York, 1901) and KING EDWARD VII —BIOGRAPHICAL AND PERSONAL SKETCHES WITH ANECDOTES (Skeffington & Son, London, 1910), a volume published immediately after the King's death, containing essays by several well-known people who knew him well.

There are a dozen or so books purporting to be biographies of George V, but only two are really worth reading. These are GEORGE V—A PERSONAL MEMOIR, by *John Gore* (Charles Scribner's Sons, New York, 1941), and KING GEORGE V, HIS LIFE AND REIGN, by *Harold Nicolson* (Constable & Co., London, 1952). Both of these are official biographies, subject to the advantages and limitations such works always have. It is a tribute to the authors that they have both made the most of their advantages and surmounted, to a great degree, their limitations. Both books manage to remain fairly objective and to give an honest three-dimensional picture of the subject. The first deals largely with the King's personal life; the second with his public career.

As might be expected, the books on monarchs long dead are more dispassionate in their treatment than books on more recent members of the royal family. Edward VII and Victoria stand out as human beings, with human strengths and weaknesses (though they, too, were presented as cardboard figures by their contemporaries). Queen Mary and her sons and granddaughters seem less believable if one takes their biographers literally. There is a whole shelf of books written during the twenties about the then Prince of Wales which outdo themselves in wholesale adulation of their subject. It is interesting to read them now in retrospect, after almost three decades, and to find that each of them is, in a sense, a defense of the Prince. "After all, he is human," is a recurring theme in most of them. But the picture presented is not that of a human being, but of a god. There is another shelf of books written during the abdication crisis, or immediately after it, and these too, for the most part, are in defense of the King. Here the facts of the crisis itself suggest that the subject is human, but the authors have done their best to maintain him as a cardboard figure. By far the best book—though by no means the definitive one—on the subject of this complicated and tragic man is the one he wrote himself with the help of Charles J. V. Murphy of *Life* magazine, A KING'S STORY, by the DUKE OF WINDSOR (G. P. Putnam's Sons, New York, 1951). It too, as might be expected, is a defense, but a much more convincing and readable one. All the same, we shall have to wait some years for the final word on Edward VIII.

We must wait, too, for a definitive and searching volume on Queen Mary. Most of the books written about her during her lifetime were scrutinized carefully by Queen Mary herself with that meticulous eye for detail for which she was noted. Thus they are accurate, but they are neither objective nor complete. The two that contain the most information are *Kathleen Woodward's* QUEEN MARY, A LIFE AND INTIMATE STUDY (Hutchinson & Co., London, 1939), which chronicles the early part of her life in fairly comprehensive detail, and *Louis Wulff's* HER MAJESTY QUEEN MARY (Sampson Low, Marston & Co., London, 1949), which contains a great amount of detail about how she lived after her husband's death. But the full story of this remarkable woman will not be known until her own diaries, which must be voluminous, are published.

We shall also have to wait for the official biography of George VI, now in preparation, before we fully understand this valiant and sincere man. For all the books written about him, and about his equally remarkable Queen, there is none worth recommending. The best published account of his character and habits is contained in *Allan A. Michie's* GOD SAVE THE QUEEN (William Sloane Associates, New York, 1953), a book that contains some useful information about royalty in general as well as good studies of Elizabeth II and her immediate family. Future biographers of the Queen will also have to consult *Marion Crawford's* famous THE LITTLE PRINCESSES (Harcourt, Brace & Company, New York, 1950; copyright by the Curtis Publishing Company), which is an invaluable source of first-hand material about the royal sisters in their childhood and teens. Miss Crawford's later books are not so useful.

The best general book on Buckingham Palace is *Marguerite D. Peacocke's* THE STORY OF BUCKINGHAM PALACE (Odhams Press Limited, London, 1951), which traces through anecdote and description the history of the palace from its purchase by George III to the present day. The furnishings and interior of the palace are described and beautifully photographed in *H. Clifford Smith's* BUCKINGHAM PALACE, ITS FURNITURE, DECORATION AND HISTORY (Country Life, London, 1931).

For much of the anthropological material contained in

my final chapter I leaned heavily upon the unabridged version of *Sir James Frazer's* THE GOLDEN BOUGH, A STUDY IN MAGIC AND RELIGION (Macmillan Company, New York, 1935), especially Part II, "Taboo and Peril," and Part III, "The Dying God," which I use with the publisher's permission. *Kingsley Martin's* intriguing little book THE MAGIC OF MONARCHY (Alfred A. Knopf, New York, 1937) was also useful.

It would be monotonous and impractical to outline the various documents that came my way and that I found useful in my researches. The George VI Funeral Number of the *Illustrated London News,* the official prospectus of Gordonstoun School, the 1937 files of *Time,* the printed itinerary of the Canadian royal tour, a Buckingham Palace menu, a BBC documentary—all these provided a sentence, a paragraph, or a page in this volume. To my wife, and to several young ladies on *Maclean's* magazine, Toronto—Miss Joan Weatherseed, Mrs. Nancy Munro, Miss Lois Harrison, Miss Janice Tyrwhitt and Miss Jean Yack—I owe thanks for help in research, checking, and typing; and to Ralph Allen, the editor of *Maclean's,* I owe a great deal for encouragement and guidance. What flaws and errors remain are, of course, my own responsibility.

INDEX

Index

iv

Index

vi

Index

This book has been set in a modern adaptation of a type designed by William Caslon, the first (1692–1766), greatest of English letter founders. The Caslon face, an artistic, easily read type, has had two centuries of ever increasing popularity in the United States—it is of interest to note that the first copies of the Declaration of Independence and the first paper currency distributed to the citizens of the new-born nation were printed in this type face.

The book was composed, printed, and bound by Kingsport Press, Inc., Kingsport, Tenn. Typography and binding design by Herbert Bayer.